food
and juice
for health

food

and juice
for
health

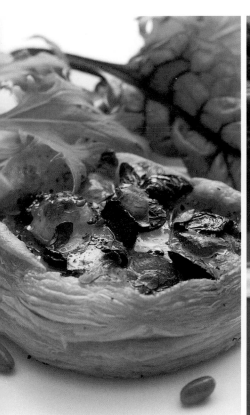

hamlyn

NOTES

Both metric and imperial measurements have been given in all recipes. Use one set of measurements only, and not a mixture of both.

Standard level spoon measurements are used in all recipes.
1 tablespoon = one 15 ml spoon
1 teaspoon = one 5 ml spoon

Eggs should be large unless otherwise stated. The Department of Health advises that eggs should not be consumed raw. This book contains dishes made with raw or lightly cooked eggs. It is prudent for more vulnerable people such as pregnant and nursing mothers, invalids, the elderly, babies and young children to avoid uncooked or lightly cooked dishes made with eggs. Once prepared, these dishes should be kept refrigerated and used promptly.

Milk should be full fat unless otherwise stated.

This book includes dishes made with nuts and nut derivatives. It is advisable for customers with known allergic reactions to nuts and nut derivatives and those who may be potentially vulnerable to these allergies, such as pregnant and nursing mothers, invalids, the elderly, babies and children, to avoid dishes made with nuts and nut oils. It is also prudent to check the labels of pre-prepared ingredients for the possible inclusion of nut derivatives.

Pepper should be freshly ground black pepper unless otherwise stated.

Fresh herbs should be used, unless otherwise stated. If unavailable, use dried herbs as an alternative, but halve the quantities stated.

Ovens should be pre-heated to the specified temperature – if using a fan-assisted oven, follow the manufacturer's instructions for adjusting the time and the temperature.

Vegetarians should look for the 'V' symbol on a cheese to ensure it is made with vegetarian rennet. There are vegetarian forms of Parmesan, feta, Cheddar, Cheshire, Red Leicester, dolcelatte and many goats' cheeses, among others.

Executive Editor: Nicola Hill
Editor: Abi Rowsell
Additional Material: Maggie O'Hanlon
                    Chris McLaughlin
Executive Art Editor: Geoff Fennell
Designer: Sue Michniewcz
Production Controller: Jo Sim
Picture Researchers: Jennifer Veall
                    Christine Junemann

First published in Great Britain in 2002 by
Hamlyn, a division of Octopus Publishing Group Ltd
2-4 Heron Quays, London E14 4JP

ISBN 0 600 60851 4

A CIP catalogue record for this book is available
from the British Library

Printed and bound in China

10 9 8 7 6 5 4 3 2 1

SAFETY NOTE

All reasonable care has been taken in the preparation of this book but the information contained in *Food and Juice for Health* should not be considered a replacement for professional medical treatment; a physician should be consulted in all matters relating to health.

NUTRITIONAL INFORMATION ON PAGES 114–189

These boxes include the amount of calories, fat, carbohydrates and fibre per serving for each recipe. The fifth amount varies and is either calcium, iron or vitamin A, depending on which features significantly in the recipe.

The following is a list of recommended daily amounts (Reference Nutrient Intakes – RNI's) for the nutrients included. Use this information to assess how beneficial each recipe will be to your daily vitamin and nutrient requirements.
Calories: 1900–1940 Kcals/7942–8109 Kj (women)/ 2550 Kcals/10,659 Kj (men).
Fat: 71 g/3 oz (women)/ 93.5 g/3½ oz (men).
Carbohydrates: 253–258 g/8 oz (women)/ 340 g/ 11½ oz (men).
Fibre: 18–24 g/¾ –1 oz (women and men).
Vitamin A: 600 mg (women)/700 mg (men). Please note that the International Units (i.u.) amount is included for use by American readers.
Iron: 14.8 mg (women)/ 8.7 mg (men).
Calcium: 700 mg (women and men).

contents

introduction

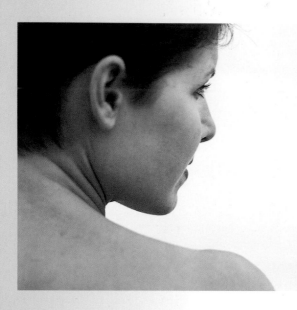

Being in good health means more than just not being ill. It is a positive state in which your body and mind are operating on full power so that you can face everything life throws at you with energy and optimism. Of course, there are bound to be times when, despite your best efforts, you do become ill or affected by stress and low moods; but, if you have been doing all you can to nurture yourself, you are likely to bounce back more quickly. What is more, by adapting your diet in such situations, you can help your body fight off illness. Of course, this does not mean you should avoid asking for help from your doctor or other health professionals at times when you really need it, but making the right lifestyle changes can often increase the effectiveness of any treatment they provide.

Above & below: A generally healthy lifestyle will safeguard you against many common ailments. Make sure you eat well and exercise daily for optimum wellbeing.

IN THE BEGINNING...

Increasingly, experts believe that many of the ills we suffer from in modern industrialized western societies are the result, in part at least, of the way we live. In particular, they point the finger at two main aspects: diet and physical activity – or, rather, lack of it. Millions of years of evolution have ensured that humans are well equipped to survive in an environment where food had to be obtained from a variety of sources – usually with the expenditure of considerable physical effort – and consumed with the minimum of preparation and cooking. Until recent times, exercise was not something you planned and fitted into your schedule when you could, but an unavoidable part of everyday life. Although most of us live very differently today, there has not been sufficient time for our bodies to adapt to the dramatic change in lifestyle, so it is no wonder that we suffer all manner of ills that would have been unfamiliar to our hard-living ancestors.

Thanks largely to modern medicine and improvements in hygiene, most of us can expect to enjoy much longer lifespans than earlier generations. Therefore we also need to do all we possibly can to protect ourselves from the physical consequences of ageing. In practice, this means looking at what we eat and drink and how our diets could be changed to meet our bodies' needs, and making physical activity a routine part of life instead of an occasional extra.

EATING FOR HEALTH

Devising a healthy eating plan is not rocket science; it just means following a few simple guidelines and accepting that this will be for life, not just a few weeks or months. The simplest way to ensure that you are eating a nutritionally sound diet is to think of your food intake in terms of a plate containing different kinds of food, such as starchy foods, fruit and vegetables, proteins and fats, in varying proportions.

starchy (carbohydrate) foods

These foods should make up the biggest portion on your plate: potatoes, wholegrain cereals, bread, pasta, rice, barley, couscous, oats and millet, for example. They are low in fat, high in fibre and rich in complex carbohydrates which are digested slowly and help sustain energy levels throughout the day.

fruit and vegetables

These should make up the next largest portion: they are low in fat, high in fibre and rich in vitamins, minerals and other plant chemicals which are believed to play an important part in preventing many illnesses common in industrialized societies, such as heart disease, diabetes and cancer.

protein

This is the third largest portion on your plate: meat, poultry, fish, lentils, pulses, dairy produce, eggs, nuts and seeds. Many of these foods are also good sources of vitamins and minerals such as calcium, iron and zinc.

Above & below: A healthy, varied diet includes foods from several different groups: cereals provide carbohydrate, fruit is rich in fibre, vitamins and minerals, and protein comes in many forms – if you wish to take the vegetarian option, lentils and pulses are a very good source.

fats

Some fat is essential, but fatty foods should make up no more than a third of your total calorie intake. Those derived from vegetable sources (polyunsaturated and monounsaturated) are a healthier option than the saturated fats in food from animal sources. Essential fatty acids, found in oily fish, nuts, seeds and vegetables, play a vital role in many bodily processes and can help protect against conditions such as heart disease.

vitamins and minerals

If you eat a varied diet, especially one that includes at least five portions of fruit and vegetables every day, you should not suffer from any serious vitamin or mineral deficiency. You may however, still not be taking in enough to resist infections and combat stress, pollution and ageing effects.

Above: Exercise needs to become an integral part of your day-to-day life. Even after a short time of following an exercise regime you will begin to see a difference in your health and fitness.

WHO NEEDS EXERCISE?

The answer is all of us, and making the necessary effort to build it into your life will soon pay enormous dividends. If exercise is not part of your regular routine at the moment, just look at what you could stand to gain by becoming more active:

● Even a short, brisk walk – one that leaves you slightly breathless and glowing at the end of it – will help your heart, circulation and lungs to work more efficiently.

● Better still, regular sessions of a more demanding exercise, such as jogging, aerobics, swimming or cycling, will strengthen your heart and lungs considerably and therefore make you less susceptible to cardiovascular diseases.

● Weight-bearing exercise, such as running, dancing, tennis or badminton, for example, helps to build bone mass and protect you against progressive bone loss which can result in osteoporosis.

● Activity that strengthens muscles and ligaments, including swimming and working with weights, will improve your stamina and help you to feel more energetic. You will also be less susceptible to back pain if the muscles in your back and abdomen are toned and strong.

● The more active you are, the greater the chances that your joints will remain mobile and flexible, so you will get fewer aches and pains and be less liable to injury.

● There is considerable research evidence that regular exercise is as effective as medication in relieving the symptoms of mild depression. A reasonably energetic session of physical activity can noticeably enhance your mood and sense of well-being, probably because it triggers the release of chemical messengers known as endorphins, the body's 'feel-good' chemicals.

● Whether you want to lose weight or just keep it under control, combining a healthy diet with regular exercise will be far more effective than diet alone. After a few weeks of exercising several times a week, you will notice a real improvement in your shape and a reduction in the amount of fat you are carrying.

● If you have a chronic condition, such as diabetes or high blood pressure, you will find it much easier to control if you combine regular exercise with the recommended changes to your diet and any medication prescribed by your doctor.

ailments

angina

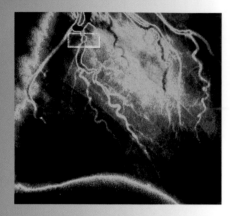

Above: Coloured angiogram showing the narrowing of a coronary artery highlighted by the yellow box (stenosis).

Although it is a warning of heart circulatory problems, angina is not a serious condition and only 2–4 per cent of cases a year progress to a heart attack. In many cases, angina can be managed by moderate adjustments to lifestyle and simple medication.

Angina is caused by a narrowing of the coronary arteries that supply the heart, which reduces the amount of blood that can flow through them, and results in an inadequate supply of oxygen to the heart muscle. The narrowing results from build-up of cholesterol deposits and the breakdown products of blood clots. The attacks most commonly occur when the heart is required to work harder than usual, for instance during periods of exercise, cold weather or strong emotion, or after large meals.

The characteristic pains of angina, although they are often severe and quite frightening, last only during the period of exercise and will disappear after a few minutes' rest, unlike the pain associated with a heart attack. The main symptom of angina is a tight, constricting pain over the heart, which typically radiates away from the heart, rising up the chest towards the jaw and often down the left arm as well. There can be odd variants, however, such as pain in one hand on exertion. Angina is more commonly found in men, although women are often affected after the menopause.

Causes of the condition include coronary heart disease and high blood pressure, both of which are exacerbated by smoking, excess weight and high cholesterol levels. Other possible causes include anaemia and diabetes.

For angina sufferers, lifestyle changes and treatment of the underlying causes are both important steps to be taken. Drugs that are used to control high blood pressure include vasodilators, which open up the arteries to the heart and thereby bring extra blood flow, and beta-blockers, which reduce the heart rate and force of contraction. Low-dose aspirin is thought to prevent heart attacks by reducing the blood's tendency to clot. Surgical options for angina include widening the narrowed coronary arteries by means of a technique called balloon angioplasty, which involves the insertion of a small tube called a stent, as well as bypass surgery.

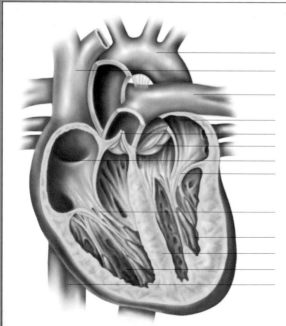

The heart

Aorta

Superior vena cava

Pulmonary artery

Left atrium
To lungs via pulmonary valve
To body via aortic valve
Right atrium
Mitral valve

Tricuspid valve

Left ventricle
Septum
Right ventricle
Inferior vena cava

eating for a healthy heart

All experts agree that the build-up of fatty deposits on the inner walls of the arteries is the cause of angina. This means that eating the right foods can really make a difference. It will certainly help to prevent the condition getting any worse, and may even improve it. Recent scientific discoveries have shown that certain foods and nutrients can help protect the heart and blood vessels against disease.

Perhaps the most important element in a diet designed to counter angina is a large intake of fresh fruit and vegetables, because these contain high levels of anti-oxidant vitamins (A, C and E). These 'mop up' free radicals – harmful molecules that damage the body's cells and play an important part in triggering narrowing of the arteries. You should also try to include foods containing the B group of vitamins in your diet every day. Recent research has shown that these may help to lower the level of an amino acid called homocysteine, which is thought to accelerate the oxidization of 'bad' cholesterol (or LDL). Try especially to include folic acid (found in liver, kidney, greens, fortified cereals and eggs), B_6 (in fish, egg yolks, wholegrain cereals, bananas, avocados, nuts and seeds) and B_{12} (in rye, sprouted seeds, pulses, eggs, kidneys, liver and milk).

As well as aiming to cut your overall fat intake, you should choose fats from non-animal sources (such as olive oil, sunflower and safflower oil and nut oils), and avoid 'trans-fats' – hydrogenated fats widely used in processed foods such as some margarines, biscuits, cakes and pies.

BENEFICIAL RECIPES & JUICES

Poached apricots with oatmeal cream
(see page 114)

•

Broccoli & red pepper fettuccine
(see page 134)

•

Watercress & mushroom frittata
(see page 154)

Apricot & pineapple smoothie
(see page 115)

•

Mixed vegetable juice
(see page 137)

•

Watercress, carrot & celery juice
(see page 157)

DIETARY TIPS

- Foods containing omega-3 fatty acids can help to prevent the accumulation of fatty deposits in the arteries – good sources are oily fish such as sardines, herrings, mackerel, salmon and tuna. Put them on your menu two or three times a week.

- 'Soluble' fibre can also help to lower levels of LDL; ideally, you should have six daily portions of fibre-rich foods including bread, cereal, pasta (all preferably wholegrain) and starchy vegetables.

- Onions and garlic contain compounds which help to tilt the balance in your body in favour of 'good' cholesterol (HDL) rather than LDL.

Above left: Nuts are a source of vitamin B_6 which helps lower levels of hymocysteine.

Below: Try to adapt your diet to include six daily portions of fibre-rich foods.

cardiovascular disease

The risk of atheroma can be reduced by stopping smoking, which increases the clotting tendencies of the blood, and lowering cholesterol levels. High blood pressure (see page 14) and diabetes (see page 36) exacerbate the problem and should be treated.

Most cardiovascular problems result from atherosclerosis, which is a degenerative disease caused by the accumulation of fatty deposits (mostly cholesterol), blood clots and their breakdown products on the inner walls of the arteries. These deposits (atheroma) narrow and weaken the artery walls, which may balloon out (aneurism) and eventually rupture. Alternatively, they may cause a complete blockage, either locally or, if they fragment, elsewhere in the arterial system.

- **stroke** is caused by obstruction of the carotid arteries supplying the brain. There is no proven treatment.

- **intermittent claudication**, or intermittent pain in the legs, typically in the calf, is caused by obstruction of the femoral arteries to the legs. The legs may feel cold and, in severe cases, the toes may develop gangrene. Regular exercise, which encourages the development of new small blood vessels, may help.

- **heart attack** is caused by obstruction of the coronary arteries. The first symptom is usually severe pain over the breastbone or left side of the chest which persists for many minutes or hours, accompanied by sweating and a grey complexion. Drug treatment includes aspirin and 'clot-busters', as well as ACE inhibitors and beta-blockers.

Below: Regular weight-bearing exercise, such as jogging, if not overdone, can boost the circulation of blood in the legs, and therefore may help in the prevention of some forms of cardiovascular disease.

- **heart failure** usually results from a heart attack. The reduced blood supply adversely affects the pumping action of the heart and damages the heart muscle. The most common symptoms of heart failure include tiredness, swollen ankles and breathlessness. In acute heart failure, the sufferer is breathless, coughs up frothy phlegm, and often turns blue. Drug treatment involves diuretics and, more recently, ACE inhibitors (see page 14).

   Other causes should be eliminated and treated if at all possible. Established obstructions can be treated surgically, for example by coronary artery bypass grafting or by replacing or bypassing the femoral arteries with man-made tubing.

a healthy eating plan

Doctors regard advice on the right kind of diet as a very important element in the care of people with cardiovascular disease because eating the right foods can help to prevent further build-up of fatty deposits in the arteries and make blood clots less likely to occur. The fatty deposits (atheroma) are made up of LDL combined with debris from cell waste, calcium and other substances. However, cholesterol in the form of HDL can help sweep these deposits away, so foods which raise levels in the body are beneficial – and among the most important are those containing omega-3 and omega-6 fatty acids.

The first type comes primarily from oily fish, while the second can be found in seeds and seed oils, such as hemp, flax, evening primrose and borage. Olive oil contains not only omega-6 but also oleic acid which has been found in some studies to protect against atherosclerosis. Oleic acid is also present in almonds and walnuts.

Anyone with a form of cardiovascular disease will be encouraged to eat lots of soluble fibre which, in practice, means pulses such as lentils and kidney beans, cereals such as rye, oats, barley and rice, and wholegrain cereals and foods made from them, such as bread and pasta. These are thought to have two main benefits: inhibiting the production of LDL in the body and increasing the proportion of fat that is excreted rather than absorbed. This type of food, together with fresh fruit and vegetables, should be the mainstay of a healthy diet, with red meat, fatty and sugary foods kept to a minimum.

Above: Oily fish are a very good source of the beneficial omega-3 fatty acids.

- Carrying excess weight is an important risk factor for cardiovascular disease, and also contributes to other risk factors such as raised blood pressure and type 2 diabetes. Shedding the pounds gradually and consistently by cutting out fatty and sugary foods, alcohol and processed foods, combined with increased physical activity, is a better approach than any kind of 'quick-fix' slimming diet.

- Drinks containing caffeine – such as coffee and cola – raise your blood pressure and are best avoided, especially if you prefer them sweetened with sugar.

- Most people consume far more salt than their bodies need, and a high intake has been linked with raised blood pressure. You can lower your intake easily if you stop adding it in cooking or at the table, and restrict your intake of salty foods and snacks.

Above left: Oils are a good source of omega-6 and oleic acid which can help to protect against atherosclerosis.

BENEFICIAL RECIPES & JUICES

Lemon & basil penne
(see page 124)

•

Mixed vegetable risotto
(see page 135)

•

Herrings with spinach & parmesan
(see page 180)

Apricot smoothie
(see page 115)

•

Watermelon & orange juice
(see page 127)

•

Wheatgerm, pineapple & banana
booster (see page 168)

high blood pressure (hypertension)

Above: Relaxation techniques, such as gentle forms of yoga, can be very helpful in reducing high blood pressure levels.

Hypertension is one of the most chronic health problems in western society, which suggests that it is linked in some way with lifestyle. Many self-help measures can be adopted, including:

- *Reducing excessive salt intake.*
- *Maintaining ideal weight.*
- *Relaxation techniques.*
- *Giving up smoking.*
- *Reducing cholesterol levels.*

Blood pressure is determined by the force and volume of the heart output at each beat and the resistance offered by the larger blood vessels. It reaches a maximum as the heart contracts (systole) and a minimum as the heart rests between beats (diastole). These pressures should be no more than 140mmHg (systolic) and 90mmHg (diastolic), depending on age and risk factors. High blood pressure, or hypertension, is a sustained rise above normal. Symptoms are rare and hypertension is often discovered during routine screening.

In 90 per cent of cases, there is no obvious underlying cause, although lifestyle factors play a role. Genetic and ethnic factors may also be involved; there is a higher incidence in Africans and it may run in families. In societies with a western-type diet and lifestyle, blood pressure rises with age. The remaining 10 per cent of cases have a recognizable cause, most commonly diabetes and other endocrine disorders, kidney disease, pregnancy and the side-effects of medication, for instance the contraceptive pill or steroids. Occasionally, hypertension can be caused by anatomical abnormalities or by rare hormonal disorders.

Prolonged hypertension can damage the arteries and lead to premature heart failure and stroke. Treatment involves lifestyle changes and, if necessary, the use of drugs. These include:

- **diuretics**, which cause the kidneys to eliminate excess fluid and reduce the resistance of the blood vessels.

- **beta-blockers**, which slow the heart rate and reduce the force of contraction of the heart muscle.

- **vasodilators**, which widen the arteries.

- **angiotensin-converting enzyme (ACE) inhibitors**, which act as both vasodilators and diuretics.

Usually lifelong treatment is required, although blood pressure sometimes returns to normal, typically on retirement, reduction of stress levels and loss of weight.

reducing blood pressure

When blood pressure is consistently higher than it should be, it puts a huge strain on your arteries. Their smooth lining becomes rough and their walls become thicker, so that they narrow and become less elastic. It is particularly important, therefore, to follow a diet that will not accelerate the build-up of fatty deposits (atheroma) inside the arteries, making them narrower still. Research has also linked high salt consumption with raised blood pressure.

Countering atheroma means eating lots of the foods which are rich in anti-oxidants, particularly beta-carotene (which the body uses to make vitamin A), vitamins C and E and the mineral selenium. Fresh fruit, salad and vegetables are the most important sources, as well as wheatgerm, nuts and seeds for vitamin E, so you should aim for at least five portions of these foods per day. The other food group which is especially important is oily fish – salmon, tuna, herrings, mackerel, sardines and pilchards, for example – as they contain essential fatty acids called omega-3, which have been found to have significant effects on blood pressure. As well as helping to lower it, they also help to clear away 'bad' cholesterol (LDL), reduce the blood's tendency to clot and have an anti-inflammatory effect. More generally, the ideal diet is one high in fibre – which means wholemeal cereals, pasta, rice and bread – and relatively low in saturated and trans-fats, found mainly in fatty meat, full-fat milk, dairy produce and processed foods such as cakes, biscuits and some margarines.

BENEFICIAL RECIPES & JUICES

Pan-fried oranges & bananas
(see page 116)

•

Brown rice pudding
(see page 171)

•

Lemon grass & tofu nuggets
(see page 185)

Avocado & banana smoothie
(see page 117)

•

Mixed fruit smoothie (see page 131)

•

Iron pick-me-up (see page 149)

•

Root juice (see page 159)

DIETARY TIPS

- Never add salt to your food – either at the table or when cooking.

- Reduce salty foods and snacks to a minimum. This includes processed meats, such as salami, bacon and ham, as well as salty snacks like crisps and salted nuts. Some processed foods such as soups, sauces and pickles also have a higher salt content than you might expect, so be cautious about these too.

- Eat foods that are rich in the mineral potassium, which helps your body get rid of salt – bananas are a particularly good source.

Below & left: If you need to increase your intake of anti-oxidants, eat plenty of fruit, vegetables and seeds.

haemorrhoids

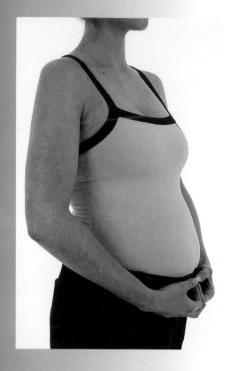

Above: Pregnancy tends to increase the pressure of blood in the abdomen, a condition that often causes the formation of piles.

Right: Constipation, which aggravates piles, can be alleviated by eating food rich in fibre and by drinking large amounts of fluids.

Mild piles are more of a nuisance than a serious problem and cause little in the way of symptoms. They are aggravated by the straining associated with constipation, so it is important to increase the amount of fibre in the diet and drink plenty of fluids.

Haemorrhoids, which are more popularly known as piles, are a common complaint. There are two types of haemorrhoids:

● **external piles**, which are visible swellings around the anus that can be felt with the fingers.

● **internal piles**, which are pillars of cushioning tissue supporting the rectum that cannot usually be felt.

Like varicose veins of the legs (see page 20), both types are veins that have become distended and varicosed. This is caused by a loss of elasticity in the veins of the anal canal and an increased pressure of blood in the abdomen. The latter is aggravated by prolonged standing, pregnancy, birth, or straining associated with chronic constipation (see page 82).

Symptoms include discomfort around the anus, itching, and sometimes bleeding or pain on defaecation. Piles are seldom a serious problem, unless they prolapse (drop through the anus). If this happens to internal piles, they become trapped by the muscles of the anus and cannot be pushed back inside. Prolapsed piles can be felt and seen as large tender swellings and may give rise to a mucous discharge. External piles may thrombose, meaning that the blood inside them clots.

Mild piles occasionally prolapse but are easily pushed back inside. No treatment is needed, apart from avoiding constipation. Prolapsed piles can be treated with rectal suppositories and creams which contain a local anaesthetic to reduce the swelling and pain. Occasionally a pile is so painful that it has to be cut open surgically to remove the blood.

The various treatments for severe piles cause the blood to clot inside the haemorrhoid, which then shrinks away. These include burning, gripping with rubber bands, freezing and injecting. However, the piles usually tend to recur and surgical removal may become necessary. Although painful, this treatment can effect a permanent cure.

reducing the risk

There are two major risk factors associated with this all-too-common problem: constipation and being overweight. Straining to pass a bowel movement raises the pressure inside your abdomen and this, in turn, causes the blood vessels around the anus to swell. Constipation is often the result of a low-fibre diet, although some medications, including certain painkillers, can cause it too. Extra weight can cause blood vessels to become compressed and losing weight may solve the problem; incidentally, this is why pregnancy piles usually disappear once the baby is born. Fortunately, both constipation and excess weight can be reduced dramatically by dietary change.

If you are making the change from a low- to a high-fibre diet, you should introduce new foods gradually, in order to give your digestive system time to adjust. Eat more fresh fruit and vegetables – unpeeled wherever possible, and raw or just lightly cooked or made into smoothies. Other high-fibre foods include pulses such as chickpeas, lentils and beans (including kidney, cannellini, butter and even baked beans). Opt for unrefined breakfast cereals, such as porridge oats, muesli and wheat biscuits, rather than sugary, refined ones. More fruit and vegetables will increase your intake of vitamin C; you can raise your consumption of vitamin E as well by eating more seeds, nuts and wheatgerm.

You will lose weight at a sensible rate if you follow a varied diet based on complex carbohydrates, vegetables and fruit, and including a minimum of fatty, sugary and processed foods.

Above: Dried chickpeas, high in fibre, should always be soaked before use.

Left: Beans of all kinds will provide another good source of fibre in your diet.

- Do not give up if your high-fibre diet gives you 'wind' at first; your system will adjust if you persevere.

- Make sure you drink plenty of water – around 2.5 litres (4 pints) a day if you can – to help keep your bowel contents bulky. Fibrous food needs more fluid to help it travel easily through your digestive system. Water used to make tea and coffee does not count – it is always better to have the water on its own.

- Chickpeas and the different varieties of beans are very economical if you buy them dried and soak before cooking, but canned ones are quicker to use and just as nutritious.

BENEFICIAL RECIPES & JUICES

Lentil, green peppercorn &
mustard dip (see page 160)
•
Nut & seed savoury cakes
(see page 172)
•
Cashew nut chicken
(see page 175)

Soothing tonic
(see page 157)
•
5-vegetable juice
(see page 163)
•
Wheatgerm tonic
(see page 169)

leg ulcers

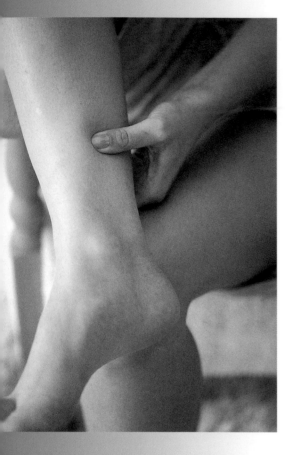

An ulcer is a breakdown of the outer layer of the skin which fails to heal within a few days. Broadly speaking, it is due to blood-flow deficiencies that create an oxygen-starved environment ripe for infection with bacteria. There are two types of leg ulcer:

- **venous ulcers** occur mainly on the lower leg and around the ankle. They have a raw core, with an irregular margin, and the surrounding skin becomes mottled from abnormal blood leakage. Venous ulcers usually result from some interference with the venous blood flow, for example by varicose veins or a previous deep-vein thrombosis. Because venous blood is both depleted of oxygen and contains waste products from the tissues, any stagnation can lead to tissue breakdown.

- **arterial ulcers** are also usually found on the legs and feet, but not around the ankles. They are smaller than venous ulcers and have sharply defined edges. They result from poor arterial blood flow caused, for example, by high blood pressure (see page 14), atherosclerosis or diabetes (see page 36).

Small ulcers can be treated with antiseptic cream, but they should be referred to a doctor if they persist. Ulcers must be kept clean with antiseptic solutions and should be treated with an antibiotic if there is a bacterial infection. A dressing that allows air to get to the ulcer and provides protection without sticking should be applied.

For venous ulcers, it is important to improve the blood flow by keeping the legs raised whenever possible and by wearing support stockings or bandages to compress the leg. Surgical treatment includes the removal of varicose veins and arterial grafts. It is also possible to apply skin grafts to resistant leg ulcers. In every case, the individual should keep active and eat a good diet to promote healing.

Above & below right: For venous leg ulcers, blood flow will be improved if you compress the affected area with a bandage, or wear a support stocking.

The high blood-sugar levels associated with diabetes eventually cause permanent damage to all blood vessels, including the small vessels of the legs, and blood flow to the legs may also be adversely affected. Consequently, diabetics are particularly prone to leg ulcers.

avoiding ulcers

Since leg ulcers generally result from problems with blood flow in both arteries and veins, it makes sense to adopt a diet that will aid the circulatory system. People who are susceptible because they have a chronic condition which increases their risk of developing ulcers (such as high blood pressure, atheroma and diabetes) will also need to take account of this factor and make the necessary adjustments to their diet.

Vitamin C has anti-oxidant properties, so it is worth increasing your consumption of citrus fruit and juices, kiwi fruit, strawberries, blackcurrants and green vegetables such as broccoli, kale and spring greens, for example. Vitamin E has similar benefits; you will get it from wheatgerm, nuts and seeds. Seeds, together with wholegrains and shellfish, are also good sources of zinc, which has beneficial effects on your blood.

All kinds of wholegrain foods, such as rice, bread, pasta and cereals, will boost your overall health. Together with other high-fibre foods such as lentils, pulses such as beans and chickpeas, and fruit and vegetables, they will help to counter a tendency to atheroma (fatty deposits in the arteries), especially as part of a low-fat diet.

If you have high blood pressure, consult the entry on this topic (see page 14), and pay particular attention to reducing the amount of salt you consume. People with diabetes need to ensure that their blood-glucose levels are well controlled – whether this be through a change in diet alone (see diabetes, page 36) or through a change in diet in conjunction with medication in the form of tablets or insulin injections.

Above: Nuts can often be very high in fat, but if you stick to the unsalted kind mixed with raisins you will increase their nutritional benefit.

- Cut down on refined and processed foods and substitute them with wholemeal and freshly prepared dishes as much as possible.

- If you need to lose weight, opt for juices made from vegetables such as carrots rather than fruit with a high sugar content, especially if you suffer from diabetes.

- Remember that, although nuts contain useful nutrients, they are relatively high in fat, so do not eat too many if you need to lose weight. Opt for the unsalted kind, especially if you have high blood pressure.

BENEFICIAL RECIPES & JUICES

Beetroot risotto
(see page 133)
●
Butter bean & tomato soup
(see page 161)
●
Mung bean & herb risotto
(see page 170)

Chicken with 40 garlic cloves
(see page 158)
●
Juice medley
(see page 159)
●
Root juice
(see page 159)

varicose veins

Varicose veins are the price we pay for standing upright. Because veins are part of a low-pressure system for returning stale blood to the heart, they are not very sturdy. Nonetheless they have to cope with a much greater pressure of blood than those of an animal that walks on all fours. As a result, their walls become stretched and distorted, forming the familiar wormlike varicosities of the legs. Anything that interferes with the return of blood through the veins, such as prolonged standing, pregnancy, constipation and excess weight, will tend to increase the pressure and therefore the predisposition to varicose veins. Varicose veins also tend to run in families, or may happen some years after a deep-vein thrombosis.

Although varicose veins are most common in the legs, especially in women, they can also occur in the oesophagus, scrotum, rectum, anus (see haemorrhoids, page 16) and vulva. The unsightly grapelike veins or flare veins may be purely a cosmetic problem. However, if there is weakness of the valves in the deep veins, or at the entrance to the deep systems, backflow into the superficial vein system occurs. Symptoms of this venous insufficiency include prominent distended veins, aching in the calves, swelling and discoloration of the leg, dry, flaky and irritable skin (varicose eczema) and a tendency to ulcers. Occasionally a varicose vein may rupture and bleed heavily.

Varicose veins of pregnancy disappear after delivery, and mild varicose veins may be relieved by losing weight. In other cases, wearing support stockings may help, but surgery may eventually be necessary. There are two main approaches: stripping out the varicose veins from groin to ankle or tying off the veins that supply deeper veins. Whatever the surgery, varicose veins tend to recur unless lifestyle changes, such as losing weight and avoiding standing, are made.

Above: Whenever you can, take the weight off your feet in order to relieve the pressure on the veins in your legs.

the right diet

As varicose veins are the result of sluggish blood flow, you may be able to alleviate the problem by eating foods which help to tone and stimulate the circulatory system and encourage blood to flow more freely. Because excess weight increases the pressure on internal organs, it can encourage the development of varicose veins, particularly around the anus (see also haemorrhoids, page 16), so it makes good sense to lose weight if this seems to be necessary.

Onions, garlic, eggs and asparagus are all rich in sulphur and appear to have a beneficial effect on blood by reducing its tendency to clot, so it is worth including more of them in your diet whenever you can. Zinc-rich foods, such as shellfish, wholegrains and seeds, will help boost your overall wellbeing, as small quantities of this mineral are required in over 200 body functions, including growth and wound healing. A balanced and varied diet which is based around fibre-rich foods, fruit, vegetables and juices may also help to slow the development of varicose veins. Vitamin C and flavonoids are especially important as they help to strengthen the walls of your blood vessels: so focus on getting plenty of fruit, particularly kiwi fruit, strawberries and citrus fruit; or try making your own juices for a change. Provided that you eat moderate portions and steer clear of high-fat and sugary foods, you should begin to lose weight at a healthy rate, especially if you become more physically active at the same time.

DIETARY TIPS

- Drink lots of water every day – 2.5 litres (4 pints) is the target you should aim for. Remember that using it to make tea and coffee does not count since these drinks are diuretic; in other words, they encourage fluid loss from the body.

- Constipation makes varicose veins more likely, especially in the form of haemorrhoids, so avoid this by eating extra fibre.

- Pregnant women are susceptible to varicose veins because of the pressure exerted on internal organs by the growing baby. Vitamin B_6 may help: good sources include cheese, eggs, peppers, apricots, dates and dried figs.

Above left: Asparagus is a rich source of sulphur which helps to prevent blood clotting.

Below: Drinking plenty of fluids, such as pure mineral water, is essential.

BENEFICIAL RECIPES & JUICES

Spiced orange & avocado salad
(see page 125)

•

Fresh lime sorbet
(see page 126)

•

Nut & seed savoury cakes
(see page 172)

Lemon rice & wild rice salad
(see page 174)

•

Orange & raspberry juice
(see page 127)

•

Root juice
(see page 159)

gout

Above: An early symptom of a gout attack is sudden pain in a joint which will then become swollen.

Right: Excess alcohol may induce an attack.

People with gout nearly always have an inherited tendency to high blood levels of uric acid, although certain drugs, notably diuretics used to treat high blood pressure, may also increase uric acid levels. Less common causes are disorders that increase cell turnover, and therefore protein load, such as certain forms of leukaemia.

Gout is caused by an excess of uric acid in the blood. Uric acid, which is a by-product of protein digestion, is usually excreted in the urine. However, if there is too much uric acid in the blood, it may be deposited as crystals inside the joints. People with a tendency to gout may find that an excess of rich foods or too much alcohol brings on an attack, possibly by generating more uric acid in the body than it can handle.

Gout occurs most commonly in middle-aged men and is very unusual in women. In young people, it may indicate an underlying blood disorder. The earliest symptom is usually sudden and extreme pain in one joint, most often the big toe, although the knees, elbows or shoulders can also be affected. The joint then becomes swollen, hot and inflamed, and painful on the slightest movement. The pain can last for several days. After repeated attacks, the joints become stiff and misshapen. If the condition is not treated, crystals can also be precipitated within the earlobes and the tissues around the joints, and in the kidneys, affecting their efficiency. Such complications are unusual nowadays, as the condition can be recognized in the early stages. The treatment is straightforward and pain relief, using anti-inflammatory drugs, is the first priority. Some adjustments to lifestyle may be sensible, such as reducing alcohol intake and eating fewer protein-rich foods.

Most people have only occasional attacks. If the attacks are frequent, however, or if there is kidney damage or persistently high uric acid levels, long-term treatment is usually advisable. The main drug used for this is allopurinol, which increases the output of uric acid in the urine by making it more water-soluble.

eating to avoid gout

People with gout are often unjustly suspected of over-indulging in alcohol and rich food, but, although this is unfair, diet and alcohol can make the symptoms worse or increase the frequency of attacks. In fact, many people are able to keep the condition more or less under control just by modifying their diet, meaning that they do not need to take medication on a regular basis.

Green, leafy vegetables such as spinach, cabbage, greens and the like are helpful, partly because of their vitamin C content but also because they contain folic acid which helps to control the level of uric acid in the blood. Vitamin C is important because it promotes the elimination of uric acid from the bloodstream via the urine. Fresh fruit and vegetables, especially watercress, celery, grapefruit, beetroot, pineapple and cherries, are all beneficial for people with gout, as are all high-fibre foods including lentils, but not other pulses such as beans and peas. However, very sweet fruit such as grapes should be eaten only in moderation, as too much fructose (fruit sugar) can actually increase the levels of uric acid.

Even more important than eating the right foods is avoiding those which exacerbate the condition. This means cutting down or avoiding entirely those which are high in purine: offal (such as liver and kidneys, including liver pâtés), red meat, fish, shellfish, oats, foods containing yeast, mushrooms and alcohol. You should also cut down on refined carbohydrates, sugar, fried foods and coffee and, if necessary, follow a weight-reducing diet, as excessive pounds make the condition worse.

BENEFICIAL RECIPES & JUICES

Spiced beetroot (see page 132)
•
Colcannon (see page 138)
•
Spinach & broccoli soup (see page 147)
•
Quick spinach (see page 146)

Chilled watercress soup (see page 155)
•
Kale & wheatgrass energizer (see page 141)
•
Iron pick-me-up (see page 149)

DIETARY TIPS

- Drink as much water as you can, but not in the form of coffee. Fluid intake is especially important in hot weather or during bouts of vigorous exercise, as dehydration may trigger an attack of gout.

- Raw vegetable juices would make a helpful addition to your diet as an alternative to fruit juices, which may contain a lot of unwelcome fructose (fruit sugar).

- Remember that vinegar may have a similar effect on your system to alcohol, so try substituting lemon juice in salad dressings.

- Vegetarians are known to be less susceptible to gout, so you may want to consider changing to a meat- and fish-free diet if your symptoms are regularly troublesome.

Above: Watercress is particularly rich in vitamin C, and therefore good for gout.

Above left: Fresh pineapple is also extremely beneficial for this condition.

Both the common cold and flu are caused by viruses and, because new strains of viruses are constantly emerging, people seldom develop any immunity. Children are more vulnerable than adults, and so are people who live or work in conditions where the virus can spread rapidly.

In the early stages, it is difficult to distinguish between a cold and flu. A cold begins with a sore throat, tiredness, aching muscles and fever, although the individual also feels cold and shivery. After 2–3 days, the nose begins to run and there is sneezing and coughing. Most colds last for 7–10 days, although it is not unusual to cough for a week or two afterwards. Children are more vulnerable to secondary infections, especially of the ear and chest. Adults sometimes develop inflamed sinuses (see sinusitis, page 28).

The early symptoms of flu are aching muscles, sometimes also with painful backache and headache, and high fever accompanied by intense shivering. A sore throat and cough often develop after a few days; unlike with colds, however, there is no sneezing or runny nose. Recovery from flu is fairly gradual, taking around 5–7 days, but post-flu tiredness may last for a period of several weeks. Occasionally, flu can lead to a serious chest infection and in extreme cases to confusion.

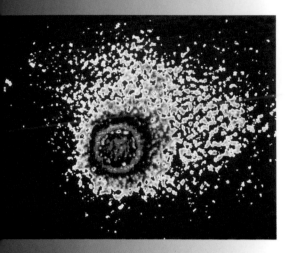

Above: A coloured transmission electron micrograph (TEM) of a rhinovirus, the cause of common cold and other respiratory diseases. Rhinoviruses are spread in the air by droplets produced by coughing and sneezing.

Right: A coloured TEM of an influenza virus.

Opposite top: Citrus fruit such as oranges are full of vitamin C, good for boosting your immune system and fighting off infections.

Opposite bottom: Making a juice using your favourite fruit and vegetables is the perfect way to ensure your daily diet is receiving all the essential nutrients and vitamins.

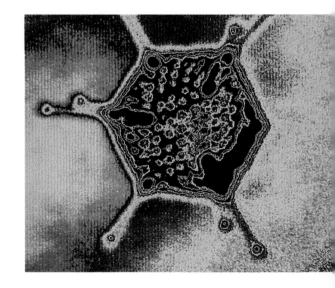

For people in a high-risk group, such as diabetics, flu vaccination is advisable. It is now offered to everyone over the age of 65 and should be considered by anyone working in an institution for the elderly or sick. The vaccine carries little risk but, because it is made from egg protein, should be avoided by anyone who is allergic to eggs.

The treatment is to rest, keep warm and drink plenty of fluids. Take aspirin (except in the case of young children) in order to reduce the fever, or paracetomol to relieve aches and pains. Over-the-counter cold cures are usually a combination of painkiller and caffeine (to lift the spirits). They may also contain a drug to relieve the runny nose and antihistamine to aid sleep and relieve stuffiness. Antibiotics are only advisable in the case of secondary infections, and in occasional cases hospital treatment may be necessary if the complications become serious.

boosting your resistance

We all get a cold from time to time, but you may be able to boost your resistance to cold viruses by eating plenty of the foods which enhance your immune system. In particular, ensure that your diet is rich in foods that contain high levels of vitamin A (or its precursor, beta-carotene) and vitamin C.

Beta-carotene, which is used in the body to make vitamin A, is found in all red, yellow and orange fruit and vegetables, especially apricots, oranges, pumpkins, sweet potatoes, carrots and red peppers, vegetables such as broccoli and salad greens like watercress.

In order to boost your vitamin C intake, opt for citrus fruit and juices, blackcurrants, strawberries, blueberries and, especially, kiwi fruit – you can combine it with other fruit in a juice if you do not enjoy it on its own. Leafy green vegetables and broccoli are also good sources, but eat them as soon after purchase as possible as the vitamin content diminishes with time. Steam or boil them for a short time to conserve vitamin C.

Garlic is said to help your immune system resist infections, so add it to stews, salad dressings, sauces or meat such as lamb whenever you can.

If you are unlucky enough to get a cold or – even worse – flu, you may not feel like eating much for a few days. However, fruit juices or hot drinks made with lemon juice, honey and water may help both to soothe your throat and to keep up your fluid intake.

DIETARY TIPS

- Some experts believe that very high intakes of vitamin C may not only help to ward off colds and flu but also shorten their duration if you do succumb to an infection. However, the suggested amounts are so high that you may not be able to reach them without taking plenty of vitamin supplements.

- Vitamins may be more effective when consumed in their natural form – that is, in fruit, vegetables and so on – because their action is enhanced by other substances which are not found in supplements, such as flavonoids.

- Complementary therapists sometimes advise avoiding milk and other dairy produce when you have a cold, on the grounds that they encourage the production of mucus; so you may like to try cutting them out while you have symptoms.

BENEFICIAL RECIPES & JUICES

Cranberry chicken stir-fry with ginger
(see page 119)

•

Cabbage bhaji
(see page 139)

•

Chunky carrot & lentil soup
(see page 142)

Breakfast smoothie
(see page 121)

•

Cabbage & carrot juice
(see page 141)

•

Red pepper & tomato tonic
(see page 145)

fever

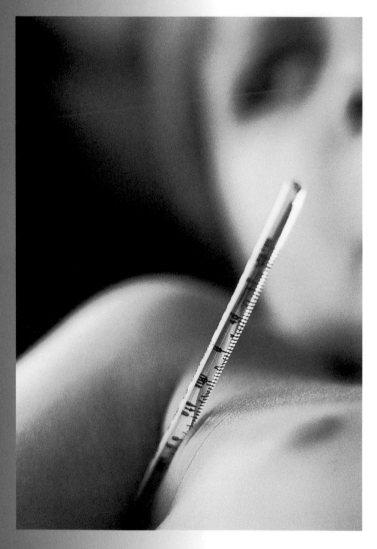

Above: The presence of a fever can be quickly confirmed by taking the sufferer's temperature with a domestic thermometer.

A rapid, high rise in temperature may provoke a febrile fit. This is a common and potentially serious hazard for children. However, fits are not dangerous if they last for less than 10 minutes, and they are linked with epilepsy in only 2–4 per cent of cases.

A body temperature of more than 37°C (98.6°F) is classed as a fever. This is an indicator of an illness, not an illness itself. Fevers that develop rapidly are usually a sign that the body is battling with an infection. The infection triggers the release of a substance called pyrogen from the defensive white blood cells. The hypothalamus of the brain then responds to the pyrogen by raising the body temperature. If the body wins the battle, the fever subsides. If the infection wins, symptoms of an illness appear. The length of the battle (the incubation period) varies: for example, from 2–4 days for the common cold to 18–21 days for chickenpox.

Unexplained fever lasting more than a week is known as pyrexia of unknown origin (PUO) and presents a major diagnostic challenge. It may be due to illnesses with a long incubation period, such as hepatitis A or unusual types of pneumonia, or tuberculosis, heart infection or chronic abdominal abscesses. In these days of foreign travel, malaria, typhoid or leishmaniasis are also a consideration. Non-infectious causes include tissue damage and autoimmune conditions, such as rheumatoid arthritis.

Common symptoms of fever include hotness, shivering and sweating, regardless of what the surrounding temperature might be. Drenching sweats may occur during the night as well. There may also be muscular aches, pains in the eyes and headache.

Although fevers may be regarded as beneficial, treatment will help improve comfort and rest, and decrease aching. Fanning, sponging with lukewarm water, removing clothing and sleeping beneath a light cotton sheet all help to reduce fever. This is particularly important for children. Aspirin is ideal for adults (but not suitable for children under 12) and paracetamol is safe for all ages. Ibuprofen is equally effective and is safe for children. In addition to these measures, the cause of the fever should be treated appropriately.

When you have a fever, you are likely to have other symptoms as well, depending on what has caused your temperature to rise. Very often, however, the underlying problem is a viral infection, such as a cold or flu, and you may not feel much like eating. While adults generally will come to no harm if they do not eat much for a day or two, it is important to keep up your fluid intake, and you may well feel a little better if you can manage to eat something.

When you simply cannot face solid food, fruit and vegetable juices make an excellent alternative. They taste good, they are easy to get down and, above all, they are rich in important vitamins and other nutrients that will speed your recovery. Some flavours may appeal more than others, but try to choose combinations that will provide a good mix of the ACE vitamins (beta-carotene, vitamin C and vitamin E). These are the so-called anti-oxidant vitamins which help to counter the damage caused by free radicals, and which will boost your resistance to illness.

Once you are feeling a bit better, you could try eating some of the same fruit and vegetables in their whole forms, raw or lightly cooked. Apricots, mangoes, carrots, sweet potatoes, red peppers, watercress and broccoli are all good sources of beta-carotene (vitamin A); citrus fruit, blackcurrants, strawberries, kiwi fruit, broccoli and other green vegetables are rich in vitamin C. Onions and garlic are also said to be helpful in fighting infection, so think about putting those on the menu too.

Above: Fruit and vegetable juices are ideal for getting the necessary nutrients and vitamins into your system when you can't face swallowing anything solid.

- As your temperature begins to drop, opt for light, easily digested meals, but steer clear of fatty or fried foods.

- When your appetite is limited, it is best to concentrate on eating nutritionally rich foods and not to fill yourself up with refined or processed foods that may have few nutritional benefits.

- It is important to take in plenty of fluids, but juices and herbal teas are better for you than caffeine-loaded drinks, such as tea, coffee and cola, or sweet fizzy drinks.

BENEFICIAL RECIPES & JUICES

Poached apricots with oatmeal cream
(see page 114)
•
Chicken with 40 garlic cloves
(see page 158)
•
Spiced orange & avocado salad
(see page 125)

Blueberry & grapefruit juice
(see page 122)
•
Cranberry & mango smoothie
(see page 123)
•
Watermelon & orange juice
(see page 127)

sinusitis

The sinuses are air-filled cavities which are situated within the bone of the face and lined with mucous membranes. Mucus flows through tiny air ducts from these cavities to the nose. Sinusitis is the inflammation of the lining of these cavities. This condition is most commonly caused by a bacterial infection that develops as a complication of a virus infection, for instance the common cold (see page 24). It may also be caused by hay fever or other types of allergy, by tooth abscesses in the upper jaw, or by nasal polyps.

As a result of this inflammation, the sinus lining swells and the channels that drain the sinus may become blocked, resulting in a build-up of mucus and pressure in the sinuses. This can be painful and may be accompanied by fever, blurred vision and swelling of the face. Typically, there is nasal congestion and a greenish yellow discharge from the nose although, in the case of allergy or hay fever, there is a very runny nose as well as streaming, puffy eyes. These symptoms are frequently accompanied by a headache and loss of the sense of smell. There may also be pain experienced around the eyes. A complete blockage of the sinuses will prevent drainage of the nasal passage.

Most cases of sinusitis last little longer than a week. Over-the-counter medicines, such as decongestant sprays, aspirin or paracetomol, will usually help to relieve the symptoms. Vaporizers or steam inhalations can also help by thinning the secretions so that they are able to drain more easily. If allergy or hay fever is thought to be the cause, antihistamines are used, but bacterial infections may require antibiotic treatment. In extreme cases, it may be necessary to wash out the sinuses, a procedure that is usually carried out under local or general anaesthetic. Polyps can be removed by endoscopic instruments.

Below: Blocked sinuses can cause the sufferer a range of unpleasant symptoms, such as nasal congestion, blurred vision and headaches.

the importance of diet

This nasty condition could be caused by an infection, in which case you will want to boost your intake of foods that help your immune system to destroy the virus or bacterium that is responsible. However, it can also be related to an allergic condition, such as hay fever, perennial rhinitis or asthma,

or a sensitivity to specific foods. In such instances, you will need to try to identify the foods which are causing the reaction, so that you can cut them out of your diet.

Foods with a high zinc content will help your body to fight off infection: good sources are shellfish, meat (including offal), eggs, wholegrains, seeds, nuts, carrots, turnips and molasses. You can also boost your resistance to infection by eating lots

of red, yellow and orange fruit and vegetables, which are high in beta-carotene, including more unusual ones such as pumpkin, sweet potatoes and mangoes, for example. You should not miss out on vitamin C either, especially if your sinusitis follows a cold, as a high intake of this vitamin may help to ease your symptoms. Choose blackcurrants, strawberries, citrus fruit, kiwi fruit and plenty of green vegetables.

If your sinusitis is related to an allergy of some kind, the list of possible suspect foods will be very long, and it may take time to identify the ones that affect you. Among the most common 'allergens' are wheat and other cereals, dairy produce, shellfish and citrus fruit.

BENEFICIAL RECIPES & JUICES

*Stir-fried broccoli with sesame seeds
(see page 136)*

•

*Nut & seed savoury cakes
(see page 172)*

•

*Griddled liver & bacon with grilled
potatoes (see page 179)*

*Carrot & banana booster
(see page 143)*

•

*Carrot & kiwi juice
(see page 143)*

•

*Spicy tomato juice
(see page 153)*

DIETARY TIPS

- Bear in mind that some hay-fever sufferers also react to foods which are related to the specific pollen that triggers their symptoms (see hay fever, page 54).

- Keeping a food and symptom diary for a few weeks may help you to identify particular foods or groups of foods which set off your sinusitis.

- If you are excluding certain food groups – such as dairy produce – from your diet, you must take care that you are not missing out on any vital nutrients. Get expert advice if you are in doubt.

Above: When undertaking an exclusion test to detect which foods, such as dairy produce, may be causing a reaction, make sure that you are still receiving all the vital vitamins and nutrients.

Above left: Increase your levels of beta-carotene by eating plenty of red fruit and vegetables, such as beetroot.

asthma

Factors that are known to trigger asthma include certain drugs, such as beta-blockers and anti-inflammatories, and allergies, particularly to dust and dead skin cells, but also to food, pollen and animal fur. Vigorous activity and changes in temperature may also provoke an attack.

Asthma is an increasingly common chronic disease of the respiratory system which now affects about 10–15 per cent of all children, as well as a high percentage of adults. Although there is no identifiable cause for some cases of asthma, others are probably related to increased air pollution and other factors that irritate the lining of the lungs.

A common early symptom is a persistent cough and a little wheezing, especially at night. In an acute attack, which can be quite dramatic, there is increasing wheeziness and breathlessness, a feeling of tightness around the chest and a struggle for air. This is caused by a tightening of the muscular walls of the small airways (bronchioles), which narrows the airways and consequently obstructs the flow of air into and out of the lungs. This causes mucus to collect, which makes the obstruction worse. The characteristic dry cough occurs as the body attempts to clear the airways.

There are three approaches to treatment:

- **removal of irritants** Asthma sufferers should not smoke and should avoid smoky atmospheres. Assiduous dusting and the use of vacuum cleaners with special dust filters will prevent the build-up of dust and dust mites in the house.

- **prevention** Inhaled steroid drugs go straight into the lungs where they reduce the sensitivity of the lung lining. The non-steroid drug cromoglycate, which works in the same way, may be effective for some people.

- **acute treatment** Drugs called bronchodilators act directly on the muscular walls of the airways, forcing them to relax and thus opening up the airways. These drugs are taken by inhaler, by injection, by nebulizer or in tablet form.

Below: False colour scanning electron micrograph (SEM) of a pollen grain of the garden hollyhock, *Althaea rosea*. Grains such as these can cause immense discomfort to hay-fever sufferers during the summer months.

Right: An asthma attack can usually be alleviated quite quickly through the use of an inhaler or a nebulizer.

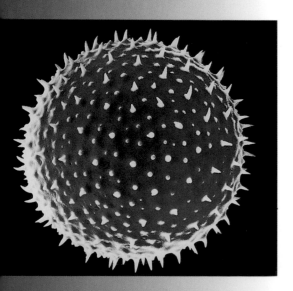

asthma and diet

Although some people with asthma believe that allergies to particular foods can trigger their attacks, most doctors believe this applies to no more than 2–3 per cent of people with the condition. A true allergy is one which produces a measurable response from the immune system and, while this may be relatively rare, food may sometimes affect people with asthma in other ways. If your doctor agrees that a food allergy may be implicated, it is possible to be tested, but the results are not always reliable. The only other way of finding out is systematically to exclude suspect foods from your diet and observe your body's response, but this process is difficult and time-consuming and needs to be carried out very carefully to avoid the risk of missing out on essential nutrients.

You should aim to follow a healthy eating programme, making sure that you eat a good variety of fruit and vegetables every day. This will ensure a good intake of the anti-oxidant vitamins A, C and E which help to fight free radicals. These chemicals are formed in the body in response partly to cigarette smoke and other pollutants and can play a part in triggering inflammation in the airways. Vitamin C may also promote good lung health and help the airways to resist narrowing. Researchers who found that eating five or more apples a week was associated with improved lung function suggested that this might result from high levels of an anti-oxidant called quercitin. As well as in apples and other hard fruit, it is found in onions, tea and red wine.

Above: Dark green vegetables, such as broccoli, can provide magnesium.

Left: Apples contain quercetin, thought to be of value to asthma sufferers.

- Magnesium may help relax the airways; asthma sufferers with low levels of this mineral may be more susceptible to attacks. Dark green vegetables, courgettes, peas, fish and sunflower seeds are good sources.

- People with asthma seem more prone to heartburn which, besides being unpleasant in itself, may trigger an attack. This probably happens because the irritated nerves in the oesophagus set off a narrowing of the airways. For how to deal with heartburn, see page 88.

- You are likely to have more attacks of asthma if you are overweight, because of your muscles' increased demand for oxygen and because the strain on your organs may make breathing in sufficient oxygen more difficult (see obesity, page 44).

BENEFICIAL RECIPES & JUICES

Strawberry & cucumber salad
(see page 118)

•

Lemon & basil penne
(see page 124)

•

Greens soup
(see page 140)

Apricot & pineapple smoothie
(see page 115)

•

Horseradish pick-me-up
(see page 127)

•

Carrot, apple & ginger juice
(see page 143)

bronchitis

Chronic bronchitis is a long-term condition resulting from constant irritation of the lungs. This is most often caused by cigarette smoking and its associated tars, but air pollution, coal and brick dust, and viruses or bacteria may also be responsible. These irritants stimulate the lining of the small airways of the lungs which respond by producing large quantities of mucus. This sticky material traps dust particles, which are then swept away by specialized cells from the narrowest parts of the lungs to the gullet, where the mucus can either be swallowed or spat out. Over decades, greater and greater quantities of mucus are produced, leading to a persistent cough. In addition, the airways narrow, causing wheezing and breathing difficulties.

The early symptoms are a persistent cough and constant bringing up of mucus. Eventually, the cough becomes permanent and there is constant breathlessness that may even put a strain on the heart.

At the earliest signs of bronchitis, it is important to give up smoking straight away and to avoid irritating dusts. This is essential in order to avoid further deterioration, although the damage that has already been done cannot be repaired.

Treatment includes the use of one of the several types of gas inhaler. These contain drugs called bronchodilators that relax the muscles in the walls of the airways, thus improving the passage of air. Inflammation of the airways can be relieved by steroids. These drugs can also be given via a nebulizer. If an underlying infection is present, it may be necessary to resort to antibiotics. If breathing is severely impaired, it may even be necessary to provide oxygen cylinders. To avoid any complications involving the lungs, flu vaccinations may be recommended.

Cypress, eucalyptus and tea tree oils, used as inhalations or chest rubs, help to free the mucus and clear the airways.

Above: Children can be just as susceptible to bronchitis as adults, and usually respond well to treatment using a gas inhaler.

Right: This illustration shows how in chronic bronchitis the airways of the lungs over-produce mucus.

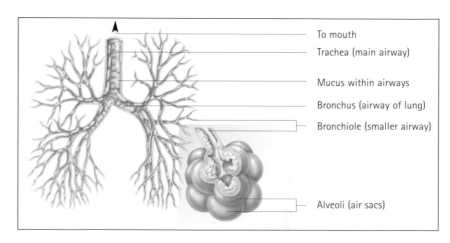

To mouth

Trachea (main airway)

Mucus within airways

Bronchus (airway of lung)

Bronchiole (smaller airway)

Alveoli (air sacs)

This can be a debilitating condition and, although what you eat cannot cure it, your diet can help to keep you in the best possible condition to cope with the symptoms. You need to build up your strength, energy and resistance to infection – the best way to do this is to eat a healthy diet with plenty of wholefoods, vegetables and fruit and a minimum of refined, sugary and fatty foods. The most important requirement is to eat plenty of foods that are rich in vitamins and minerals, especially beta-carotene (vitamin A), vitamin C and zinc, because these nutrients will provide overall health benefits at the same time as boosting your immune system.

For beta-carotene, opt for orange, red and yellow fruit and vegetables – including apricots, mangoes, citrus fruit, carrots, sweet potatoes, pumpkins and red peppers – avocados, green vegetables such as broccoli and cabbage, meat, offal, and wholegrains. Foods that are rich in vitamin C include citrus fruit (especially the peel and pith), bananas, pineapples, blackcurrants, kiwi fruit, apricots, strawberries, cabbage, carrots and offal. If you have never been much of a fruit and vegetable fan, you may enjoy them more when they are combined in delicious juices.

There is evidence that quercetin, a substance found in hard fruit such as apples and pears, as well as in tea, red wine and onions, may help to improve lung function. You should try to eat plenty of zinc-rich foods, because a low level may increase your susceptibility to infection; good sources include shellfish, wholegrains and seeds.

Above: Yellow fruit, such as apricots, contain good amounts of beta-carotene (vitamin A) to boost your immune system.

- Some people believe that milk and other dairy produce can increase mucus in the lungs and, while there is no scientific evidence for this, you might wish to try cutting them out to see whether it helps. However, if you do so for more than a short time, make sure you have alternative sources of calcium in your diet.

- Steer clear of sugar and sugary foods that have no nutritional value and can contribute to weight gain.

- Fatty and fried foods are not good for your general health, and also make it more likely that you will be overweight, so putting unnecessary strain on your lungs.

BENEFICIAL RECIPES & JUICES

Mixed vegetable risotto
(see page 135)

•

Roasted pepper soup
(see page 144)

•

Penne with chicken livers
(see page 178)

Banana & almond smoothie
(see page 117)

•

Green vegetable juice
(see page 137)

•

Sweet & sour smoothie
(see page 145)

chronic fatigue
syndrome

The term chronic fatigue syndrome (CFS) is preferable to myalgic encephalomyelitis (ME), which implies some understanding of this condition. This is not the case. There seems to be no single cause of CFS, although viral infection may trigger it. Glandular fever virus is a prime suspect, but there is no evidence to prove this. Current research is directed at abnormal cell metabolism and the hypothalamic/pituitary axis, but no firm conclusions have yet been drawn.

It is clear that prolonged tiredness after a viral infection may acquire psychological overtones. In short, although a physical event may trigger CFS, it is almost certainly psychological factors that prolong it. The agreed criteria for CFS are at least six months of fatigue associated with inability to function at work or at home, often accompanied by muscle aches and irritability. Tiredness characteristically alternates with bursts of activity, which result in increased fatigue and muscle pain. There are often sleep and mood disturbances but no true depression. A full medical examination and comprehensive blood tests to rule out diabetes, thyroid disease and hormonal disturbances are necessary to make the diagnosis acceptable.

Before treatment can proceed, both doctor and patient must accept that there is a problem. Until a cause is recognized, the current thinking is for patients to accept that their own psychological approach is the key to overcoming the problem. To begin with, the patient should identify possible contributory factors, such as work, relationships and general dissatisfaction with life. A level of activity should be agreed on that is sufficient to stimulate but not enough to exhaust. This replaces the vicious circle of rest and activity. Sleeping during the day is discouraged in the interests of getting a better night's rest. Drugs used to treat CFS include antidepressants and modern selective serotin reuptake inhibitors (SSRIs), which have a slight stimulant effect.

Surveys suggest that up to 1 in 200 people suffers from chronic fatigue syndrome. Many more have similar symptoms but accompanied by clinical depression.

- *It is most common in women between the ages of 20 and 40.*
- *About 70 per cent have not recovered after a year.*
- *Children recover faster than adults.*

Below: Gentle massage helps to relieve aching muscles and joints and relax your whole body and mind, allowing you to function more consistently and effectively.

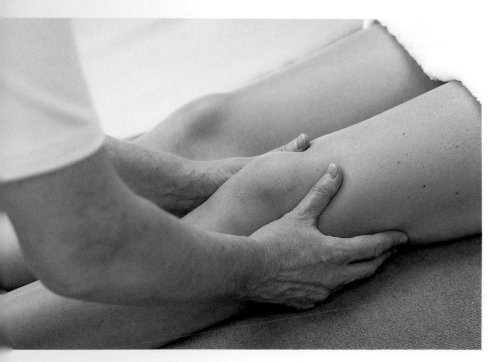

eating to replenish energy

People with CFS often receive contradictory dietary advice from different health professionals. This may be partly because the condition – and how best to treat it – are not yet fully understood, and partly because different approaches work for different people. As you will almost certainly know if you are a sufferer, finding out what works for you can be time consuming and may vary during different phases of the condition.

As a general rule, you will probably need a nutrient-dense diet to replenish your energy stores, so do not fill yourself up with refined and processed foods, especially if your appetite is limited, as they have a relatively low nutritional content. Biscuits, cakes, pastries and all sugary and fatty or fried foods are best avoided, so you can concentrate on eating foods that will benefit you as well as stimulating your taste buds.

Wholegrain foods, such as pasta, bread, rice and cereals, fruit, vegetables, lentils, beans and other pulses, should be the mainstays of your diet, but you may need to supplement them with fish and some animal protein. Meat, including offal, and poultry will provide this, along with important vitamins and minerals, and regular meals including oily fish, such as salmon, mackerel, herrings and pilchards, will ensure that you get a good intake of the essential fatty acid (EFA) omega-3. Omega-6, the other important EFA, is found mainly in seeds and seed oils, and in olive oil. If you eat a wide range of fruit, vegetables, nuts and seeds, you should be supplying your body with enough vitamins – do not forget to try new combinations in the form of juices, to give you some variety.

Above: Fizzy drinks contain high amounts of caffiene and can interfere with the body's absorption of nutrients.

- Avoid tea, coffee, cola and other fizzy drinks, as they may interfere with your body's efficient absorption of nutrients and their stimulant effect can exacerbate feelings of anxiety.

- You may find you get on better by eating small, frequent meals rather than the standard two or three larger ones per day.

- Some people with CFS have food sensitivities: among the most common are additives, dairy produce, monosodium glutamate (MSG) and gluten (the protein found in wheat). If you suspect any particular food is making your symptoms worse, try cutting out it for a week or two in order to assess the effects.

BENEFICIAL RECIPES & JUICES

Date & orange fool
(see page 128)

•

Spinach & lemon risotto
(see page 148)

•

Bean & tomato couscous
(see page 162)

Boiled eggs with anchovy soldiers
(see page 181)

•

Tuna & red pepper chowder
(see page 182)

•

Iron pick-me-up
(see page 149)

---

diabetes

Above: Regular exercise will help you control your weight, lessening your risk of diabetes.

Excessive dosage of drugs or insulin will result in low blood-sugar levels, a condition called hypoglycaemia. It starts with light-headedness, followed by confusion, sweating and unconsciousness. Diabetics and their companions should learn to recognize the early signs. Treatment is a sweet drink or an injection of glugagon, which will rapidly restore the blood-sugar level to normal.

The body's intake of sugar is controlled by the hormone insulin, which is produced by the pancreas. Too little sugar in the blood leads to light-headedness and tiredness; too much leads to diabetes, of which there are two types:

- **type I** (insulin-dependent or juvenile-onset) occurs in people under the age of 35. Onset is rapid and insulin levels may be very low, or even absent, and may lead to diabetic coma and death.

- **type II** (non-insulin-dependent or maturity-onset) usually occurs in people over the age of 40, especially if they are overweight. Onset is gradual and insulin levels are not as low as those in type I.

The symptoms, in both types of diabetes, include excessive urine output and thirst, tiredness, weight loss and an increased susceptibility to bacterial infections. If they are left untreated, high blood-sugar levels can permanently damage blood vessels, eventually leading to blindness, ulcers, kidney failure, heart disease and stroke. Treatment aims to maintain the blood-sugar level within acceptable limits. It can be checked by analysing finger-prick samples of blood, or, in type II diabetes, testing the urine for sugar. There are three approaches to treatment:

- **diet** A regular, balanced intake of fat, protein and sugar is important for diabetics. The sugar should be natural and unrefined, as found in fruit and vegetables. It is also important to lose any excess weight.

- **drugs** If diet proves insufficient, two classes of drugs are used: sulfonylureas, which stimulate the release of insulin from the pancreas, and biguanides, which are a kind of insulin substitute.

- **insulin** For severe diabetics, there is no substitute for insulin, and the process of self-injection has been greatly simplified in recent years.

following a healthy eating plan

Although diabetes has a genetic component, type II is more likely to affect adults who are overweight. Therefore, it is worth avoiding foods that are most likely to promote weight gain, such as those with a high fat and/or sugar content, especially if you have any close relatives with the condition. If you need to lose some weight, it is best to do it slowly by following a healthy eating plan rather than going for a 'quick-fix' diet, because with the latter you will almost certainly regain what you have lost after you stop dieting.

The belief that people with diabetes should avoid sugar completely is outdated: small amounts will do no harm, though it is best to have any sweet foods as part of a meal or as an occasional treat. The recommended diet is one that includes plenty of complex carbohydrates, such as wholemeal bread, pasta and rice, fresh fruit, salads and vegetables, pulses – such as lentils and chickpeas – seeds and nuts, while keeping animal fats to a minimum. Try to eat plenty of foods containing chromium; this mineral plays a role in the way the body regulates blood-glucose levels and is thought to enhance the effects of insulin. Chromium-rich foods include brewer's yeast, lean red meat, wholegrains and cheese.

Experts advise against so-called 'diabetic foods' such as sugar-free chocolate; it is better to eat a few squares of good-quality chocolate now and again. Also watch your alcohol intake. Small amounts will do no harm, but do not drink on an empty stomach. Alcohol can also cause blood-glucose levels to drop.

BENEFICIAL RECIPES & JUICES

Butter bean & tomato soup
(see page 161)

•

Roasted peppers with millet & basil
(see page 165)

Mushroom, couscous & herb
sausages (see page 166)

•

Berry fruit scones (see page 164)

•

Brown rice pudding (see page 171)

DIETARY TIPS

- It is vital to eat breakfast, as your blood-glucose levels are likely to be low first thing: opt for unsweetened cereals, such as wholewheat biscuits or porridge with semi-skimmed milk.

- People who have diabetes should make a point of sticking to regular mealtimes whenever possible, especially if their condition is being treated with insulin or a medication which makes them susceptible to hypoglycaemia.

- Remember that many fruits, such as grapes, contain a lot of natural sugars in the form of fructose, so it is best to space out your intake over the whole day rather than eating a large amount all at once.

Below & left: Fruit juices and wholegrain rice should be used as part of an overall healthy diet to combat the effects of diabetes.

hangovers

A hangover results from drinking too much alcohol. Those people with a low body weight, and therefore smaller amounts of body fluids, or a low ratio of fat to lean tissue, are more vulnerable. So are women and young people, who have smaller amounts of the stomach enzymes that break down alcohol. The time and nature of the last meal also have an effect.

The principal cause of a hangover is dehydration. Alcohol is a diuretic, and loss of body fluid in the urine causes the classic symptoms of headache, nausea, vertigo and depression. Severity is largely determined by the amount and nature of the alcohol consumed. Brandy, champagne and whisky contain congeners, which exacerbate the symptoms of hangover. Red wine contains tyramine, which causes headaches. Gin, vodka and white wine are the least likely candidates to cause hangover symptoms so stick to these when possible.

Prevention is always better than cure:

- Eat a good meal and drink a glass of milk before you embark on the consumption of any alcohol. Fatty, oily food will slow down the absorption of alcohol. Drink plenty of water with the meal.

- Intersperse alcoholic drinks with soft drinks. This helps to prevent dehydration as well as reducing alcohol intake.

- Choose your drinks carefully, avoiding those containing congeners, and do not mix drinks.

Afterwards, it is wise to drink more water before going to bed, preferably with a soluble vitamin C tablet. Alcohol is a stimulant, so drinking a glass of warm milk before bed will help to encourage sleep.

On the morning after, drink plenty more fluids, preferably in the form of water, dilute fruit juice or skimmed milk. Solutions of rehydrating powders for diarrhoea may also be helpful. Avoid coffee and tea as the caffeine they contain is a stimulant and will exacerbate any jittery feelings. Eating, even a banana, will boost low blood-sugar levels, which may be causing irritability, dizziness and tiredness. Proprietary painkillers will relieve headaches, but hangover cures containing alcohol should be studiously avoided.

The consumption of alcohol is measured in units:

- *A glass of wine = 1 unit*

- *A measure of spirits = 1 unit*

- *A pint of beer = 2 units*

The current recommendations of maximum alcohol intake per week are 28 units for men and 21 units for women.

Below: White wine is less likely to give you a hangover than some other forms of alcohol, as long as you don't overdo it.

DIETARY TIPS

A hangover tells you that alcohol and/or the chemicals contained in your drinks are toxic to your system. The various unpleasant symptoms relate to the specific consequences which have affected various organs and systems within the body but, together with a painkiller, food and fluids can help you get over the worst relatively quickly.

You will almost certainly be suffering from dehydration – this is responsible for the dry throat and, in part, for the headache. Your first priority, therefore, must be lots of liquid. The traditional sobering-up cup of black coffee is actually not a good idea because coffee is a diuretic – in other words, it encourages the body to get rid of even more fluid. It is much better to have plenty of plain water and juices made from fruit rich in vitamin C, such as strawberries, blackcurrants, citrus fruit (include the zest), kiwi fruit and apples, plus vegetables such as carrots and celery. An additional benefit of juice is that it will contain plenty of fruit sugars, and if you have a hangover you almost certainly have low blood-sugar levels.

The traditional fried breakfast is not a very good idea either. You would do much better to have some wholegrain cereal or oat porridge, as this will release glucose into your bloodstream at a controlled rate and help you avoid a sudden rise in blood-sugar level, followed by a steep drop which would make you feel many times worse. If the idea of protein appeals to you, however, try a poached egg on wholemeal or rye toast – perhaps with a few sliced, grilled tomatoes.

Above: Porridge with some added fruit will be much better for you than a fried breakfast.

- Ginger is a good remedy for nausea; try making tea with boiling water and a piece of stem ginger, or nibble on some good-quality ginger biscuits.

- If you can remember to make yourself drink several glasses of water after you have been drinking, you may avoid the worst of a hangover. Of course, the best preventive measure is always to drink in moderation.

- Do not be tempted to try any of the so-called 'hangover cures' which feature quantities of alcohol – usually spirits. They may be effective in the short term, but the effects will wear off and, in any case, that can be the first step on the road to alcohol dependency.

BENEFICIAL RECIPES & JUICES

Really fruity flapjacks
(see page 129)

•

Orange & raspberry juice
(see page 127)

•

Cabbage & carrot juice
(see page 141)

Carrot & banana booster
(see page 143)

•

Carrot, apple & ginger juice
(see page 143)

•

Tomato & apple pick-me-up
(see page 153)

iron deficiency

Above: Iron deficiency can result in lethargy and breathlessness – if you combat the causes you will soon be able to exercise regularly.

Anaemia is a symptom rather than a disease in itself and iron deficiency is only one of a number of causes. Pernicious anaemia is caused by vitamin B$_{12}$ deficiency, while sickle-cell anaemia and thalassaemia are both inherited anaemias. Bone-marrow disorders, such as leukaemia, and chronic diseases such as tuberculosis and rheumatoid arthritis, may also cause anaemia.

Iron plays an important role in the formation of red blood cells and is a vital component of haemoglobin, the pigment which carries oxygen to the cells of the body and carbon dioxide away from them. It is also involved in the formation of another pigment, myoglobin, which stores oxygen in the muscles for use during exercise. In addition, it is an essential component of some enzymes and is involved in the uptake of oxygen by cells and the conversion of blood sugar into energy.

Red blood cells are made in the body's bone marrow from protein, iron and certain trace elements, such as vitamin B$_{12}$. Normally there is a balance between this production of new red blood cells and the destruction of old blood cells in the spleen. This balance may be upset or disturbed if too little iron is taken in or too much is lost.

Iron deficiency most commonly results from an inadequate diet or failure to absorb iron from the food. Vegetarians and vegans are more likely to suffer from iron deficiency because the high-fibre foods in their diet, such as pulses and wholegrains, bind iron and this makes absorption difficult. Also, their iron intake tends to be less than that of people who eat animal products. Iron deficiency may also result from excessive blood loss, for example heavy menstrual periods or bleeding from peptic ulcers, piles or bowel cancer. There is also a small loss of iron during pregnancy.

Iron deficiency leads to anaemia, which is indicated by general tiredness, breathlessness, headaches and dizziness, sometimes accompanied by apathy, irritability and a lowered resistance to infection.

Treatment involves an iron-rich diet and iron and vitamin supplements. Because iron can be stored in the body, it is important not to exceed the recommended dose – always read the dosage instructions on supplement bottles.

getting enough iron

Many people still think of spinach as being the prime source of iron in the diet and, while this has some basis in reality, there are many other foods which will help to boost your intake of this essential mineral. For non-vegetarians, one of the best ways of guaranteeing a healthy iron intake is to eat red meat. This does not just mean beef and lamb, but also liver, pork, duck, rabbit and the more unusual varieties now in most supermarkets, such as game birds and venison. The other bonus of red meat is that the iron it contains is readily accessible and easily absorbed by the body, which is not the case with some other iron-rich foods. If you do eat meat, remember that, for the sake of your general health, you should choose lean rather than fatty cuts, and remove as much visible fat as you can before cooking. The fat in meat is generally of the saturated type, and a healthy diet means keeping that to a minimum.

For vegetarians and those who prefer not to eat a lot of red meat, other useful sources of iron include all green leafy vegetables (including spinach), cereals, eggs, seeds, dried fruit, lentils, beans and other pulses. Whenever you can, eat vegetables raw or only very lightly cooked, and as fresh as possible, to make sure you get the full benefit of their iron content. Iron from these sources will be better absorbed if you have some vitamin C at the same time – say a glass of orange or other fruit juice with your breakfast cereal. Opt for the kinds of cereal that do not contain added sugar and are fortified with iron.

Above: To maximize your chances of absorbing the iron in your diet, eat onions or garlic together with foods that contain plenty of iron.

- Onions and garlic aid in absorption of iron, so remember to combine these with iron-rich foods.

- Avoid drinking coffee, tea or cola with your meal, or for an hour before or after it, as they will affect your body's ability to absorb iron.

- Dried fruit, especially apricots and dates, are good sources of iron and can add more interest to your diet.

- If you are a very strict vegetarian or a vegan, you may think it worth consulting a nutritionist, especially if you have symptoms of anaemia, in order to check that your dietary intake of iron is adequate.

BENEFICIAL RECIPES & JUICES

Watercress & couscous filled cannelloni (see page 156)

•

Tabbouleh with fruit & nuts (see page 167)

•

Stuffed guinea fowl (see page 176)

Orange & apricot juice (see page 115)

•

Watermelon & orange juice (see page 127)

•

Mixed vegetable juice (see page 137)

---

thyroid problems

The thyroid gland, which is situated on either side of the windpipe, is probably the most important gland in the whole body because it regulates the body's activity, also referred to as its metabolic rate.

The major thyroid problems are:

- **hypothyroidism**, in which the gland is underactive and produces too little thyroxine, thus slowing down the metabolic rate.

- **hyperthyroidism**, in which the gland is overactive and produces too much thyroxine, thus speeding up the metabolic rate.

The balance can be shifted either way by thyroid disease.

Thyroid disease is usually caused by an autoimmune response of the body to the cells of the thyroid gland, which results in an increase or decrease in both its activity and the production of thyroxine. Hypothyroidism may also be caused by congenital disorders and a deficiency of iodine, which is an essential ingredient for the formation of thyroxine.

Symptoms of hypothyroidism include a heart rate below 60 beats a minute, sluggishness, tiredness, constipation and weight gain unrelated to food intake. The face becomes coarse and puffy and the skin feels rough and cool to the touch. If it is left untreated, this disease can lead to severe hypothermia (very low body temperature), apathy, self-neglect and heart failure.

In hyperthyroidism, the heart rate is well above the normal 60–90 beats a minute and there are palpitations, anxiety and a fine tremor in the hands. Weight loss is rapid although the appetite is good. Without treatment, the disease leads to exhaustion and heart failure.

Treatment aims at regulating the amount of thyroxine produced. Hypothyroidism is treated with daily tablets of thyroxine. Blood tests monitor the thyroxine level and the dose is gradually built up until the condition is stable. Treatment then continues for life. Hyperthyroidism is treated with drugs that reduce the levels of thyroxine. If this fails, the options are to remove part of the thyroid gland surgically or to destroy it using radioactive iodine.

Below: Your thyroid gland is located in your throat, on each side of your windpipe.

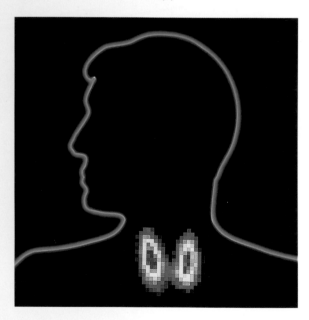

In some cases of thyroid disease, the thyroid gland swells to produce a goitre, which may be of considerable size. A staring gaze, caused by abnormal tissue deposited behind the eyes, is associated with hyperthyroidism.

what to eat and what to avoid

The changes you need to make to your diet will depend on whether your symptoms are caused by an overactive (hyper-) or underactive (hypo-) thyroid gland. You may be given nutritional advice by your doctor or a dietician in the course of your treatment.

If your problem stems from too little thyroid hormone, you may benefit from foods rich in iodine, such as seaweed, seafood and fish. You should also

include on your menu dairy produce of all kinds, brown rice, seeds – especially sunflower, pumpkin and sesame seeds – and nuts, particularly walnuts. Oils made from nuts and seeds are also beneficial, including linseed oil. Some nutritional therapists recommend a detoxification diet, but you should only try this under professional supervision. People with an underactive thyroid should steer clear of vegetables such as cauliflowers, cabbages, kale and turnips as well as soya and peanuts. This means you need to be extra careful to have plenty of other vegetables and fruit to maintain your vitamin levels.

For an overactive thyroid, you should avoid the foods that contain iodine and make sure you have a reasonable intake of protein at each meal. All kinds of meat and dairy produce are fine, but you should avoid fish and shellfish (as well as seaweed). Unlike those with hypothyroidism, you can eat as much cauliflower, broccoli, cabbage and kale as you like, along with other fruit and vegetables of your choice. All types of nuts and seeds are good too, including oils made from them.

BENEFICIAL RECIPES & JUICES

Cabbage bhaji
(see page 139)

•

Nut koftas with minted yogurt
(see page 173)

•

Lemon rice and wild rice salad
(see page 174)

Salmon & courgette brochettes
(see page 183)

•

Kale and wheatgrass energizer
(see page 141)

•

Cabbage & carrot juice
(see page 141)

DIETARY TIPS

- When buying nut or seed oils, opt for the cold-pressed kind. Although slightly more expensive, they retain more of the nutrients present in the nuts and seeds they are made from.

- Thyroid disease can be difficult to treat and you may need to reconsider your diet if medication or surgery alters your levels of thyroid hormones.

- Do not attempt to lose weight on a drastic slimming diet if you have a hypothyroid condition, because the problem will resolve itself once the treatment takes effect.

Above: Sesame seeds make an excellent cold-pressed oil as mentioned above.

Above left: With an overactive thyroid problem, you can eat plenty of vegetables like cabbage and kale.

obesity

Above: Regular exercise combined with healthy eating is the best way to control your weight.

Tables of average weights are misleading because if everyone is already overweight, these averages do not represent ideal weights. A better indicator is the body mass index (BMI). This can be calculated using the following formula: weight (in kilograms) divided by height (in metres) squared. For example, $62 \div (1.7 \times 1.7) = 62 \div 2.9 = 21.4$. A normal BMI for a woman is 19–24 and for a man 20–25. A BMI above 30 indicates obesity.

Basically, if energy intake (in the form of calories) exceeds energy expenditure (in the form of exercise), the excess will be turned into fat and stored by the body, resulting in weight gain. Anyone who is 20 per cent or more over the maximum desirable weight for their height is described as obese. Although nearly half the population in Britain is overweight, only 10 per cent are obese.

Some people are more prone to obesity, such as those with a low basal metabolic rate. Evidence also shows that obesity may run in families; children of obese parents are ten times more likely to be obese, but whether this is genetic or a result of upbringing remains to be seen. More rarely, obesity results from metabolic disorders, such as thyroid problems, or the use of appetite-stimulating drugs.

The long-term risks associated with obesity include a variety of medical problems. Obese people are twice as likely to suffer from high blood pressure and stroke and five times more likely to suffer from mature-onset diabetes. Obesity also places a strain on the joints and the back, and can aggravate osteoarthritis. Obese women are more likely to get cancer of the breast or uterus.

The recommended answer is to follow a diet of about 1,000–1,200 calories a day, which should lead to a weight loss of up to 1kg (2lb) per week. Excess fat can only be lost by losing weight slowly, so crash diets are to be avoided, as they usually only result in loss of water rather than fat. Exercise is also important, as it serves to burn off surplus calories as well as to raise the metabolic rate.

Appetite-suppressant drugs are now seldom used because their effects are temporary and they can be addictive. In extreme cases, surgical intervention, such as stapling the stomach, may become necessary.

ACTIVITY AND ENERGY USE	
Activity	Calories/hour
Cycling	400
Dancing	300
Gardening	250
Golf	250
Jogging	500
Running	900
Swimming	500
Walking	250

losing weight

While it is true that you have to burn more calories (energy) than you consume to lose weight, you may find it more difficult to shed excess pounds on a diet that is high in refined and processed foods even if you keep your total calorie intake down to

the recommended level. Unrefined foods are more filling, so you need to eat a smaller amount of them in order to feel satisfied. You will also struggle if you do not exercise: not only does physical activity burn calories, but it also raises your metabolic rate and, as you gain more muscle, you will burn more calories to 'feed' it even when you are at rest.

Decreasing the amount of fat in your diet is likely to have a noticeable effect on your weight. Eat more vegetable protein in place of fatty meat and meat products such as sausages; increase your consumption of low-fat meat such as poultry (with the skin removed), fish and eggs, and either cut out dairy produce or opt for the low-fat versions. Do not use oil or fat in cooking, apart from minimal amounts of olive, vegetable nut or seed oils in dressings. Remember that fat is likely to be present in many ready-made foods, including pies, cakes and biscuits, as well as in takeaways such as burgers and many Indian dishes.

DIETARY TIPS

- If you have a sweet tooth, keep chocolate and other 'temptations' as an occasional treat, and try to avoid all kinds of sweetened foods as much as possible. Get used to checking labels – you may be surprised at the amount of sugar present in foods such as baked beans, canned soups, pickles and sauces, for example.

- It will help you to stick to a weight-reducing diet if you plan your menus ahead and, if it is practical, do not keep tempting items such as crisps, cakes, biscuits and chocolate in your cupboards at all.

- Try to think of your weight-loss plan as a whole new way of eating rather than as a short-term diet. Do not expect to lose a lot each week – slowly but surely is a far healthier approach, and you will be less likely to regain what you have lost if you do it gradually.

- Alcohol is relatively high in calories so restrict your intake while you are losing weight; you will be able to enjoy moderate drinking again once you have reached your target.

Above left & below: Eggs and fish will provide protein without high levels of fat.

BENEFICIAL RECIPES & JUICES

Stir-fried chicken with pineapple
(see page 130)

•

Chicken with 40 garlic cloves
(see page 158)

•

Herrings with spinach & parmesan
(see page 180)

Boiled eggs with anchovy soldiers
(see page 181)

•

Tuna & red pepper chowder
(see page 182)

•

Mixed fruit smoothie
(see page 131)

---

sleeping problems

Sleep patterns vary enormously; for example, babies sleep for more than 16 hours a day, most adults need about 8 hours, and the elderly may manage with just 5 hours. It is only when the pattern deviates from what is normal for an individual that there may be a problem.

Insomnia, an inability to fall asleep or difficulty in remaining asleep, affects one in three adults at some time in their lives. Even the loss of one night's sleep can cause a serious fall in the performance of tasks involving skill and judgement. Prolonged insomnia results in constant tiredness and daytime drowsiness, with poor concentration, tension and irritability.

The most common cause is worry, including worry about getting to sleep; consequently a run of bad nights can be self-perpetuating. However, although worry may stop people getting off to sleep initially, once they are asleep they usually get a reasonable night's rest. On the other hand, people with depression usually have no difficulty in getting to sleep but wake up in the early hours and keep themselves awake worrying – a pattern that is also seen in old age.

Measures can be taken to deal with some of the more obvious causes; for example, using heavy curtains or a sleep mask to exclude light, wearing earplugs or installing double glazing to counteract noise from neighbours or traffic, and improving ventilation or adjusting central-heating levels. Insomniacs should avoid heavy meals and stimulants, such as alcohol and coffee, before bedtime and also avoid daytime snoozes. If getting up in the night to pass urine is a problem, it is best not to drink too much before retiring. A pre-bedtime ritual of a bath and a warm drink may also help.

In those cases where a physical disorder, such as a chronic cough, pain, prostate problems or sleep apnoea, is the root cause, medical advice should be sought to deal with the problem. Depression and anxiety, which may also cause insomnia, are less easy to treat. Hypnotic drugs can give short-term relief but may be addictive and do not tackle the basic problem.

Above: Worry is the most common cause of insomnia and can leave you feeling frustrated and depressed.

Right: Having a bath with essential oils before you go to bed will help you to relax and hopefully reduce the chances of insomnia.

diet and eating habits

There are a number of ways in which what you eat and drink can affect your ability to get a good night's sleep, but changing your diet can certainly help. First, though, consider whether the pattern of your eating may be playing a role. For instance, a large, fatty or spicy meal may stop you falling asleep, especially if you eat it relatively late in the evening. Conversely, a light meal taken relatively early could mean you wake with hunger pangs in the middle of the night or early in the morning. If you are prone to insomnia, try cutting out coffee, tea and cola, which all contain the stimulant caffeine; some people find it is sufficient to avoid them in the evening, others may need to steer clear of them from the middle of the day. Alcohol in anything other than small quantities may help you to fall asleep quickly, but you are also likely to have a disturbed night or wake in the early hours after drinking a lot the previous evening.

Pay attention to your intake of minerals, especially magnesium and calcium, as low levels of these may contribute to sleeping problems. For calcium, eat plenty of dairy produce, green vegetables, soya, muesli, prawns, and oily fish such as sardines and pilchards; good sources of magnesium are wholegrains, seafood, green vegetables, nuts and seeds.

Cheese late at night was traditionally linked with nightmares. If there is a grain of truth in this, it may be that protein is harder to digest than some other types of food and so is best avoided just before bedtime.

DIETARY TIPS

- Tryptophan is a substance present in certain foods which seems to encourage sleep: bananas, dates, bread and hazelnuts all contain it and these are worth trying as a bedtime snack.

- You could combine your snack with a soothing herbal tea: valerian has been shown to help ease insomnia, particularly when it is the result of stress.

- Avoid foods which you know from experience give you indigestion or heartburn, however much you enjoy them. Digestive problems are a common cause of sleep disturbance.

Above left: Fresh peas will increase your intake of calcium.

Below: Eat a banana before you go to bed and it may help you to avoid insomnia.

BENEFICIAL RECIPES & JUICES

Broccoli & red pepper fettuccine
(see page 134)

•

Stir-fried broccoli with sesame seeds
(see page 136)

•

Mung bean & herb risotto
(see page 170)

Banana & almond smoothie
(see page 117)

•

Banana & peanut butter smoothie
(see page 117)

•

Carrot & banana booster
(see page 143)

stress

Above: Commuting by car or train is one way in which stress levels can build up even before you arrive at your place of work.

Right: Relaxation techniques can help both your body and your mind to cope with stress.

Although a certain amount of stress is beneficial in providing challenge and stimulation, the body is not designed to cope with the long-term stresses imposed by our modern lifestyle. These include problems associated with work, financial affairs, relationships, noise, commuting, information overload and, on a more personal level, moving house, death of a close family member, study and examinations.

Certain people respond positively to stress. Others find it debilitating, both physically and mentally, and succumb to a variety of stress-related illnesses, such as heart disease and high blood pressure, disorders of the digestive system, allergies and skin complaints. Fortunately, it is becoming increasingly recognized that unreasonable levels of stress lead to poor performance, which is ultimately counterproductive to family life, society in general and to employers in particular.

Under stress, the body produces more adrenaline, noradrenaline and corticosteroids, the 'fight or flight' hormones, which cause the muscles to tense and breathing and heart rates to increase. Prolonged stress results in anxiety, general worry and poor concentration and is manifested by physical symptoms ranging from headaches and fatigue, tremors and sweating, to abdominal pains and indigestion. As stress increases, anxiety becomes more pronounced and the individual becomes trapped in a vicious circle of worry about doing something wrong, neglect of tasks and poor performance, which can deteriorate into depression and a nervous breakdown.

Gentle exercise and relaxation techniques, as well as developing interests outside work, are more important than drugs, which can merely provide short-term relief. However, the problem can only be overcome by radical changes in lifestyle. Recognizing and alleviating the causes of stress are both paramount – for example, rearranging schedules, working shorter hours, setting priorities and generally managing your time more effectively.

The production of 'fight or flight' hormones is the body's response to an immediate danger or threat. The energy they provide would usually be dissipated during the reaction to the threat, but this is not the case in long-term stress.

stress-busting foods

Although tackling long-term stress is a complex task, paying attention to your diet can play its part in alleviating some of the symptoms. When your body is under strain, it is vital that you eat the right kind of foods to give it a fighting chance of coping and remaining in good health. This means basing your main meals around wholefoods, including unrefined cereals and cereal-based food such as bread, pasta and rice, and ensuring that you have at least five portions of fruit and vegetables every day. Take these raw when you can, including in the form of juices. Making citrus fruit juices is worthwhile, because you can include the pith and zest which contain flavonoids – these help to counteract the cell damage caused by oxygen molecules called free radicals. Tea, apples, green beans, red wine and onions are other good sources of flavonoids, which

also strengthen blood-vessel walls and so may protect against heart disease, for which stress is a risk factor. For the same reason, you should substitute fat from non-animal sources for saturated fats, while aiming to keep down your overall consumption of fat. Choose skinned chicken, eggs, low-fat dairy produce and, especially, oily fish as protein alternatives to meat, together with pulses, lentils and nuts.

A stressful lifestyle can often mean eating lots of takeaways and 'junk' food, leaving you deprived of essential vitamins and minerals you would get from natural wholefoods. Try to make time to eat unrefined wholefoods, even if it is a wholemeal sandwich, fruit and a live yogurt rather than a cooked meal.

- Resist grabbing a caffeine-rich drink such as tea, coffee or cola to give you a lift and help you cope; ultimately they can make anxiety and stress worse. Water or herbal tea are much healthier options.

- Sugar and sugary foods will quickly boost your blood-glucose levels, so giving you an energy boost; but the effect is short-lived and your levels will drop as fast as they rose, leaving you feeling worse than before.

- Do not soothe your frazzled nerves with more than the odd alcoholic drink, as this may have adverse effects on your general health in the longer term.

Left: Onions contain flavonoids to strengthen blood-vessel walls.

Below: Fruit should form a major part of your diet.

BENEFICIAL RECIPES & JUICES

Beetroot risotto
(see page 133)

●

Penne with chicken livers
(see page 178)

●

Cashew nut chicken
(see page 175)

Salmon & courgette brochettes
(see page 183)

●

Avocado & banana smoothie
(see page 117)

●

Red pepper & tomato tonic
(see page 145)

arthritis

Above: Exercise such as walking will ease the pain of arthritis and improve general health.

Below: An x-ray of a normal pair of hands. In osteoarthritis, extra bone forms around the joints, causing distortion.

In both types of arthritis, gentle exercise, such as swimming, will keep the joints moving freely as well as strengthening the supporting muscles. Losing any excess weight will reduce the strain on the joints.

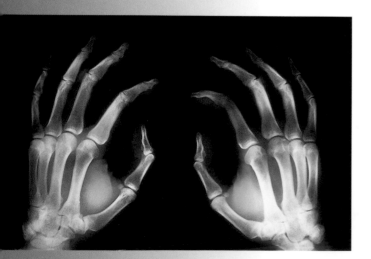

There are two forms of arthritis:

● **osteoarthritis**, a non-inflammatory degenerative condition.

● **rheumatoid arthritis**, an aggressive autoimmune disease characterized by inflammation and distortion of the joints.

Osteoarthritis involves wear and tear of the cartilage capping the bones rather than the bone itself. The joints lose their natural lubrication and the cartilage eventually splits and degenerates until bone rubs against bone. It most commonly affects the hips, knees, neck, back and finger joints, which all stiffen and creak. The condition is worse in the morning and exacerbated by damp weather. Bone growing around the joints may cause distortion of the fingers and knees. Flare-ups of pain and stiffness are common and the joints occasionally swell.

Pain relief ranges from the mildest effective painkiller to non-steroidal anti-inflammatory drugs (NAIDs) in instances where the pain is severe or prolonged. In certain extreme cases, surgical replacement of the hip or knee joint may be advised.

In rheumatoid arthritis there is swelling of the synovial membrane which lines the joints and provides lubrication. Nearby cartilage is also affected, leading to deformation of the joints; spindly fingers and distortion of the toes at the sides are typical. The early signs are discomfort or swelling of the small joints of first one hand or foot, then both. Pain and stiffness are worse in the morning and can last for several hours. The knees, shoulders and hips may also be affected, but not the back. Tendons may snap. Other symptoms include general malaise, skin nodules and rashes, fluid accumulation in the lungs, anaemia, heart, kidney and nervous system problems, and inflamed or dry eyes.

Pain relief is afforded by NAIDs. Other drugs have superseded the more powerful oral steroids and appear to affect the condition fundamentally rather than just reducing the symptoms. However, they need careful monitoring for side-effects. Surgical treatment includes repair of ruptured tendons, injection of steroids into the joints to reduce inflammation and joint replacement.

foods that can help

There is now considerable research evidence to show that omega-3 fatty acids, found mainly in oily fish, may help to alleviate the symptoms of arthritis for some people. These essential fatty acids, which must be obtained from your diet because the body is unable to manufacture them otherwise, seem to reduce inflammation, pain and swelling, especially in people with rheumatoid arthritis, osteoarthritis and gout (see page 22). It is worth putting fish such as mackerel, herrings, trout, salmon, pilchards, sardines and halibut, on your menu several times a week. Other good sources of omega-3 fatty acids are walnuts, chestnuts, linseeds and wild greens, such as purslane and sorrel.

Since some fats in oily fish may promote free radical damage, you should balance your increased intake with foods rich in anti-oxidants, especially vitamin E. This is found in nuts, seeds, sweet potatoes, avocados and nut and seed oils. Other anti-oxidants include vitamins A and C, found in fruit and vegetables, and minerals such as iron, zinc, copper, manganese and selenium.

In a minority of people with some forms of arthritis, the condition may be triggered or exacerbated by a reaction to certain foods. The commonest culprits include corn, wheat, dairy produce, citrus fruit, preserved meats, chocolate, peanuts and tomatoes. Finding out whether you are sensitive to any of these can be difficult and time-consuming, and is best done under the guidance of a nutritionist.

Some complementary therapists believe that foods belonging to the nightshade family may have an adverse effect on people with arthritis, and would advise cutting out members of this family, including tomatoes, peppers, aubergines and potatoes.

DIETARY TIPS

Above: Green, leafy vegetables are an excellent source of B vitamins.

- Attempt to lose any excess weight, especially if you have osteoarthritis, as carrying surplus weight increases the strain on any damaged joints, especially the knees.

- Aim to eat as varied a diet as you possibly can, since this will boost your overall health and wellbeing and will also help to build up your resistance to infection.

- Check with your doctor as to whether any of the medications you are taking for your arthritis could be depleting your body of essential nutrients; if so, increase your intake of foods containing these nutrients.

- Some people with arthritis appear to have low levels of some B vitamins (found in wholemeal bread and brown rice, nuts, offal, poultry, fish, soya, green leafy vegetables and eggs), vitamin E (found in nuts and seeds), magnesium (found in green vegetables, wheat, oats, walnuts and almonds) and zinc (found in orange fruit, wheatgerm, brewer's yeast, cocoa and pumpkin seeds).

BENEFICIAL RECIPES & JUICES

Stir-fried chicken with pineapple
(see page 130)

•

Spinach & broccoli soup
(see page 147)

•

Caldo verde & smoked tofu soup
(see page 184)

Breakfast smoothie
(see page 121)

•

Mixed fruit smoothie
(see page 131)

•

Blackberry & pineapple juice
(see page 131)

osteoporosis

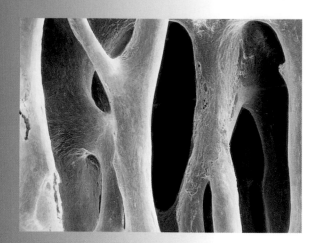

Above & below: Healthy dense bones (above) become increasingly porous and brittle (below) when osteoporosis takes hold.

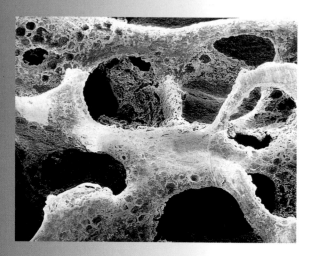

The following preventive measures will

delay or minimize the onset of osteoporosis,

especially if adopted early:

• Weight-bearing exercise, such as walking

and weight-training.

• A diet rich in calcium.

• Vitamin D and calcium supplements.

• Giving up smoking and limiting alcohol intake.

Bone consists mainly of calcium and phosphorus, and its formation is regulated by a complex system involving parathyroid hormone and vitamin D, which is associated with calcium uptake by the body. In addition, the sex hormones testosterone and oestrogen have a direct effect by reducing the rate at which bone is reabsorbed by the body.

Before the age of about 30, some 20 per cent of the calcium in bones is replaced annually. After this, the body creates less new bone and becomes less efficient at absorbing calcium. As a result, about 1 per cent of bone mass is lost each year. With increasing age, the bones become thinner, more porous and more brittle and are more likely to break. This is called osteoporosis.

Osteoporosis is a particular problem for women, who not only start with 30 per cent less bone mass than men but also experience falling oestrogen levels after the menopause. (Calcium and phosphorus levels fall rapidly for ten years after the menopause.) Taking oral steroids, little exposure to sunlight and a poor calcium intake will also increase the risk of osteoporosis taking hold.

There are no symptoms and osteoporosis is usually only revealed when a weakened bone fractures. If this happens in the spine, there is sudden, severe backache. Other common sites of osteoporotic fractures are the hips and wrists. Shrinkage of the intervertebral discs results in loss of height and the back bends into the so-called 'dowager's hump'. Bone scans can monitor the extent and progress of osteoporosis.

Exercise and a diet that is rich in calcium and vitamin D will help maintain the density and mass of your bones. However, lost bone cannot be fully restored, although slow rebuilding may be possible. Hormone replacement therapy (HRT) can prevent further bone loss caused by lack of oestrogen, but the effect only lasts while it is being taken. Drugs containing phosphorus, such as etidronate, may help to improve the condition.

calcium in the diet

As calcium is essential to the formation of bone, it makes sense to ensure that you are getting enough of this vital mineral. Dairy foods, including milk, cheese and yogurt, are among the richest sources, but you will also get some from green vegetables, soya products and fish. The sooner in life you begin a calcium-rich diet, the more you are protecting yourself against the risk of developing this condition in the future, which is one reason why it is unwise for young women in particular to avoid milk and dairy produce in the hope of becoming or remaining slim. Skimmed or semi-skimmed milk are just as good from a calcium point of view as full-fat versions, and are better from an overall health perspective because of their reduced fat content. Cereal with semi-skimmed milk is a great start to the day.

However, in order for your body to make optimum use of the calcium in your food, you need to combine a high intake with other nutrients, especially vitamins C and D and zinc. Vitamin C aids calcium absorption, so have plenty of leafy green vegetables, fruit and juices (particularly citrus fruit, blackcurrants, strawberries, plums and kiwi fruit). Zinc encourages acid production, which is also necessary for calcium absorption; you will find it in chicken, mushrooms, pineapples, pears, cherries, dried figs and dates, molasses, butter and yeast extract.

Vegetarians appear to be less prone to osteoporosis. This may be related to the fact that animal protein seems to interfere with the absorption of calcium. It may also be because they have a high intake of plant oestrogens (or phyto-oestrogens) – substances which are related to the female hormone oestrogen which is known to protect pre-menopausal women from rapid bone loss.

BENEFICIAL RECIPES & JUICES

Strawberry & cucumber salad
(see page 118)

•

Figs with blackberries on toast
(see page 120)

•

Chicken tzatziki
(see page 188)

Blueberry & grapefruit juice
(see page 122)

•

Cranberry yogurt smoothie
(see page 189)

•

Yogurt & buttermilk
fruit medley (see page 189)

DIETARY TIPS

Above: Soya products, such as tofu, are good sources of calcium which will protect your bones against osteoporosis.

- Pulses, seeds and, particularly, soya beans and foods made from them, like tofu, are rich in phyto-oestrogens, as are grains and many fruit and vegetables; all of these may help to protect against osteoporosis.

- Caffeine, sugar and sugary foods, and fatty foods may all interfere with calcium absorption, so keep them to a minimum.

- Vitamin D – the 'sunshine vitamin' – is produced in the body when your skin is exposed to ultra-violet light, but you can also consume it in foods such as eggs, fish and cottage cheese. Make sure you get enough to help promote healthy bones.

hay fever

Allergy testing is rarely useful. Desensitization, which involves giving increasingly stronger doses of the allergen, is no longer recommended because of the risk of provoking a severe allergic response.

Right: Close up of an ear of rye showing the dangling, pollen-bearing stamens which can cause great discomfort to hay-fever sufferers.

Below: Fields of rape which produces vast amounts of pollen, are now a common sight in the countryside.

Hay fever is a response to substances that provoke an allergic reaction (allergens). These substances include pollen from flowers, trees and grasses, fragments of skin or hair from animals, and chemicals that are released into the air from fumes or pollution. For some people, hay fever, or allergic rhinitis, is a seasonal problem, while others who are allergic to a number of allergens suffer all year round.

The most common symptoms are itchy eyes and a runny nose, and sometimes also a tickle in the throat. In severe cases, these may be accompanied by a persistent cough or wheezing. The severity of the symptoms varies from being a mild nuisance to a constant battle against breathlessness and discomfort. Fortunately, there is a tendency to grow out of hay fever in adult life.

The main treatment consists of antihistamines. These reduce the severity of the allergic response and a single tablet may be sufficient to relieve the symptoms. Modern antihistamines are taken once or twice a day and, unlike earlier forms of the drug, rarely cause drowsiness. They are available in liquid form for children. Anti-allergy eyedrops contain substances such as cromoglycates which block the allergic response and are extremely safe, although they need to be applied several times a day for full effect. Nasal sprays can also be used. These contain either the same anti-allergy substances used in eyedrops or low doses of steroids. They are safe for long-term use because the steroids are absorbed within the nose rather than by the body as a whole.

Preventive measures include avoiding bright sunlight and keeping windows closed. Contact with animals should also be avoided. If standard remedies have no effect, surgery is a possibility. This involves removing the lining of the nose, thus relieving persistent stuffiness and discharge.

reducing symptoms with diet

When you are experiencing the misery of hay-fever symptoms, you need to do everything you can to boost your general health by eating a balanced, nutrient-rich diet. If your throat is raw and your senses of smell and taste are disturbed because of nasal symptoms, you may find juices, soups and highly flavoured foods more appetising than dry or bland dishes. Try to ensure that you get a good range of vitamins, especially vitamins C and A; you can do that by putting lots of fresh fruit and vegetables on the menu. The flavonoids in fruit such as citrus fruit, strawberries, kiwi fruit, blackcurrants and other berries can help your immune system to work as it should.

However, it is worth knowing that some foods may exacerbate the symptoms of hay fever in certain individuals, probably because they are related to the plant whose pollen triggers your allergic response. Many people know which pollens affect them because of the time when their symptoms begin: tree pollens appear in the spring, grass pollens in summer and yeast and mould spores in late summer and autumn.

One of the commonest of what are called 'cross-reactions' is that people who are allergic to birch pollen may also be sensitive to apples and, less frequently, to other fruit such as pears, peaches, plums, cherries, nectarines and apricots, and to potatoes and hazelnuts. Ragweed allergy may be linked to a sensitivity to bananas or melons, and mugwort allergy to celery.

DIETARY TIPS

- The body produces a substance called histamine as part of the allergic response, and a few people find that foods containing it exacerbate their symptoms. If you suspect this applies to you, trying cutting out histamine-containing foods such as mature or ripe cheeses, tuna, salami and similar processed meats and wine.

- Some people suspect that milk and dairy produce may encourage mucus production, although there is no hard scientific evidence of this. You can see whether avoiding such foods helps you, but take care to keep up your calcium intake in other ways.

- Apart from the cross-reactions mentioned (see left), there are no foods you need to avoid specifically; it is more important to ensure you have a generally healthy diet.

Above left: Being allergic to birch pollen could mean that you are also sensitive to fruits such as apricots.

Below: Highly flavoured juices can still be palatable when you are suffering.

BENEFICIAL RECIPES & JUICES

Lemon & basil penne
(see page 124)

•

Colcannon
(see page 138)

•

Chunky carrot & lentil soup
(see page 142)

Apricot & pineapple smoothie
(see page 115)

•

Horseradish pick-me-up
(see page 127)

•

Carrot & kiwi juice
(see page 143)

hives

Above: Eating various types of shellfish may provoke an allergic reaction.

Right: Strawberries are another possible cause of hives or nettle rash if they have recently been eaten by the sufferer.

People who know that they may develop anaphylaxis, because they are allergic to nuts or insect stings, should wear a medical bracelet to announce the fact. They should also carry a self-injection kit for administering adrenaline.

Hives, also known as nettle rash or urticaria, is a response by the skin to an allergen, something that causes an allergic reaction. It is most common in young children and may be caused by something that has been eaten, such as strawberries, shellfish or an aspirin-related drug, or something that has come into contact with the skin. In most cases, the cause remains obscure, even after allergy testing. Other causes of urticaria are emotion and exercise, or reactions to cold, sunlight or even water. There are also a few rarer causes that should be identified because of long-term implications.

The allergic reaction usually occurs within minutes of exposure. The skin feels itchy and swells into a weal that is pale in the middle and red around the margins. There may be a few large weals or a number of small ones, commonly called hives. The weals wax and wane very quickly and may last from a few minutes to a few days.

If the allergic response is widespread, the lips and eyes may swell and in severe cases there may be swelling of the soft tissues of the throat and trachea, causing breathing difficulties. In the most extreme response, anaphylaxis, there is a total collapse of blood pressure due to the release of antihistamine-type substances throughout the body. This is mostly due to insect stings or eating nuts.

Mild urticaria is treated with antihistamines, either in tablet form or by injection. Soothing lotions, such as calamine, may help to relieve the symptoms in children. Anaphylaxis is a medical emergency which requires immediate injections of adrenaline to restore blood pressure, followed by treatment with steroids and antihistamines.

Those people who develop an instant and dramatic outbreak of hives very soon after eating a particular food may find it relatively easy to identify the origin of their problem. Very often, the first attack occurs relatively early in life, perhaps even on the first occasion when a child eats the trigger food, so a little detective work will usually pinpoint the culprit. In future, the individual will need to make every effort to avoid that food, both in its natural state and as a constituent of other prepared foods: for example, both strawberries themselves and yogurts or drinks containing natural strawberry flavouring or juice. Such people will often show a positive response to a skin or blood test for allergic reaction to that food, because their immune system releases chemicals designed to destroy the 'allergen', and these can be measured.

Sometimes, however, the link may be less obvious and harder to identify. For people who have what is sometimes called 'chronic urticaria', skin and blood tests may fail to pick up any signs of a direct immune-system response, even though they develop a rash which comes and goes without any easily detectable cause. One possibility is that they may be responding to foods which have a relatively high histamine content, so they might want to try cutting them out to see whether this helps. It would mean avoiding very ripe cheeses, sausages such as salami, mackerel and tuna (especially tinned varieties), sauerkraut and some alcoholic drinks, particularly red wine.

Above: Include live yogurt in your daily diet to help rebalance the natural bacteria in the gut.

- Because gut bacteria can produce histamine in response to large amounts of starch, reducing your intake of starchy fruit and vegetables may help.

- Live yogurt can help to rebalance the natural bacteria in the gut and consequently make it less likely to respond abnormally.

- If you do reduce your consumption of starchy fruit and vegetables, make sure to keep up your vitamin intake with leafy vegetables and salad, and fruit such as blackcurrants, kiwi fruit, oranges and grapefruit.

BENEFICIAL RECIPES & JUICES

Spiced orange & avodcado salad
(see page 125)

•

Nut koftas with minted yogurt
(see page 173)

•

Blueberry & grapefruit juice
(see page 122)

Watermelon & orange juice
(see page 127)

•

Carrot & kiwi juice
(see page 143)

•

Yogurt & buttermilk fruit medley
(see page 189)

depression

The majority of mothers experience mild post-natal depression when faced with coping with a new baby and all the domestic responsibilities. This usually passes but about 10 per cent become persistently depressed, either immediately after the birth or within the first three months. In the most severe cases, they may harbour thoughts of harming the baby.

Depression is a natural response to the problems of life, such as bereavement, divorce or financial worries. It has an obvious cause and is usually short-lived. This so-called reactive depression should not be confused with true (endogenous or psychotic) depression, which is a mental illness.

Such depression may be a response to an underlying problem, such as alcoholism. In the elderly, it may be a reaction to physical and mental deterioration, especially in the early stages of dementia. It is also common after childbirth, when it is known as post-natal depression. In young people true depression may be associated with the onset of schizophrenia. More rarely, it can be the result of brain disease. It is believed to be linked with neurotransmitters in the brain. Several of these, including noradrenaline, serotonin and dopamine, seem to be associated with moderate and severe depression.

Symptoms include an overwhelming feeling of emptiness and despair, mood swings, irritability, obsessional behaviour, insomnia and fatigue. Low self-esteem may lead to self-neglect and loss of appetite and libido. Physical symptoms include aches and pains, digestive disorders and palpitations. As the depression deepens, there may be anxiety attacks and the sufferer may become increasingly withdrawn, apathetic and eventually suicidal. Some 10–15 per cent of sufferers do attempt suicide.

Treatment involves counselling, psychotherapy and drugs, in various combinations. Drug treatment has the benefit of bringing sufferers to the point where they can discuss their problems rationally. Two types of antidepressant are used:

Above: Most new mothers soon recover from post-natal depression, but if the symptoms persist treatment may be necessary, to help the mother as well as protect her baby.

- **tricyclics**, which alter the level of neurotransmitters in the brain. Side-effects include drowsiness, dry mouth and blurred vision. An overdose can cause dangerous irregularities of the heart rhythm.

- **selective serotonin reuptake inhibitors (SSRIs)**, which act on the neurotransmitter serotonin. These are becoming increasingly popular because they produce fewer side-effects and are much safer in overdose than the tricyclics.

mood-lifting foods

It is common to lose your appetite and your enjoyment of food when you are depressed, so you need to make a special effort to remain well nourished. It may help to opt for smaller, more frequent meals or snacks rather than being defeated by the prospect of three, normal-sized meals a day. You (or someone else, if possible) should aim to present food attractively and opt for any foods which do appeal to you. Some depressed people crave carbohydrates, possibly as a result of low levels of the brain chemical serotonin which is known to influence mood. To counter this, try to eat more foods containing tryptophan which helps boost serotonin levels, such as bread, potatoes, cauliflowers, bananas, dates and hazelnuts. You should also make sure that you are getting enough B vitamins, especially B_6 which is also needed for serotonin production. Good sources include meat, offal, chicken, wholegrain cereals, pulses, most vegetables, seeds and nuts, wheatgerm and yeast.

If your appetite is small, avoid sating it with processed, sugary or fatty foods which are not good for your general wellbeing and may contain fewer valuable nutrients than whole, fresh foods. Vitamin C is important too – so choose fresh green vegetables and salads, blackcurrants, strawberries, citrus fruit and kiwi fruit; you may find them more appealing made into juices if you do not feel much like eating. Some people feel better if they increase the protein content of their diet; if this works for you, choose oily fish, poultry or non-fatty meats and offal rather than processed meats such as sausages.

Above: Caffeine should be excluded from the diet, so try herbal teas instead.

- Always resist the temptation to use alcohol to 'drown your sorrows'. This does not work in the long term because alcohol depresses the central nervous system, and too much may cause other damage, especially to the liver.

- Caffeine does not help either and may also make matters worse, so try drinking juices or herbal teas – borage, camomile flower and mint, for example – rather than coffee, tea or cola drinks.

- Do eat regularly and, especially, do not skip breakfast. Low blood sugar can contribute to feelings of depression. For the same reason, avoid lots of sugary foods as these will cause your blood glucose to rise rapidly, then drop equally fast.

BENEFICIAL RECIPES & JUICES

Mixed vegetable risotto
(see page 135)
•
Penne with chicken livers
(see page 178)
•
Chicken tzatziki
(see page 188)

Banana & almond smoothie
(see page 117)
•
Green vegetable juice
(see page 137)
•
5-vegetable juice
(see page 163)

---

alzheimer's disease

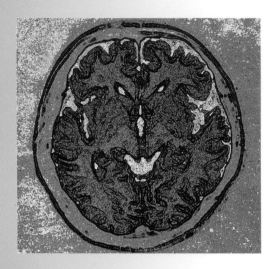

Alzheimer's is a progressive brain disease that affects 2–3 per cent of people between the ages of 65 and 75, and about 20 per cent of people over the age of 80. It is caused by a degeneration of the interconnections between the brain cells. As these connections become progressively more tangled, the personality of the sufferer increasingly disappears. This seems to be associated with a decrease in acetylcholine, one of the transmitter substances in the brain.

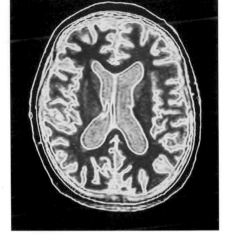

Above: A coloured magnetic resonance imaging (MRI) scan of an axial section through a healthy human brain. The brain is divided into two hemispheres. The hemispheres are made up of grey matter (pink) and white matter (orange). The grey matter consists largely of nerve cells, and the white matter is mainly nerve fibres. The blue area (centre) is a ventricle, which is filled with cerebro-spinal fluid.

Above right: An MRI scan of an axial section through a brain with Alzheimer's disease. In this condition there is widespread destruction of brain tissue leading to abnormally deep folding and shrinkage of the brain (red). Two of the brain's fluid-filled ventricles (blue, centre) have become enlarged.

The basic symptom is loss of short-term memory, although events of many years ago can be clearly recalled. Early signs, such as mislaid spectacles or not recognizing people, can easily be mistaken for forgetfulness. Eventually, it becomes obvious that there is a deeper problem as sufferers fail to recognize their children, wander away from home and drift into a permanent state of confusion.

It is important to identify the condition in case it is treatable. Blood tests can rule out anaemia, thyroid disease and syphilis, and a brain scan can exclude blood clots or brain tumours. Drugs should also be reviewed in case they are implicated. Otherwise diagnosis rests on demonstrating that the symptoms of loss of short-term memory and confusion are present during clear consciousness and are not due to drowsiness or a comatose state.

Premature dementia, that is, dementia that occurs before the age of 60, should always be thoroughly investigated in case it is due to a treatable disorder. A number of other types of dementia have been recognized but as yet they can only be differentiated by post-mortem examination.

There is no recognized treatment for Alzheimer's disease. It is important to stimulate Alzheimer's sufferers for as long as possible by reading out loud, talking to them and taking them out. Asking about daily activities and where they live will increase their awareness of time and place and a regular routine will provide them with some anchor in reality. Ultimately, however, constant nursing supervision and help with all aspects of day-to-day living may be necessary. Sedation may be necessary if agitation and wandering off become major problems.

maintaining a balanced diet

As far as anyone knows, there are no foods or food constituents which can actually reverse the brain changes which occur in people with Alzheimer's disease, nor can the specific neurological symptoms be significantly affected by diet. However, this is not to say that diet is unimportant for someone with this distressing and progressive condition. It is vital that they are encouraged to eat a varied, nutritionally balanced and nourishing diet to ensure that their general state of health remains as good as possible and that their symptoms are not exacerbated by nutritional deficiencies.

As the condition becomes more advanced, it is likely that someone – whether they are a family member, a friend or a health professional – takes responsibility for ensuring that the confused person does eat regularly, otherwise they may forget when they last ate, or forget to eat at all. Missing meals can result in low blood-glucose levels, which can make the confusion caused by the condition itself still worse.

To give the brain the best possible chance of functioning as well as it is able, it must receive what it needs: water, proteins, carbohydrates, fats, vitamins and minerals. In practice, this means a wide-ranging diet, designed to appeal to the individual's taste and appetite. This may mean a certain amount of experimenting – a person who refuses fresh fruit may enjoy it when juiced, or may prefer vegetables turned into soup rather than served as an accompaniment, for example.

DIETARY TIPS

Above: Plenty of fluids are essential or dehydration may make symptoms worse.

Below left: Brown rice is a source of slow-release carbohydrate which the brain needs for energy.

- The essential fatty acids omega-3 and omega-6 are vital for brain function and cannot be made in the body. Good food sources include all kinds of oily fish, such as mackerel, herring and salmon, and nuts and seeds.

- The brain requires a constant supply of glucose to meet its energy needs, but ideally this should arrive in a steady stream rather than in bursts. A diet that is based on complex carbohydrates such as bread, pasta, rice and other cereals is the best way to achieve this, together with a minimum of high-sugar foods.

- A confused person can easily become dehydrated if they forget to drink frequently and this will add to their mental difficulties. Plenty of water and a minimum of alcohol are the best ways to balance fluid levels.

BENEFICIAL RECIPES & JUICES

Spiced beetroot
(see page 132)

•

Stir-fried broccoli with sesame seeds
(see page 136)

•

Brown rice pudding
(see page 170)

Lemon rice & wild rice salad
(see page 174)

•

Herrings with spinach & parmesan
(see page 180)

•

Runa & red pepper chowder
(see page 182)

migraines

Some foods, such as cheese, chocolate, bananas, oranges and nuts, as well as red wine and coffee, provoke attacks. It is worth keeping a diary to see whether your migraines are linked with any particular foods or with any particular activity.

Above: As soon as you feel the first signs of a migraine coming on, you should start appropriate treatment.

Right: Once the migraine has set in, it may be too late to prevent its worst effects taking hold and it could last up to a few days.

Everyone gets a headache occasionally and, although the causes of most headaches are uncertain, many are clearly associated with tension in the muscles of the neck. Migraine is a particular type of headache, caused by an abnormal widening of the blood vessels within the skull and around the brain, and its effects can be particularly debilitating.

The early symptoms of classic migraine are a sense of foreboding of something happening within the head, often accompanied by nausea, and shimmering in the field of vision, known as the fortification spectrum. Some people also experience visual disturbances in one eye or odd sensations in one limb; they may also develop slurred speech and have an increased sensitivity to light or sound. These symptoms are followed by a severe headache that affects only one side of the head. This may last anything from just a few hours to a few days.

Certain drugs, such as those used in contraception and hormone replacement therapy (HRT), and calcium-channel blockers (for high blood pressure), can trigger migraine and it may be advisable not to take them. Other triggers include overtiredness, overexcitement, eyestrain or tension and certain foods.

Drugs known as triptans are effective at cutting short the symptoms of severe migraine. It is very important to take these drugs at the first signs of an attack because, once nausea sets in, they are poorly absorbed from the stomach. People who have frequent migraines may also find preventive treatment worthwhile; beta-blockers, which have a mild calming effect, are the most widely used drug. Both must be taken every day for full benefit.

identifying trigger foods

All kinds of foods can trigger a migraine attack in susceptible people, although they may sometimes be able to get away with eating small amounts of their trigger foods. Identifying those which affect you personally can be difficult, especially if the symptoms only appear many hours later rather than immediately after eating. Probably the best way to establish any links between what you eat and a migraine is to keep a detailed food diary for a week, noting in detail everything you eat and drink, the time you do so and the timing and nature of any migraine attacks.

There are a number of triggers which are known to cause reactions in many people with migraine, including: caffeine, chocolate, preserved meats, fermented foods and alcohol (especially red wine, brandy, whisky and sherry). A more comprehensive list would also feature citrus fruit and juices, yeast extracts and products, bananas, smoked fish, shellfish, wheat-based foods and dairy produce. However, your personal triggers may not appear on either of these lists, so you need to do your own detective work.

The reason why some foods trigger migraine is that they contain a group of natural chemicals known as vasoactive amines, such as tyramine. These substances act on the blood vessels, causing them to widen or narrow. It is this change in the size of the blood vessels that triggers the cycle of pain. Different types of amines are found in some cheeses, red wine, yeast extracts, chocolate, some sausages and citrus fruit.

DIETARY TIPS

- Other chemicals besides amines may be triggers for certain individuals, especially nitrates and nitrites, which occur naturally in many foods. These include beetroot, lettuce, celery, spinach, radishes and rhubarb. They are also present in processed meats such as bacon, salami, frankfurters and pepperoni.

- Soft, cream and cottage cheeses do not contain tyramine, unlike many other cheeses, especially blue and mature ones, so you may be able to eat them without any ill effects.

- If you identify several different types of food which set off your migraine and decide to cut them out, make sure you are still getting a sufficiently wide range of essential nutrients from other sources.

Above: Cheese is a common trigger food.

Below: Unsuspected foods, such as radishes, contain chemicals that can also act as triggers.

BENEFICIAL RECIPES & JUICES

Baked vine tomatoes (see page 150)
•
Nut koftas with minted yogurt (see page 173)
•
Mung bean & herb risotto (see page 170)
•
Butterbean & tomato soup (see page 161)

Brown rice pudding (see page 171)
•
Cabbage bhaji (see page 139)
•
Kale & wheatgrass energizer (see page 141)
•
Cabbage & carrot juice (see page 141)

ear infections

Above & right: Children are very susceptible to ear infections, but usually grow out of them as the passages in their ears and nose get larger. It can be quite upsetting to see your child with an ear infection as they will change from being naturally active and boisterous to withdrawn and upset.

Some children suffer from 'glue ear', in which there is persistent mucus in the ear that affects hearing. If this involves both ears, it lasts for a number of months and causes considerable hearing loss. Most ear, nose and throat (ENT) surgeons would remove the adenoids and insert grommets in the eardrums.

The ear is made up of three distinct parts – the outer, middle and inner ears – all of which may become infected. Ear infections tend to occur more frequently in children, although adults commonly suffer from eczema of the outer ear.

The outer ear is prone to skin disorders, such as eczema and fungal infections. These cause itching and a watery discharge, and scaling may spread from the ear canal onto the ear itself. Boils also occur and, however small, may be extremely painful. Antibiotic or antifungal drops settle most minor infections and eczema. More serious infections, especially boils, require antibiotics by mouth. Chronic infections, including eczema, require specialized treatment to remove the debris and to pack the ear canal with antiseptic gauze.

The middle ear is the most common site of infections, which are usually spread from the mouth or throat via the Eustachian tube. If the tube becomes blocked, secretions accumulate and become infected. The build-up of pressure results in intense pain and may even rupture the eardrum, releasing the infected matter and relieving both the pressure and the pain. Treatment of middle-ear infection varies from painkillers to antibiotics. A ruptured eardrum should be checked after a few weeks to see whether it has healed.

Inner-ear infections are usually caused by viruses. They may be a complication of colds, flu or mumps, or they may spread from the middle ear. Viral infections usually tend to clear within a few days, but antihistamine drugs may be given to alleviate the symptoms.

Children often outgrow ear complaints as their nose and ear passages enlarge. In some cases of chronic ear infection, however, it may be advisable to remove the adenoids and insert grommets in the eardrums; these allow secretions to pass out of the ear passage and air to flow in.

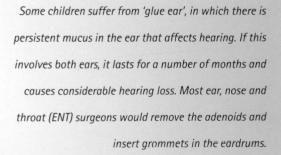

fighting infection with food

Ears may be directly infected, or problems may develop as a result of an upper respiratory tract infection with a virus, such as a cold, which then causes infected mucus to build up in the ears. Either way, you need to follow a diet which will encourage your immune system to fight the infection and reduce the accumulated mucus.

You need to ensure that you eat a good, varied diet to improve your resistance to infection, paying particular attention to your zinc intake. Steer clear of sugar and sugary foods, caffeine and alcohol, because all of these can lower your zinc levels. Foods that are high in zinc include meat, especially offal such as liver and kidneys, all kinds of fish and shellfish, wholegrain cereals, pulses such as peas, beans and soya, cabbages and seeds. Make sure that you get plenty of vitamins too – especially vitamin A, B and C vitamins. This means lots of fresh fruit and vegetables; red and orange ones are good for vitamin A – carrots, apricots, red peppers, pumpkins and sweet potatoes, for example – while citrus fruit, strawberries, blackcurrants, kiwi fruit and green vegetables such as broccoli are high in vitamin C. Both garlic and onions are said to have properties that help the body fight against infection, so try to have some of each every day.

Some experts believe that milk and other dairy produce may encourage the production of mucus, so it may be worth cutting these out while you have the infection, to see whether it helps.

Above: Red peppers will provide you with a boost of vitamin A.

- An ear infection can make you feel quite unwell, especially if it is combined with a bad cold; so, if your appetite is poor, you may find juices and soups more appealing than solid food.

- If the ear infection is a result of some other condition, such as eczema, it may be that you need to consider whether a food allergy is playing a part. Some children with eczema might be reacting to cows' milk and/or dairy produce, but you should consult a doctor or health visitor before restricting a child's diet.

- The herb echinacea is often recommended as a means of fighting cold-type infections – and you can use it to make a soothing tea.

BENEFICIAL RECIPES & JUICES

Poached apricots with oatmeal cream
(see page 114)

•

Cabbage bhaji
(see page 139)

•

Lentil, green peppercorn &
mustard dip (see page 160)

Carrot & kiwi juice
(see page 143)

•

Juice medley
(see page 159)

•

Root juice
(see page 159)

---

tonsillitis

Right: Treatment for tonsillitis will often come in the form of penicillin antibiotics or painkilling medicine. Children will often need to take this in the form of a medicine instead of tablets, which will actually be easier on the throat.

Below: It may be necessary for your doctor to take a throat swab in order to decide on the most appropriate treatment.

The tonsils are located on either side of the back of the throat. Together with the adenoids, they are part of a ring of specialized tissue that surrounds the throat and nasal passage and serves to trap any infectious organisms before they get into the lungs or gullet. As a result of this activity, the tonsils sometimes become severely inflamed and swollen and very painful.

Symptoms include a mild sore throat, which rapidly becomes painful and makes swallowing difficult, headache and fever. Often there is pain in the ears and bad breath. The tonsils themselves may be covered in white spots or a white slough and the lymph nodes of the neck may also swell, making the whole neck tender.

Tonsillitis is most common in children, although it may occur at any age. In teenagers, it is often caused by glandular fever, but is more usually due to a viral or bacterial infection. Few cases are dangerous but, in cases of severe bacterial infection (the so-called 'strep throat'), the sufferer may feel extremely ill. Complications are rare but include inner-ear infections, rheumatic fever, kidney inflammation and septicaemia (which is also known as blood poisoning).

Painkillers reduce the fever and pain and there are several preparations that act as a local anaesthetic, making eating and drinking less uncomfortable. Throat sweets can give relief. It may be necessary to take a throat swab in order to identify the cause of the infection. Bacterial infections are usually treated with penicillin antibiotics. For recurrent bouts of tonsillitis, a blood test may be necessary to exclude glandular fever or a blood disorder. Chronic tonsillitis may require the removal of the tonsils surgically (tonsillectomy).

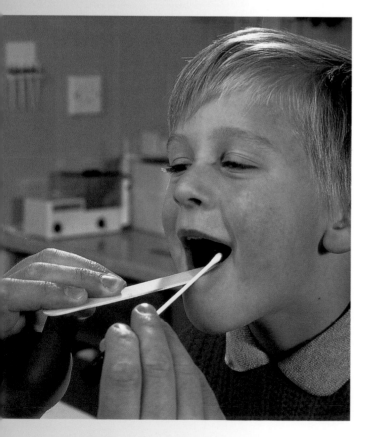

soothing foods

When your throat is painful, anything sharp or solid can irritate the inflamed area, making eating difficult. Nevertheless, it is important to maintain your intake of vital nutrients to help your body fight the virus or bacterium that is the root cause of your symptoms. You need to maintain a good intake of vitamins and flavonoids to help your immune system battle the infection and reduce inflammation; a good intake of minerals – especially zinc – will also help. You will probably find it more comfortable to meet your nutritional needs by opting for juices and soups which will be much easier and less uncomfortable to swallow. If acid fruit hurts your throat, try juices incorporating vegetables such as carrots and beetroot; tomatoes may be best avoided too while your throat is sore.

Look for recipes that include plenty of ingredients rich in vitamin A, such as apricots, mangoes, red peppers, pumpkins, sweet potatoes,

carrots, watercress and broccoli. If you can manage to eat oily fish, such as herrings, salmon, mackerel, sardines and so on, you will be getting the benefit of the omega-3 fatty acids they contain, together with their vitamin A content. Fruit such as apples and citrus fruit, green beans, onions and tea are the best sources of flavonoids; they are also present in red wine, but you might find that hard to take while you are feeling bad. Dairy produce has a reputation for increasing mucus, so you may want to avoid it for the time being.

BENEFICIAL RECIPES & JUICES

Stir-fried broccoli with sesame seeds
(see page 136)

•

Chilled watercress soup
(see page 155)

•

Herrings with spinach & parmesan
(see page 180)

Apricot smoothie
(see page 115)

•

Cranberry & mango smoothie
(see page 123)

•

Watercress, carrot & celery juice
(see page 157)

DIETARY TIPS

- Traditionally, children with tonsillitis were encouraged to eat ice cream which does not irritate the throat; it is better to give them one made with natural ingredients if possible as these have more nutritional value than cheaper commercial varieties.

- While sugary foods may give you a brief energy boost, their nutrient content is often limited. They are best avoided if your appetite is small, because you may then not want to eat much else.

- You may find herbal teas soothing for your throat – try mint or camomile – but remember not to drink it too hot.

Above left: Pumpkins are a rich source of vitamin A and would be ideal eaten in a soup.

Below: Ice cream has always been a traditional aid to soothing the discomfort of tonsillitis in children. Ensure that you give your child a homemade version that is relatively low in fat and sugar.

motion sickness

Some people are sensitive to repetitive movements of the whole body and may suffer from motion sickness, or travel sickness as it is also known. The symptoms include headache, pallor, sweating and heavy breathing, discomfort in the abdomen, nausea and vomiting. Because of this, many people dread the prospect of travelling by car, boat or aeroplane, and even going on funfair rides or going up and down in a lift.

Motion sickness is thought to be associated with the balancing mechanisms within the ear, which help the brain coordinate information about space and movement. As well as physical causes, there can also be a psychological cause, brought on by fear of movements over which the person has no control. For example, it is usually the passengers in a car that suffer from motion sickness rather than the driver, who is in charge of the motion.

Sufferers should avoid eating a rich or heavy meal before setting out on a journey. They may find it helpful to sit in the passenger seat of a car rather than the back, or near the centre of a boat, where the motion is less.

Various over-the-counter drugs are available but sufferers may have to try several before finding one that suits them. It is important to take the drug an hour before setting out on the journey; if it is taken while travelling, it may be vomited out of the system. These drugs usually contain atropine and antihistamines, which can have a sedative effect; it is important to avoid drinking alcohol when taking them. Occasionally they have side-effects, such as blurred vision. For long journeys, or for people who suffer badly, a doctor may prescribe stronger drugs.

Applying pressure to an acupuncture point on the inner wrist, about three fingers' width above the wrist crease and in line with the middle finger, may help to alleviate travel sickness. This is the principle behind the wristbands that are available from pharmacies.

Above: Being a passenger in a car is a very common cause of motion sickness. Your suffering can be lessened if you sit in a passenger seat instead of the back of the car.

Right: You can try to help yourself during bouts of motion sickness by applying pressure to a specific point in your wrist (see above).

limiting the effects

While there are various remedies available to treat the symptoms of motion sickness, you may make yourself less vulnerable to them in the first place by making adjustments to your diet. If you are planning a lengthy journey, ban sugary and fatty foods from your plate for at least 24 hours before you are due to set off from home. Instead, have only small, light meals and, in particular, avoid having a substantial meal in the hour or so before your departure.

When you are on the road, resist the 'chips with everything' menus in motorway service stations. When travelling by air, you may find it helps to pack a light picnic meal to eat on the plane rather than eating whatever the airline provides. If you have to wait for a plane, resist any temptation to have a couple of drinks in the hope that they will settle your stomach, and do not drink alcohol during the flight. It may upset your digestive system and simply make matters worse.

Keep your fluid intake up before and during the journey: water is best, or opt for herbal teas such as camomile or peppermint. Ginger has a reputation as an anti-nausea remedy, so it might help to drink tea made with hot water and root ginger before you set off. Good-quality ginger biscuits, made with a minimum of sugar, make a handy mid-journey snack. You may not feel like anything at all, but if you can manage light snacks you will feel better than you will on an empty stomach.

Above: Root ginger can help alleviate nausea, and is best taken in a hot tea.

- If it is practical, consider taking a vacuum flask of ginger tea with you to drink on the journey – as well as being refreshing it will help to stave off any nauseous sensations.

- Dry, wholegrain crackers may not be particularly appetising, but they will help to settle a complaining stomach and their blandness may make them acceptable when you simply cannot face the thought of anything else.

- Do not be tempted to soothe a child prone to motion sickness with sweets or chocolate bars – the sugar content will only add to their problems. The same applies to fizzy sweet drinks – fruit juice is a much better choice.

BENEFICIAL RECIPES & JUICES

Greens soup
(see page 140)

•

Tomato & orange soup
(see page 152)

•

Carrot, apple & ginger smoothie
(see page 143)

Breakfast smoothie
(see page 121)

•

Blueberry & grapefruit juice
(see page 122)

•

Banana tofu smoothie
(see page 187)

---

acne

Above: Taking care of your skin, and not applying too much greasy make-up, should help reduce the effects of acne.

The role of food in the development of acne is debatable. There is no scientific evidence to suggest that excess fat in the diet and certain foods, such as cheese and chocolate, are implicated, but individual experience may suggest otherwise. The answer is to keep a record.

This very common skin disorder affects mainly adolescents and young adults, both males and females, and occurs mainly on the face, chest and back. The condition is caused by an overproduction of an oily secretion (sebum) by the sebaceous glands, which is stimulated by increases in the levels of male hormones (androgens).

The sebum becomes trapped in the sebaceous gland and changes colour, forming a blackhead. This attracts bacteria which gradually build up until the surrounding area becomes inflamed and swells to form a characteristic red pimple with a yellow tip. Small pimples disappear in a few days, but large ones may pit and scar the skin.

Acne may be aggravated by excessive sweating, some drugs, such as steroids and contraceptives, and face creams and greasy cosmetics. There is also some evidence to suggest that it may be a hereditary condition. Exposure to sunlight or ultra-violet light may lead to an improvement.

Lotions or creams containing benzoyl peroxide will help to unblock the pores and remove the sebum, thus reducing the formation of blackheads. Retinoic acid, which is a more powerful agent, has a similar effect to this, but should never be used during pregnancy.

Extensive or resistant acne may require long-term antibiotic treatment, in either lotion or tablet form, but there is no proof that this reduces colonization by acne-producing bacteria. For severe acne, retinoic acid tablets are now available, but they have certain side-effects, such as dry skin and liver upsets.

Women may find that taking contraceptive pills, which regulate hormone levels, helps to reduce acne. Changing brands of contraceptive pill can also help because different brands vary in their natural antiandrogen activity. Discuss this with your doctor.

The unsightly scars left by acne can be reduced by dermabrasion (removing the top layer of skin) and collagen treatment can plump up the pitting.

healthy foods for healthy skin

Most doctors now dismiss as an old wives' tale the idea that eating chocolate and fatty foods is a cause of acne, although a diet consisting mainly of 'junk food' certainly will not help the condition. Nevertheless, some people are sure that particular foods have an adverse effect on their skin, in particular, chocolate, cheese, wheat-based foods such as bread, pasta and some cereals, and almonds. If you suspect this might apply to you, try cutting out each one for a while to see whether there is any improvement in your acne. Do not exclude them all at the same time or you will not know whether it is just one or all of the foods that is making your skin worse.

To give your system the best possible chance of battling acne, you should eat a diet that is based around lots of complex carbohydrates (such as wholemeal bread and pasta, and brown rice), plus plenty of fresh vegetables, salads and fruit. Keep processed foods to a minimum and, if necessary, cut down your intake of saturated fats. Most of the fat in your diet should be polyunsaturated or monounsaturated; that is to say, those from vegetable and plant rather than animal sources, as well as essential fatty acids. The best source of these is oily fish such as mackerel, herrings, salmon, sardines. Try to get a lot of your protein intake from non-animal sources; pulses, lentils and soya, for example. Anti-oxidant vitamins are important too, especially beta-carotene which the body turns into vitamin A; opt for red and orange fruit and vegetables.

DIETARY TIPS

• Sulphur-rich foods can help your skin improve – so try to eat some garlic and onions every day. Eggs are another good source.

• If you find it difficult to eat lots of fruit and vegetables every day, try making juices from different combinations of ingredients.

• Keep up your fluid intake by drinking as much water as you can, and keep alcohol to a minimum.

• Make sure your diet is rich in both vitamins and minerals, especially zinc. Fish, shellfish, wholegrains and seeds are all good sources.

Above left: Carrots provide the essential anti-oxidant vitamin, beta-carotene.

Below: Garlic provides sulphur, which is good for your skin.

BENEFICIAL RECIPES & JUICES

Broccoli & red pepper fettuccine (see page 134)

•

Bean & tomato couscous (see page 162)

•

Nut & seed savoury cakes (see page 172)

Cabbage & carrot juice (see page 141)

•

Carrot & kiwi juice (see page 143)

•

Red pepper & tomato tonic (see page 145)

burns, cuts
& bruises

Accidents occur most commonly in the home, but the majority are fairly minor. Many involve the following soft-tissue injuries.

Burns are caused by exposure to dry heat, such as fire, electricity and strong sunlight or wet heat, such as boiling liquids. Mild burns (first degree) are painful but seldom dangerous. The damage is restricted to the outer layer of skin and there is redness, soreness, heat and sometimes blistering. Sunburn produces first-degree burns and may also cause fever and swelling of the affected area. More serious burns (second degree) affect the lower layers of the skin, producing blisters. The most serious burns (third degree) affect the tissue and nervous system deep below the skin. Shock may accompany both second- and third-degree burns. All burns should be bathed in cold water for 10–15 minutes and covered with a clean dressing.

Seek medical advice if the burn is extensive or fails to heal.

Cuts are usually minor and only damage the capillaries. Some blood may be lost into the tissues or escape from the wound, but it should soon clot. To stop any bleeding, apply pressure and raise the affected area. A loose dressing will keep the cut clean, although exposure to air may help the healing process. Severe or deep cuts may need stitching.

Bruises are caused by an impact to the body that ruptures the capillaries. Blood then leaks into the tissues under the skin, forming a characteristic blue-purple bruise. A cold compress should alleviate minor bruising. A badly bruised limb may need to be rested for 24–48 hours, preferably raised on pillows to reduce the blood flow to the affected area. Spontaneous bruising is generally due to a benign condition, but may be indicative of haemophilia. No medical help is required unless the bruising has no apparent cause or has not cleared up within the space of a fortnight.

Many accidents around the home can be avoided by simple precautions. These include:

- *Taking extra care in the kitchen if there is boiling water or fat around.*
- *Storing knives and sharp instruments out of the reach of children.*
- *Removing obstacles from floors, tacking down loose carpets and providing good lighting.*

Right: Boiling water can cause serious scalds, so you should take extra care, especially if there are children in the kitchen.

Below: Take care with sharp implements, and store where children cannot get hold of them.

foods & juices for tissue repair

Your body will heal itself in time, provided that the damage is not severe enough to need medical treatment; in the mean time you need to supply it with all the nutrients it needs to repair itself as quickly as possible. As well as eating the right kind of foods, make sure you drink plenty of water to help make up any loss of fluid and encourage the clearance of any debris around the injury.

To promote tissue repair, the most important components of your diet should be vitamin A (or beta-carotene), vitamin C, zinc and sulphur-rich foods. This means lots of fruit and vegetables, but these will be just as effective in the form of juices as raw or lightly cooked. For beta-carotene, remember it is mostly red and orange fruit and vegetables you need: opt for apricots, mangoes, pumpkins, sweet potatoes, carrots and red peppers, plus oily fish (herrings, mackerel, sardines, salmon and pilchards, for example), watercress and broccoli.

Good sources of vitamin C include citrus fruit, blackcurrants, strawberries, kiwi fruit, pineapples, tomatoes, broccoli and other green, leafy vegetables, avocados, mushrooms and sprouted seeds. All kinds of fish (including shellfish), meat (particularly offal), chicken, eggs and wholegrain cereals will boost your zinc levels, while onions and garlic should be included in your diet for their sulphur content.

BENEFICIAL RECIPES & JUICES

Spiced orange & avocado salad
(see page 125)
•
Watercress & mushroom frittata (see page 154)
•
Mushroom, couscous & herb sausages (see page 166)

Mixed fruit smoothie
(see page 131)
•
Blackberry & pineapple juice
(see page 131)
•
Soothing tonic
(see page 157)

DIETARY TIPS

- Foods with a high vitamin C content, those containing flavonoids – such as apples, green beans and tea – and zinc-rich foods may help to ensure that, as a wound heals, the new skin will be supple and healthy.

- Steer clear of too many processed or fried foods – you will get more useful nutrients from raw or lightly cooked ingredients.

- Make sure you eat a good variety of foods each day, because then you are unlikely to miss out on any of the essential nutrients.

Above left: Avocados are one of a number of foods that will provide you with good levels of vitamin E to help repair damaged tissues.

Above: Citrus fruit is also well known as a good source of vitamin C.

cold sores

Although cold sores are not harmful, they are unsightly and highly contagious. They are caused by the *Herpes simplex* type 1 virus and are usually passed from person to person, often through kissing.

After the first attack, many people succeed in developing a natural immunity to the virus. In those who are less fortunate, the virus lies dormant in the nerve cells until it is reactivated by illness, stress or the state of being generally run down. Exposure to strong sunlight or high winds may also activate the virus.

Cold sores and genital herpes are both caused by the Herpes simplex *virus, although genital herpes usually results from a different strain (type 2). Nevertheless, it is possible to transmit cold sores to the genitalia.*

The first symptom is a tingling sensation, typically on one lip. This is followed by small raised blisters, which eventually burst, releasing a pale yellow fluid that forms a crust. The blisters usually occur around the mouth, often in clusters. They are itchy and painful and take 10–14 days to disappear. Secondary infections by bacteria are not unusual, and may lead to swelling of the affected area.

The pain and duration of the attack can be reduced by treatment with acyclovir, a modern antiviral drug. This is supplied as an ointment or, for severe cases, in the form of tablets. It is important to apply the ointment to the affected area as soon as the tingling begins, because it is at this time that the viruses are multiplying. If a secondary infection develops, it may be necessary to use a separate antibiotic cream.

In time, the attacks will become progressively less severe, until they eventually stop altogether.

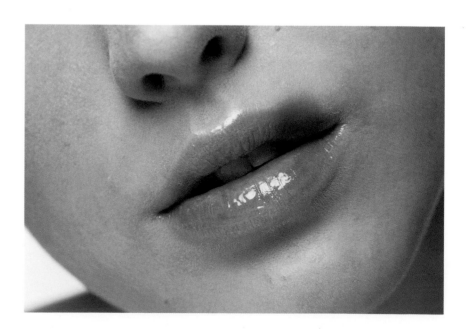

Right: Cold sores are highly contagious, and if you develop one you should refrain from kissing other people until the condition has been successfully treated.

avoiding cold sores

If you are one of those people who tend to develop cold sores when you are run down or under stress, you need to eat foods that build up your immune system and your ability to resist infection.

It could also be that outbreaks are triggered by sensitivity to certain foods – you will need to experiment to find whether this applies to you. Very often you will find that, if you are prone to cold sores, you are more likely to get them when you have a cold or upper respiratory tract infection, so anything that helps you to avoid catching cold viruses will lessen cold-sore attacks too.

Two particular amino acids – which are the building blocks of protein – may also play an important role in whether you get lots of cold sores. The first, lysine, is thought to have a protective effect, preventing recurrences of sores as well as easing the symptoms. The other, arginine, is believed to play a role in the synthesis of the herpes virus which causes cold sores. Some of the 21 amino acids can be made by the body itself, but these two have to be obtained through the foods we eat. By eating more lysine-containing foods and less of those containing arginine, you may be able to reduce the number of cold-sore attacks. This means eating more chicken, turkey, eggs and fish, and lower amounts of beans, lentils, nuts, seeds, raisins, chocolate and foods containing gelatine.

DIETARY TIPS

- Boost your resistance to infection with a vitamin-rich diet, paying special attention to vitamin C, found in blackcurrants, strawberries, pineapples, kiwi fruit, citrus fruit, broccoli, cabbages and other green, leafy vegetables.

- Zinc-containing foods will also help boost your resistance, so eat plenty of fish, shellfish, meat, offal, wholegrain cereals and seeds.

- Garlic is a good source of several important minerals, including sulphur, also found in onions.

Above left: Seeds, such as sesame seeds, contain arginine, which could trigger cold sore attacks.

Above: Fish contains zinc, which will help your ability to resist infection.

BENEFICIAL RECIPES & JUICES

Cranberry & chicken stir-fry with ginger (see page 119)

•

Mixed vegetable risotto (see page 135)

•

Boiled eggs with anchovy soldiers (see page 181)

Apricot & pineapple smoothie (see page 115)

•

Green vegetable juice (see page 137)

•

Wheatgerm, pineapple & banana booster (see page 168)

dermatitis

Dermatitis is a general term meaning inflammation of the skin, and it tends to imply a reaction to a chemical. Several different types of dermatitis have been identified:

● **primary irritant dermatitis** This is caused by chemicals, such as industrial solvents, detergents and household cleaners, that remove the natural lubricants in the skin. Cleaners and hairdressers are often affected by this condition. Exposure causes the skin to become dry, fissured and cracked.

● **allergic contact dermatitis** This form consists of an immune reaction by the skin to a chemical to which the body has become sensitized. Once developed, the sensitivity is lifelong. It is more common in people with eczema, and the hands are particularly affected. Common sensitizers include dyes, cosmetics, rubber, elastic, leathers, nickel in jewellery and preservatives in skin creams. There is irritation, redness, and scaling or blistering at the site of contact. The rash may spread, and affect the whole body.

● **asteotic dermatitis** Most common in the elderly, this type of dermatitis causes dry skin and irritation, which worsen if soap is used too frequently. The condition improves if soap substitutes are used and emollients are applied regularly.

● **photodermatitis** Clusters of blisters or spots appear on areas exposed to sunlight or ultra-violet light. Sensitivity may be triggered by chemicals in perfumes, some antibiotics, and contact with plants, such as wild parsley and rue.

Above: There are several different forms of dermatits, but most result from an allergic reaction to some kind of liquid, such as perfumes and cosmetics.

In skin testing, a small amount of allergen is dropped on to the skin and a puncture is made below it with a fine needle. A small red weal will appear at this spot if there is an allergy to the substance. In this way, several allergens can be tested at the same time.

All forms of dermatitis have similar symptoms, which may vary in severity. The itching and burning leads to a strong impulse to scratch which can result in an infection that prolongs the condition.

Once the offending agent is recognized, contact can be avoided, for instance by wearing gloves or using a barrier cream. Skin testing helps to identify the less obvious irritants. Symptoms respond to moisturizing creams or steroid creams and antihistamines will relieve itching.

feeding your skin

Your main defence against dermatitis will consist of trying to steer clear of the substances or situations that trigger it, but following the right eating programme will be good for the general health of your skin and of your whole body. Although the terms eczema and dermatitis are sometimes used interchangeably, the kind of skin problem which is more likely to be a reaction to food is treated in a separate section (see eczema, page 78).

You should aim for a varied diet, based on unrefined carbohydrates, including bread, pasta, brown rice and starchy fruit and vegetables, such as potatoes, squashes and bananas. As far as possible, opt for fresh foods in preference to fatty or sugary processed foods which are likely to contain far fewer nutrients.

Fruit and vegetables are important because they ensure a good supply of anti-oxidant vitamins, especially vitamin C: so eat plenty of citrus fruit, strawberries, blackcurrants, kiwi fruit, green, leafy vegetables and red, orange and yellow vegetables such as peppers, carrots, tomatoes and sweet potatoes. Another group of nutrients in fruit and vegetables, known as quercetins, is said to stabilize cell membranes and block the allergic response. The mineral zinc is important for healthy skin, and good sources include oysters, clams, eggs, hazelnuts, Brazil nuts and pumpkin seeds.

Although you should try to eat only small amounts of saturated fats (which come mainly from animal sources), so-called essential fatty acids may be helpful because they may reduce any tendency you have to dry skin, as well as countering inflammation. Eat plenty of oily fish – sardines, mackerel or herrings – plus nuts and seeds, and use nut and seed oils for salad dressings.

DIETARY TIPS

- Try substituting water or herbal teas for drinks containing caffeine, such as coffee, normal tea and cola, as too much caffeine may diminish the body's ability to make full use of the nutrients in your diet.

- Saturated fats (including those found in fatty meat foods such as sausages, dairy produce, cakes and pastries) may stop your body making effective use of the essential fatty acids omega-3 and omega-6, so cut down on these types of foods.

- It is unlikely that specific reactions to food are playing any part in triggering dermatitis, so it is not worth cutting out any particular food that you like and which is otherwise good for you.

Below: Cake is high in saturated fats which can prevent your body making use of essential fatty acids.

BENEFICIAL RECIPES & JUICES

Strawberry & cucumber salad
(see page 118)

•

Baked vine tomatoes
(see page 150)

•

Tomato, oregano & mozzarella
tartlets (see page 151)

Brown rice pudding
(see page 171)

•

Banana & peanut butter smoothie
(see page 117)

•

Tomato & apple pick-me-up
(see page 153)

eczema

Eczema most commonly occurs in people who have a heightened immune system and who also suffer from hay fever and asthma. It is becoming increasingly prevalent and now affects one in twelve people. It is often inherited and children of parents who both have eczema have a 60 per cent chance of getting it. The condition may be exacerbated by dry skin, food intolerance, non-specific stimuli (such as temperature, humidity, stress, sweating) and direct contact with allergens (jewellery, for example).

A number of self-help measures can prevent an outbreak of eczema. These include:

• Avoiding soaps, detergents and heavily perfumed or lanolin-based toilet preparations.

• Wearing absorbent cotton clothing and using non-biological detergents for all laundry.

• Avoiding substances that are known to cause allergic reactions.

The skin becomes dry, red and flaky and, in severe cases, blisters may form, burst open and develop into sores. There is extreme itching, even pain, and persistent scratching can lead to infection. The condition may be quite unsightly, but it is not contagious.

Eczema can begin within a few weeks of birth, affecting the scalp, eyebrows, cheeks, chest and groin of the baby. With age, the skin becomes less greasy-looking, redder and drier. The areas most affected are the creases of the elbows and the knees. Where there is particular irritation, the skin becomes thickened and cracked, a process that is called 'lichenification'. The condition improves in 50 per cent of children by the age of five, and in 80–95 per cent by the time they reach adolescence.

Below: Keeping vulnerable and affected areas of skin well moisturized with an appropriate lotion will help relieve the effects of eczema.

Adults who have had lifelong eczema will have areas of red, dry, lichenified skin that vary in severity according to external factors. They may also have eczema of the palms of the hands and soles of the feet, in the form of tiny, itchy, fluid-filled lesions. In some cases, eczema can also accompany varicose veins (see page 20).

Treatment is aimed primarily at keeping the skin moisturized and avoiding contact with any obvious irritants. Antihistamines will reduce the itching. For regular long-term treatment, mild hydrocortisone preparations are safe for all ages, while steroid creams or ointments are reserved for acute flare-ups. Steroid/antibiotic preparations are used in cases of infection.

how can diet help?

A tendency to allergic conditions runs in some families, who are said to be 'atopic'. Individual members may have asthma, hay fever or eczema, or, in some unfortunate cases, more than one of these conditions. The first signs of atopic eczema usually appear in the first weeks or months of a child's life. Even if you suspect that food may be a factor in triggering the condition, you should always seek professional advice before restricting a child's diet.

While many children eventually grow out of eczema, it can sometimes persist into adulthood. There are two aspects to tackling the role of food in your condition. The first is to eat a balanced diet that ensures your body is getting all the nutrients it needs to keep you in optimum health; the second is to discover whether particular foods exacerbate your condition so that you can avoid them if necessary.

As a first step, make sure your diet contains a wide range of vitamins and minerals by making it as varied as possible. This means lots of fruit, salad and vegetables – juices can play a part here – and keeping saturated fats and sugary or processed foods to a minimum. Build up your consumption of starchy foods, including pulses, lentils, nuts and seeds, as well as pasta, bread and brown rice, and cut down on drinks containing caffeine. Oily fish should appear on your menu several times a week to ensure a good intake of essential fatty acids.

If you want to try excluding certain foods, do so one at a time, noting the reaction, if any, before moving on to the next.

Above: Corn can be a trigger food for an attack of eczema.

- The most likely trigger foods in eczema include: wheat, rye, oats and corn; dairy produce and eggs; beef; poultry; fish or shellfish; chocolate, tea and coffee; food additives; yeast; pork; peanuts; nuts; citrus fruit; bananas; soya beans; and alcohol.

- It is possible to be tested at an allergy clinic for specific allergies, although the results are not always completely reliable. Medical allergy specialists advise against the tests offered by many complementary practitioners, as there is no evidence yet that they work.

- If you suspect food is implicated in your eczema, try keeping a detailed diary of everything you eat and drink to see whether there is a link with the state of your skin.

BENEFICIAL RECIPES & JUICES

Butter bean & tomato soup
(see page 161)

•

Nut koftas with minted yogurt
(see page 173)

•

Lemon rice & wild rice salad
(see page 174)

Cashew nut chicken
(see page 175)

•

Salmon & courgette brochettes
(see page 183)

•

Red pepper & tomato tonic
(see page 145)

---

coeliac disease

Above: Cereal grains such as wheat have become a staple part of most people's diet, but many may not realize that they are allergic to the protein gluten.

Food allergies can sometimes be identified by following an exclusion diet. This begins with a simple diet of just a few foods. If the symptoms disappear, a single food is then introduced every two weeks until one provokes symptoms. However, this is a lengthy process, interpretation of the effects is difficult and a long-term exclusion diet may be nutritionally deficient.

Coeliac disease is an allergy to gluten, which is a protein found in most cereals, particularly wheat and rye. This leads to destruction of the food-absorbing surface in the small intestine. The disease affects at least 1 in 1,500 to 1 in 2,000 of Caucasians, but is rare in non-Caucasians. It is more common in women and also far more common in some areas; for example, it affects 1 in 300 people in Ireland. It tends to run in families, which suggests that there is a genetic association. The disease was first recognized in the Netherlands during the Second World War, when bread was scarce. As a result, the health of certain children improved because they were no longer exposed to gluten.

Digested food passes from the stomach along the intestinal tract and the products of digestion are normally absorbed in the small intestine. To increase the surface area available for food absorption, the lining of the small intestine is covered with tiny, finger-like protrusions called villi. Hypersensitivity to gluten causes these villi to disappear, thus greatly reducing the surface area of the small intestine and leading to malabsorption of food. The exact mechanism whereby gluten affects the villi has yet to be determined.

In children, the onset of coeliac disease coincides with the introduction of cereals into the diet and there is failure to grow. Adults may experience abdominal pains and diarrhoea, although it is likely that many are just anaemic. Investigation may reveal anaemia and mouth ulcers. A biopsy of the small intestine will confirm the diagnosis. A blood test, which is useful in screening, shows antibodies to parts of the bowel.

Treatment involves following a lifelong gluten-free diet. Fortunately, a wide range of gluten-free products is now available. The surface of the small intestine will recover within 3–4 months of starting this diet.

avoiding gluten

The only remedy for coeliac disease is to avoid consuming gluten, the protein which triggers the damage to the small intestine and produces the symptoms. It is found in wheat, rye, barley and, in lesser amounts, in oats. It may sound simple enough, but in fact it is very difficult to do without expert advice from a dietician. This is because gluten is found in various forms in all sorts of foods and drinks and, often, you cannot be sure it is not there unless you have prepared or cooked the food yourself.

It is simple enough to recognize the more obvious gluten-containing foods: anything made from wheat, rye or barley, or flour made from them, such as bread, breakfast cereals, pasta, cakes, biscuits, pies and pizzas, for example. However, you also need to bear in mind that gluten is also likely to be present in many sauces, sausages, ready-made soups and fishcakes, as well as a wide range of processed foods. Eating out in restaurants can be more trouble than it is worth: you have to check whether an innocent-looking dish may have had some flour added, even when it is not obvious.

However, the good news is that there are lots of delicious foods you can eat and, if you choose, you can buy a range of gluten-free foods and ingredients to make dishes you might otherwise be unable to eat.

You will need to make a special effort to ensure that you get a good intake of vitamins and minerals; the cereal foods you cannot have are rich in many essential nutrients and it makes sense to get professional advice. All fruit, vegetables, salads, lentils, pulses, meat and fish should feature prominently on your menus, as can most dairy produce, though you may need to check on some milk- or yogurt-based desserts in case any flour has been incorporated into them.

BENEFICIAL RECIPES & JUICES

Mixed vegetable risotto
(see page 135)

•

Berry fruit scones
(see page 164)

•

Roasted red peppers with millet
& basil (see page 165)

Brown rice pudding
(see page 171)

•

Mung bean & herb risotto
(see page 170)

•

Lemon rice and wild rice salad
(see page 174)

DIETARY TIPS

- You may find traces of gluten in some surprising places – some mustards, margarines and salad dressings, for example – so check labels extremely carefully.

- Beer is on the forbidden list because it is made from barley, as well as North American whisky (or bourbon), which is made from rye.

- Some people with coeliac disease find they can eat oats without problems; others cannot. Alternative cereals that are safe include rice and corn.

Top: Dairy produce should not cause any problems for people with coeliac disease. Above: If you can't eat oats, substitute with rice or corn cereals.

constipation

People's bowel habits vary from having one bowel action every day to one a week. Constipation is defined by reference to usual bowel habit and not by any fixed rules. If the bowels are opened only infrequently but without straining there is no reason for concern.

Bowel habits vary greatly, but difficult and infrequent passing of dry, hard faeces is described as constipation. Although usually harmless, this can indicate an underlying disorder, especially in people over 40. Regularity and ease of passage is generally more important than frequency, but any noticeable change in bowel habits should be reported to a doctor.

Constipation results from the accumulation of faeces in the large intestine. The longer they remain, the more water is extracted and the harder they become. This accumulation may be caused by a reduction in the rhythmic bowel contractions that normally push food through the system or by a bowel obstruction. Constipation may be associated with pregnancy, an underactive thyroid gland (see page 42), irritable bowel syndrome (see page 92) and depression (see page 58), as well as the use of painkillers and a diet that is low in fibre. In children, it may be caused by emotional disorders. The elderly are more prone to constipation because they tend to eat smaller quantities of less bulky foods, and exercise less.

Symptoms of constipation include pain on defaecation and a feeling that the bowel has not been completely emptied. Persistent constipation in older people may indicate a growth in the large bowel, especially if this is accompanied by pain and bleeding. In the case of children, it may be due to a congenital malformation of the bowel. Sudden constipation together with pain and distension of the abdomen indicates an obstruction in the bowel and requires emergency treatment.

All constipation benefits from an increased intake of fibre and fluids. Laxatives may also provide occasional relief although they should not be used regularly. There are three types:

Above & below: Foods with a high fibre content, such as beans and pulses, will help to alleviate the discomfort of constipation.

● **stimulants**, which affect the muscular movements of the bowel and speed up the passage of the faeces. These may lead to cramps.

● **fluid retainers**, which draw water back into the faeces. These are safer for long-term use.

● **suppositories** stimulate the bowel quickly, while enemas will wash out the contents of the bowel.

Unless constipation is the result of an underlying condition which needs appropriate diagnosis and treatment, it usually responds well to dietary measures. In most cases, constipation is largely a result of eating a diet that includes a lot of refined and processed foods and relatively small amounts of fibre. Making the change from the old habits to eating a high-fibre diet is best done gradually so that your digestive system (and your taste buds) have time to adapt.

Fibre comes from the cell walls of plants, and is an important component of a healthy diet because it adds bulk to the stools and accelerates the progress of waste material through the digestive system. However, if your body is not used to a large intake, you may suffer initially from wind or discomfort if you overdo fibre-rich food. Start by increasing your consumption of fruit, vegetables and salads – and try some of the delicious juice combinations you will find in the recipe section. You can then begin to introduce complex carbohydrates, such as wholemeal bread instead of white, pasta, rice, potatoes, lentils, pulses and wholemeal cereals, including oats.

As you get used to the new way of eating, try to base all your meals around such high-fibre foods – think in terms of a baked potato or pasta accompanied by a topping or sauce made of vegetables or a little meat, rather than treating meat as the main component of your meal with the odd vegetable as an accompaniment.

Above: Make a baked potato, with a tasty sauce, the main focus of your meal rather than just something to eat with meat.

- Fibre absorbs a lot of water as it passes through your system, so make a point of drinking more than you are used to; juices, pure water and herbal teas are healthier choices than tea, coffee, cola or alcohol.

- Wean yourself away from highly refined foods such as white bread, cakes, biscuits and pastries. As well as being low in fibre, many such processed foods contain high levels of sugar, fat and salt, and are not as rich in important nutrients as unprocessed foods.

- 'Traditional' remedies to combat constipation, such as figs and prunes, really do work, but remember to treat them as part of a varied, balanced diet rather than as the occasional 'instant fix' when your constipation is troubling you.

BENEFICIAL RECIPES & JUICES

Really fruity flapjacks
(see page 129)

•

Spinach & lemon risotto
(see page 148)

•

Tofu, cinnamon & honey pockets
(see page 186)

Sweet & sour smoothie
(see page 145)

•

Banana tofu smoothie
(see page 187)

•

Tofu fruit smoothie
(see page 187)

diarrhoea

Above & below: Bowel infections leading to diarrhoea are commonly caused by poor hygiene in the kitchen, so take extra care.

Foreign travel brings people into contact with unfamiliar foods and unfamiliar organisms, which may result in diarrhoea. It is a wise precaution to use only bottled water for drinking and cleaning your teeth. Freshly cooked foods are preferable to mass-produced foods or foods that have been kept in a warm cabinet.

Food passes through most of the intestinal tract as a liquid slurry. When it reaches the bowel, the water is reabsorbed to produce solid or semi-solid motions that are then evacuated from the body. If the fluid is not reabsorbed, the motions remain liquid, resulting in diarrhoea. A number of conditions affect the reabsorption process.

Infections may cause temporary inflammation of the bowel. Typhus and cholera are rare in the developed world but can rapidly lead to a dangerously high fluid loss. Gastroenteritis, or food poisoning, is caused by a particular organism or toxin in food that does not infect the bowel but makes it overactive. Less common causes are worry, malabsorption and an overactive thyroid gland (see page 42). Persistent diarrhoea may be a sign of inflammatory bowel disease or, in an older person, a growth in the bowel.

Symptoms include abdominal cramps that are relieved by opening the bowels, urgently and many times a day. The motions are semi-formed or liquid. Blood in the motions is not uncommon in the case of gastroenteritis. A combination of recurrent blood or mucus, persistent diarrhoea at night, abdominal pains and weight loss indicates inflammatory bowel disease or a growth. Prolonged diarrhoea accompanied by thirst and tiredness suggests a serious loss of fluids and minerals.

Most cases of diarrhoea resolve themselves within a few days. It is advisable to drink 2–3 litres (3½–5 pints) a day of water to replace lost fluids. Milk and sweet drinks aggravate the condition and are best avoided. Children and the elderly should take rehydrating fluids to restore the mineral balance. Various remedies work by slowing down the muscular action of the bowels and are useful in the short term. Diarrhoea lasting for more than a few days should be referred to a doctor. A stool analysis may reveal an infection that requires antibiotic treatment.

coping with diarrhoea

If diarrhoea is more than an occasional problem or lasts more than a day, you should consult your doctor to establish the cause and find out whether any treatment is necessary. More often than not, however, it is more of an unpleasant nuisance for a day or so, and will clear up on its own relatively quickly, provided you follow a few sensible rules about what you eat and drink.

When something, be it food, an infection or even a bout of serious stress, has upset your normal bowel movements, you need to avoid eating or drinking anything that will irritate it still further. While symptoms are raging, the safest things are bland, easily digested foods such as plain boiled white rice, dry white toast, apples and relatively bland vegetable juices, made from ingredients such as carrots and celery. It is unlikely that you will feel like eating much anyway, but, even if you are hungry, steer clear especially of high-fat or spicy meals, dairy produce, milk, sugar and sweet foods, tea, coffee and alcohol.

Do not forget that, because the products of your digestion are passing through your system much more quickly than usual, you will not be reabsorbing liquid from your stools before they are excreted. This extra fluid loss is why diarrhoea can result in dehydration, especially in babies and older people. The answer is to drink lots of water or mild herbal teas.

DIETARY TIPS

- If your fluid loss is really severe, try one of the rehydration fluids which you can buy from the chemist. These contain additional ingredients which help to rebalance your body chemistry and make up for any deficiencies resulting from the diarrhoea.

- Once the worst is over, make the move back to your normal diet gradually. You might start with easily digested foods such as white fish, chicken and soup, for example, but leave it a while before having curry or steak and chips!

- Live yogurt containing lactobacilli may help to rebalance your gut flora, but wait until your symptoms have settled before trying it.

Above left: Bland food, such as plain boiled white rice will be easily digested.

Below: Rehydrate your system by drinking copious amounts of fluids.

BENEFICIAL RECIPES & JUICES

Banana & almond smoothie
(see page 117)

•

Banana & peanut butter smoothie
(see page 117)

•

Cabbage & carrot juice
(see page 141)

Carrot & kiwi juice
(see page 143)

•

Cranberry yogurt smoothie
(see page 189)

•

Yogurt & buttermilk fruit medley
(see page 189)

gallstones

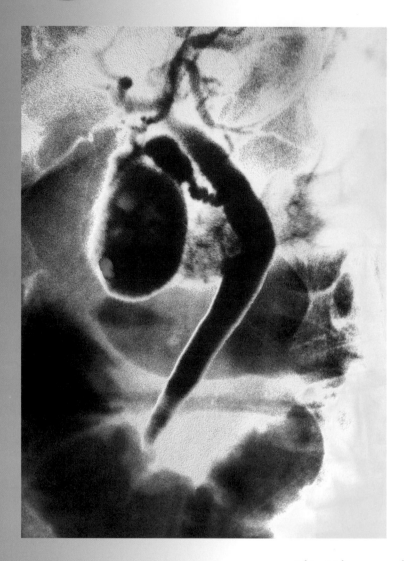

Above: A coloured x-ray showing gallstones within the gall bladder (red, pear-shaped). The gallstones are seen as green areas in the gall bladder.

The technology exists to break up gallstones without the need for surgery. Shockwaves can be used to shatter the stones, which then pass harmlessly out of the body. Stones may also be broken up by passing a tube into the gall bladder, through which is flushed a solution that dissolves cholesterol.

Gallstones are extremely common and are present in about 10–20 per cent of the population. They occur more frequently in women, until later in life, when they become equally common in both men and women.

Gallstones form within the gallbladder as a result of precipitation of cholesterol and salts from bile. Bile plays an important role in the absorption of fats from the intestinal tract because it makes fats soluble. Most bile, about 1 litre (1¾ pints) a day, is formed in the liver and is a mixture of cholesterol and pigments from old red blood cells. A few rare conditions can lead to an excessive load of bile pigments, which increases the risk of gallstones.

Fewer than 20 per cent of gallstones cause any problems to the sufferer, even after 15 years, so treatment is generally unnecessary. However, a stone that obstructs the gallbladder will cause waves of severe pain in the upper right side of the abdomen. Another classic symptom is a mild intermittent pain under the right ribs, which is worse after eating, especially after indulging in particularly fatty foods. Complete obstruction invariably causes infection of the gallbladder within 24 hours, resulting in fever and jaundice.

If there is pain, most surgeons recommend removal of the stones because there is a much higher chance of a complete obstruction. In acute cases of complete obstruction, analgesics will deaden the pain until the gallstone leaves the bile duct. This usually takes a few hours. Any infection is treated with antibiotics.

Surgical opinion is divided about whether to remove the gallbladder immediately after an acute attack has settled or to wait a few months. It is possible to dissolve gallstones with drugs, but this takes up to two years of continuous treatment, after which there is a 50 per cent chance of the gallstones recurring. This treatment is now rarely used because surgery is so safe.

reducing the risk of gallstones

Changing your diet may decrease the chances of gallstones recurring and, if you are seriously overweight, it will also be worth making an effort to shed the excess. People who are within the normal weight range for their height are less prone to this condition. You can work towards both of these objectives by cutting down (dramatically if necessary) the amount of saturated fat – from animal sources – you eat, and reducing your intake of fried and unrefined foods, which are often high in fat and sugar.

There is evidence that vegetarians are less susceptible to gallstones than meat-eaters, so you might want to consider replacing some or all of the animal protein in your diet with that derived from alternative sources. You could do this by eating more lentils and pulses, fish, nuts and low-fat dairy produce such as yogurt. Fruit and vegetables should be an important part of your daily diet, especially those containing salicylates; good sources include beetroot, apples, apricots, peaches, plums, pineapples, grapefruit, avocados, broccoli, green beans and many other vegetables.

If you eat a good selection of unrefined foods, including fruit and vegetables, you should be ensuring that you have a satisfactory vitamin and mineral intake, as well as a high fibre intake, all of which will be helpful. In particular, fibre – together with plenty of fluids – will help discourage any tendency to constipation (see page 82) which can make you more prone to gallstones.

Above: Drinking lots of fluids in the form of juices or water aids in preventing constipation, and can therefore minimize the risk of gallstones forming.

- A minority of people with gallstones may be suffering from food sensitivity: keeping a food and symptom diary may provide some evidence of possible suspect foods. Among those most often implicated are onions, eggs and pork.

- Steer clear of spicy foods. Remember that many Indian dishes also contain relatively large amounts of saturated fats and sugar, even though they are not immediately obvious.

- Cut down your coffee intake and try substituting herbal teas, such as those made with camomile and dandelion, for example.

BENEFICIAL RECIPES & JUICES

Poached apricots with oatmeal cream
(see page 114)
•
Spiced beetroot
(see page 132)
•
Beetroot risotto (see page 133)
•
Tuna & red pepper chowder
(see page 182)

Apricot smoothie (see page 115)
•
Blueberry & grapefruit juice
(see page 122)
•
Carrot, apple & ginger juice
(see page 143)
•
5-vegetable juice
(see page 163)

heartburn

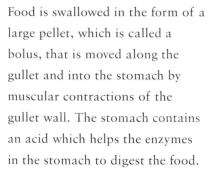

Food is swallowed in the form of a large pellet, which is called a bolus, that is moved along the gullet and into the stomach by muscular contractions of the gullet wall. The stomach contains an acid which helps the enzymes in the stomach to digest the food.

The gullet and stomach are separated by a sphincter valve that should prevent any backflow of the contents of the stomach into the oesophagus. This mechanism frequently fails, however, and, as a result, strong stomach acid flows back into the gullet, causing heartburn. This is characterized by a burning sensation that spreads across the front of the chest behind the breastbone not long after eating. It is often accompanied by belching and acid may rise into the mouth. This acid has a hot, sour taste.

About a quarter of all adults in Britain regularly suffer from heartburn. The most obvious remedy is to avoid all those foods which can cause heartburn, such as acidic foods and alcohol. It is also important to eat regular, unhurried meals. If late meals cannot be avoided, placing an extra pillow or two on the bed to raise the head and chest during the night may help to reduce the incidence of heartburn for many people.

Heartburn can be relieved by one of the many simple antacids that are readily available over the counter. These work by neutralizing the stomach contents and providing a protective coating to the wall of the gullet. In severe cases, acid-blocking drugs may be needed.

Sometimes the wall of the gullet becomes inflamed spontaneously, a condition called oesophagitis, and mere swallowing will cause discomfort.

Below & right: The acid in citrus fruit and tomatoes, for example, may trigger an attack of heartburn by irritating the oesophagus.

It is important to distinguish the pain associated with eating from that caused by exertion, which may be angina. Indeed, the first attack of heartburn in older people can be indistinguishable from angina, and doctors may order heart checks. Generally, the close association with eating will decide the diagnosis.

Unfortunately, in order to reduce or eliminate the unpleasant symptoms of heartburn, you may have to stop eating some of the foods that you particularly enjoy, as well as changing your overall meal pattern. Many people find that they have fewer problems, for example, if they eat several smaller meals rather than two or three normal ones, and also if their biggest meal is either in the middle of the day or early (rather than late) in the evening. Some people also find that giving up drinking wine with their food, or even cutting alcohol out almost completely, is worth the sacrifice in terms of gaining relief from heartburn.

Although people with heartburn all tend to have a weakness of the valve at the top of the stomach, they will not all find that the same foods trigger their symptoms. Often it is a question of employing a system of trial and error in order to discover which are the main culprits in your own particular case. Nevertheless, the majority of heartburn sufferers do benefit from avoiding very fatty foods and dishes, including most fried foods. Any highly spiced dish is more likely to cause problems than blander ones, although herb flavourings are usually acceptable.

Acidity can sometimes be an important factor – white wine may irritate the oesophagus, as may vinegar, citrus fruit or very sharp juices, although some people are able to tolerate these quite well. Substituting wholefoods for some or most of the refined or highly processed ones in your diet may help too, possibly because processed foods frequently have a very high fat and sugar content.

Above: The nautral enzymes in papaya can help to ease heartburn as it aids digestion.

- Adding pineapples and papaya to your menus – on their own or in juices – can ease heartburn, probably because they contain natural enzymes which aid digestion.

- If it is not obvious which foods give you heartburn, try keeping a food and symptom diary for a few weeks, and you should then be able to recognize any links.

- Herbal teas – in particular mint and ginger – may relieve symptoms and may be a better choice to finish your meal than coffee.

BENEFICIAL RECIPES & JUICES

Stir-fried chicken with pineapple
(see page 130)

•

Lemon rice & wild rice salad
(see page 174)

•

Apricot & pineapple smoothie
(see page 115)

Orange & apricot juice
(see page 115)

•

Carrot, apple & ginger juice
(see page 143)

•

Wheatgerm, pineapple & banana
booster (see page 168)

indigestion

Below: A coloured TEM of a *Helicobacter pylori* bacterium. Colonies of this bacteria occur on the stomach mucous membrane and are a contributing factor for gastric cancer and stomach ulcers.

Stomach cancer begins in the glands of the stomach lining and the early symptoms are indistinguishable from indigestion. Therefore, anyone over 40 with unusual or persistent indigestion should consult a doctor. Biopsy of a stomach ulcer will determine whether or not it is malignant. Duodenal ulcers are invariably benign.

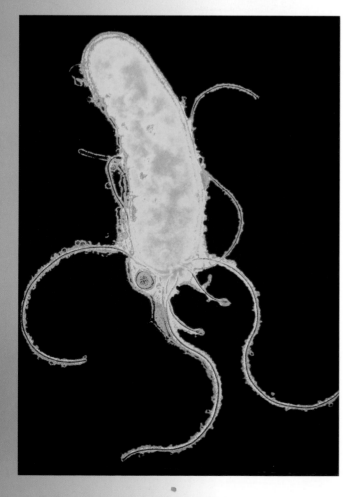

Indigestion is very common, and only rarely leads to peptic ulcers of the stomach and duodenum. It is caused by excessive hydrochloric acid in the stomach. The acid, which sterilizes food and aids the digestive process, is secreted by the stomach wall. Usually, the stomach wall is protected by a thick coating of mucus. Persistently high levels of acid cause this coating to break down, and the acid can attack the stomach wall, causing indigestion.

Alcohol and acidic foods, and certain drugs, particularly anti-inflammatories, can further irritate the stomach wall. The bacterium *Helicobacter pylori* is now a recognized source of gastric irritation, peptic ulcers and possibly also stomach cancer.

In mild cases of indigestion, there is a burning, gnawing sensation in the stomach, which may be either provoked or relieved by eating. Acid may escape into the gullet, causing heartburn (see page 88), or into the duodenum, where it may cause ulceration. A peptic ulcer causes persistent pain that seems to gnaw into the back. The diagnosis involves an endoscopy, a breath test to detect *H. pylori*, which gives off a characteristic gas, or biopsy of the ulcer.

If the ulcer eats through a blood vessel, there may be vomiting of blood or blood in the stools, which appear jet black. If untreated, the ulcer can erode the stomach or duodenal wall, becoming a perforated peptic ulcer. This causes severe upper abdominal pain and peritonitis, and is a medical emergency.

Mild indigestion usually responds to antacids, which neutralize the acid and reduce the burning sensation. A more efficient treatment is to block the formation of acid with drugs called H2-blockers or the more powerful, rapidly acting proton-pump inhibitors. Current treatment directed at *H. pylori* combines antibiotics with a powerful antacid. This cures about 90 per cent of peptic ulcers for at least a year. Bleeding or perforated peptic ulcers, however, will require urgent surgery.

changing your diet

Although excessive acid is the usual cause of indigestion, specific foods may cause a problem in individual cases; such people can often eat anything other than their personal culprit foods with no problems whatsoever. Onions, sardines, strong or blue cheese, spicy foods, coffee and alcohol are among the foods which often cause problems. You may be able to pinpoint your own trigger foods by keeping a food and symptom diary for a few weeks.

If you do not turn up anything specific, making some general changes to your diet may help. Try eating more wholefoods in place of those which have been heavily refined or processed – substitute wholemeal bread and rice for white, eat more potatoes, pasta, lentils, beans and other pulses, as well as plenty of fresh fruit and vegetables, including juices. Pineapples and papaya, eaten daily, may ease digestive symptoms.

Most people find that it helps to reduce their intake of fatty – including fried – foods, as well as those containing lots of sugar. Remember that many processed foods, such as cakes, pies, pastries and biscuits, can be high in both sugar and fat.

While a glass of wine with a meal may be good for your digestion, some people find its acidity irritating to their digestive system; spirits frequently have a similar effect, especially if taken on an empty stomach.

Bear in mind that it may be the way you eat rather than what you eat that triggers indigestion; try to eat slowly, sitting down rather than 'on the go', and in a stress-free environment if you possibly can.

BENEFICIAL RECIPES & JUICES

Lemon & basil penne
(see page 124)

•

Cabbage bhaji
(see page 139)

•

Tomato & orange soup
(see page 152)

Kale & wheatgrass energizer
(see page 141)

•

Red pepper & tomato tonic
(see page 145)

•

Spicy tomato juice
(see page 153)

DIETARY TIPS

- Ginger is a traditional and effective remedy for indigestion. Try it in recipes, or make a tea using hot water and a little root ginger.

- Although people with ulcers were once advised to drink lots of milk, this can actually make symptoms worse. Try switching to a low-fat variety or, if that does not work, cut milk out altogether for a while.

- Caffeine can cause indigestion, so try avoiding tea, cola and chocolate as well as coffee.

Above left: Blue cheese is a common trigger for indigestion.

Below: Drinking lots of milk used to be common advice for people suffering with ulcers. Be careful though as it can sometimes make symptoms worse.

irritable bowel syndrome

Irritable bowel syndrome (IBS) is a blanket term applied to the many abdominal disturbances for which no direct cause has been found. It appears to be a disorder of the nerves in the wall of the bowel that make the bowel muscle contract, and is associated with stress and depression (see pages 48 and 58). Given the number of cases worldwide that have come to the attention of gastroenterologists, it seems unlikely that some simple cause has been overlooked.

It occurs most frequently in young women. The typical symptoms are recurrent abdominal pains, often accompanied by minor changes in bowel habit, ranging from constipation to diarrhoea (see pages 82 and 84). The pains are consistently relieved by defaecation and made worse by stress. The motions may be pellet-like, and there is a frequent need to open the bowels. In addition, the abdomen feels distended and bloated. Symptoms are experienced for months, even years, but there is no weight loss and the individual looks well. Apart from a non-specific abdominal tenderness, there are no other abnormalities.

Basic investigations will exclude other diseases and reassure the patient that the problem is being taken seriously. Blood tests will reveal any inflammation and inspection of the lower bowel (sigmoidoscopy) and biopsies of the bowel wall will reveal any more serious conditions. For people under 30, a reasonably confident diagnosis can be made with minimal investigation. Testing of older individuals may be more extensive because of the increased risk of cancer.

Treatment is difficult because the causes are unknown. Some cases may respond to reassurance and a high-fibre diet. Bowel-relaxant drugs benefit some people, but not others. Antidepressants may help if there are symptoms of stress or depression. Specialists have recently been dividing IBS into separate syndromes, which may lead to a more focused treatment of the problem.

Above: At times of stress, IBS can cause pain and discomfort in the abdomen.

Right: Simple massage techniques on the area in distress can be used to help relieve pain and discomfort.

improving your symptoms with diet

Unfortunately, there is no one eating programme that will suit everyone who has irritable bowel syndrome, and it may be a question of using trial and error before you find the balance of foods that suits you best.

Unless you already know which foods make your symptoms worse, you should aim for an all-round healthy diet based around fresh, raw or lightly cooked foods, keeping processed foods to an absolute minimum, as they may contain hidden ingredients that could trigger your symptoms. If you can, you should try to base your diet around starchy foods, such as potatoes, wholegrain cereals, bread, pasta, fruit and vegetables, although you may discover that you are one of the many people with IBS who are sensitive to the gluten in wheat-based foods. Include as many fruit and vegetables as possible – if they cause you any problems, you may find that they are more digestible when cooked.

Juices may be better tolerated when diluted with water. Some people find that sulphur-containing foods upset them – these include onions, bread, eggs and most fried foods. Opt for poultry, very lean meat or fish to meet your protein requirements; fatty meat and some pulses may make your symptoms worse.

Milk and dairy produce can be problematic: many people with IBS are sensitive to or cannot digest lactose, the protein in milk, although yogurt is more easily tolerated; you could try seeing whether goats' and sheep's milk, and products made with them, suit you better. You may need to experiment with cutting out suspect food groups in order to find those which trigger your symptoms, but be careful that you do not end up eating so small a range of foods that you miss out on essential nutrients.

BENEFICIAL RECIPES & JUICES

Chunky carrot & lentil soup
(see page 142)

•

*Watercress & couscous filled
cannelloni (see page 156)*

•

*Berry fruit scones
(see page 164)*

*Cabbage & carrot juice
(see page 141)*

•

*Carrot & banana booster
(see page 143)*

•

*Carrot & kiwi juice
(see page 143)*

DIETARY TIPS

Above: Soluble fibre can be found in dried fruits.

• You will almost certainly have to steer clear of highly spiced meals, as these are very likely to upset your digestive system.

• Doctors no longer routinely recommend a low-fibre diet for people with IBS as they once did, but some people may find it difficult to tolerate insoluble fibre – found in grains and the skins of certain fruit and vegetables. The soluble type may be easier to digest: this is found in oats, barley, pulses and dried fruit.

• Drink plenty of water, especially if you are on a relatively high-fibre diet, as this will help to keep your stools soft and bulky. Alcohol, tea and coffee, on the other hand, may make symptoms worse.

• If you cannot easily identify which foods upset you, keep a food and symptoms diary for a few weeks to see whether there is a pattern.

worms

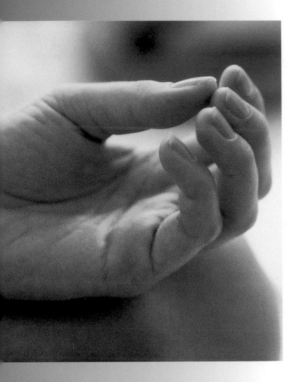

Above & right: Worm eggs lodge beneath the fingernails, and may be ingested by sucking the fingers, especially in children.

To reduce the risk of reinfection, fingernails should be kept short and hands should be washed thoroughly several times a day. As the worms lay their eggs at night, a bath or shower each morning should wash away the eggs. Towels should be changed frequently.

Three types of worm infect human beings – threadworms, tapeworms and roundworms – but threadworms (*Enterobius vermicularis*) are by far the most common in temperate climates.

Children from the cleanest of homes can contract threadworms, and they usually become infected at school. The most likely source of the initial infection is soil. Children habitually get their hands dirty and then suck their fingers; thus any worm eggs that have been trapped beneath their fingernails will be transferred to the mouth. More rarely, worms are acquired from infected meat that has not been cooked thoroughly.

Once the eggs have been swallowed, they hatch out in the large intestine, and some worms may be passed out of the body in the faeces. They resemble thin, white threads about 5mm (¼ in) long. At night the worms emerge and congregate around the anus, where they lay their eggs. This causes intense irritation which leads to scratching. As a result, more eggs are trapped beneath the fingernails, the fingers are sucked, the eggs are ingested, and the whole cycle begins again. Both sexes may be affected, although in girls the worms may also crawl into the vagina and set up further irritation.

Ointments are available to relieve the irritation and inflammation caused by scratching. One dose of an antiworming drug is usually sufficient to cure the infection, but it is advisable to repeat the treatment after two weeks. Ideally the whole family should be treated at the same time to prevent cross-infection between family members. Raw garlic is toxic to worms but few children can be persuaded to eat it. Carrots and pumpkin seeds can also help to clear infections.

choosing the right diet

Good hygiene, combined with appropriate treatment, is the most effective way to deal with an infestation of worms, but attention to the right kind of diet can also play its part. The first person to be infected in any family is usually a child, although the problem can then spread to other members; so everyone should be treated at the same time. Young children are often choosy about what they will and will not eat, so it may need a certain amount of ingenuity on their parents' part to persuade them to try unfamiliar foods that might be helpful in eradicating worms.

Raw garlic has a reputation for helping to fight such infestations, but few children (and few adults) will be enthusiastic about chewing uncooked cloves. You may find it is more acceptable when crushed and mixed into a salad dressing or scattered into a casserole – at least it is worth a try. Pumpkin seeds may go down better: try mixing them with sultanas and raisins or nuts, or adding them to breakfast cereal. Too much fruit should be avoided until the infestation has cleared, with the exception of pineapples and figs.

A diet rich in fibre will help to keep the digestive system working effectively, so include starchy and green vegetables, lentils, beans and other pulses, oats and wholegrain foods such as bread, rice and pasta on the daily menu. Children who are fussy about vegetables may be more willing to consume them in the form of juices.

Above: Try drinking nutritious vegetable juices instead of sugary fizzy drinks.

- Until the worm infestation has been thoroughly cleared, it is best to steer clear of all dairy produce, with the exception of live yogurt containing lactobacilli, which help to rebalance gut flora.

- Cut out sugar and sugary foods, including fizzy drinks and squashes as well as juices with a high content of natural fruit sugar. Opt for vegetable juices instead.

- Although most people find the idea of worm infestation disgusting, try to remember that it is not serious and does not reflect badly on the individuals affected.

BENEFICIAL RECIPES & JUICES

Figs with blackberries on toast
(see page 120)

•

Stir-fried chicken with pineapple
(see page 130)

•

Stir-fried broccoli with sesame seeds
(see page 136)

•

Roasted peppers with millet & basil
(see page 165)

Apricot & pineapple smoothie
(see page 115)

•

Juice medley
(see page 159)

•

Root juice
(see page 159)

•

5-vegetable juice
(see page 163)

prostate gland problems

The prostate gland surrounds the urethra, the tube that runs from the bladder to the penis. Problems include:

- **inflammation (prostatitis)** More frequent in younger men, this is usually caused by an infection, particularly of chlamydia.

- **enlargement** A slow, benign (non-cancerous) enlargement of the gland occurs naturally in all men after middle age, and is by far the most common prostate problem. It is associated with changes in the levels of testosterone and oestrogen, and in the nature of the testosterone.

- **prostate cancer** Currently the third commonest cause of death in men, this now accounts for about 7 per cent of all cancers in the UK. Male sex hormones are partly responsible, but heredity and diet also have a role in its care.

The symptoms of prostatitis are similar to those of cystitis (see page 106), with the addition of lower back pain, painful ejaculation and inflamed testes. Treatment involves antibiotics and alpha-blockers.

Enlargement of the prostate, whether benign or cancerous, exerts pressure on the urethra, constricting it and reducing the flow of urine, often to a mere dribble. The urine accumulates, increasing the risk of infection and distending the bladder. The back-pressure may extend to the kidneys and cause aching loins.

A rectal examination will reveal whether the enlargement is smooth (benign) or hard with irregular areas (cancerous). There is a useful blood test for detecting malignancy, and the use of rectal biopsies or ultra-sound scans will serve to confirm the diagnosis.

Drug treatment for benign prostate enlargements includes the use of alpha-blockers, to alleviate the symptoms, in conjunction with alpha-reductase inhibitors, to shrink the gland. If such treatment proves to be unsuccessful, or if there is complete blockage, the gland is removed by laser surgery.

Treatment of cancerous enlargements of the prostate involves the removal or irradiation of the gland. Both microsurgery and the use of radioactive implants have greatly reduced the risks that are associated with these treatments.

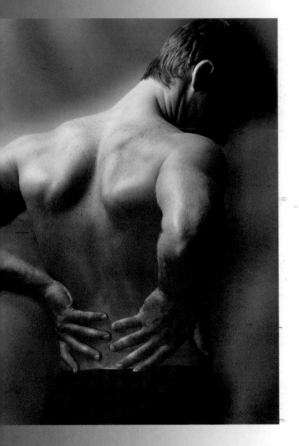

Above: Lower back pain, when combined with other specific symptoms, can be indicative of an inflamed prostate gland.

The discovery of prostate specific antigen (PSA) opened up new prospects in the screening for prostate cancer. Its value is still controversial but, nonetheless, men over the age of 50 are increasingly asking for an annual rectal examination and PSA test.

useful foods

Treatment of prostate disease sometimes includes the female hormone oestrogen, and so it is thought that eating foods which are high in plant oestrogens (phyto-oestrogens) may have a similarly beneficial effect. This means including plant foods rich in these substances, such as soya beans and soya products (such as tofu), chickpeas, lentils, peas, garlic, fennel, celery, rhubarb and all kinds of wholegrains.

The form in which you have them makes no difference, so it is worth experimenting with soups, juices and spreads, such as hummus, to add variety to your menus.

Another food which has recently come into prominence with respect to prostate disease is tomatoes. The reason for this is that food scientists have discovered that they are a particularly rich source of lycopene, a phyto-chemical that is thought to have a protective effect against heart disease and some forms of cancer, including prostate cancer. It does not matter whether you take your tomatoes raw, cooked, out of a can or as juice, and, in fact, tomato purée and even tomato ketchup are excellent sources of lycopene.

Protein derived from vegetable rather than animal sources is also important, because it contains amino acids that may play a role in countering enlargement of the prostate gland. You should try to eat plenty of lentils, beans and other pulses, as well as nuts and good amounts of fibre-rich foods such as wholegrains, oats and brown rice. A good mineral intake is very important, too, and therefore you should take particular care to get sufficient zinc, which is found in fish, shellfish, seeds, eggs and molasses.

BENEFICIAL RECIPES & JUICES

Baked vine tomatoes
(see page 150)

•

Tomato, oregano & mozzarella
tartlets (see page 151)

•

Chicken with 40 garlic cloves
(see page 158)

Lemon grass & tofu nuggets
(see page 185)

•

Banana tofu smoothie
(see page 187)

•

Tofu fruit smoothie
(see page 187)

DIETARY TIPS

- The main source of protein in your diet should come from vegetable sources and fish rather than meat or dairy produce.

- Switch from refined to unrefined versions of foods whenever you can – opt for wholegrain bread, rice and pasta rather than the white versions – and remember to cut down on all types of processed food.

- Seeds and nuts of all kinds are a useful addition to your diet as they contain a range of minerals and other important nutrients.

Below: Fennel, with it's peppery taste, is rich in plant oestrogens, which can be used to treat prostate problems.

fibroids

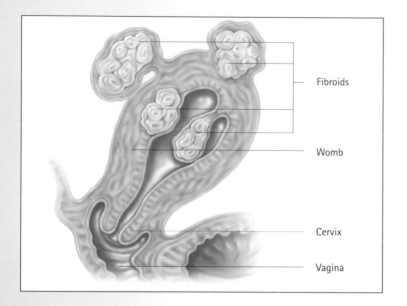

Fibroids
Womb
Cervix
Vagina

Above: Fibroids of various sizes within and outside the womb. Symptoms can range from none to heavy, painful periods.

Right: The appearance of fibroids is most common in women who have no children or have delayed having children until after the age of 30.

The walls of the womb consist mostly of tough muscle, designed to cope with pregnancy and labour. In some instances, a number of the cells in this muscle start to expand and grow into a tumour within the surrounding healthy muscle. This tumour, or fibroid, is entirely benign and is not associated with any cancerous process.

Fibroids grow very slowly and there are often several of varying sizes within the womb. They seldom give rise to any symptoms until they are large enough to distort the womb. They are present in about 20 per cent of women and, if untreated, can reach as much as 20kg (44lb) in weight.

What exactly stimulates fibroid formation is unclear, but prolonged exposure to oestrogen may play a part. This is borne out by the fact that fibroids are more common in women who have no children or who have delayed having children until after the age of 30. Moreover, fibroids tend to shrink after the menopause, when oestrogen levels fall.

Fibroids are seldom painful unless they outgrow their blood supply and degenerate. Large ones, perhaps the size of a small melon, most commonly cause heavy and irregular periods. The largest fibroids result in abdominal swelling and, because they exert pressure on the bladder, they can lead to a constant desire to pass urine.

Treatment is only necessary if the fibroids are causing symptoms or might interfere with an intended pregnancy. It is possible to remove one or several fibroids in an operation known as a myomectomy. However, many women who have completed their families opt for removal of the entire womb (hysterectomy) to avoid the 10–15 per cent chance of the fibroids regrowing.

Drugs such as goserelin, which act by reducing oestrogen levels, are currently being used to treat endometriosis. In future it may be possible to use similar drugs to shrink fibroids.

The fact that fibroids cause increased menstrual flow may mean that affected women become anaemic or simply feel debilitated by excessive blood loss. Such symptoms can be eased by eating a balanced, nutrient-rich diet which places emphasis on wholefoods and a rich supply of essential vitamins and minerals. Refined and processed foods make little contribution to good nutrition, so start by excluding as many of them as possible from your daily diet. Replace white bread, pasta and rice with wholegrain versions and choose wholegrain cereals made with wheat, oats and nuts rather than the sugary, highly processed kind. These will also increase your fibre intake, as will starchy vegetables, fruit and juices made from them, lentils, beans and other pulses, and peas.

If you suspect you may be anaemic, you need to make sure you are getting sufficient iron. Rich sources include red meat of all kinds, including pork, liver and kidneys, dark green, leafy vegetables such as spinach and kale, and salad vegetables such as watercress. Try to eat your vegetables raw whenever possible, as you will then get more of their iron content than if they were cooked. Iron is more readily absorbed from meat, but having vitamin C in plant sources will help to encourage more efficient absorption of iron.

It is a good idea to have a juice made from fruit that are high in vitamin C – such as blackcurrants, strawberries, citrus fruit, kiwi fruit – with a meal rather than tea or coffee. Avoid both of the latter for an hour before and after meals, since they inhibit iron absorption.

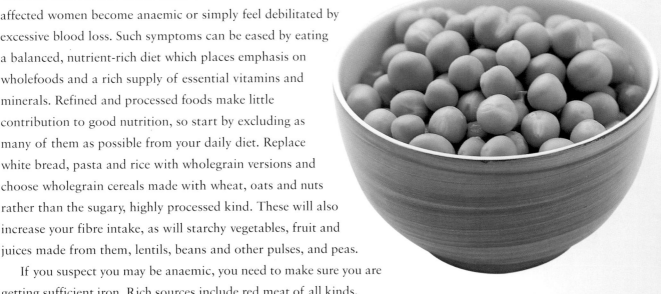

Above: Peas are a good source of phyto-oestrogens, which will help to restore hormonal balance.

- Although fibroids flourish in the presence of oestrogen, eating foods containing so-called phyto-oestrogens may help to restore hormonal balance. Opt for soya beans and foods made from them. Chickpeas, lentils, garlic, peas, fennel, celery, rhubarb and wholegrains are good sources.

- Nuts and seeds provide a good supply of several important minerals, especially zinc, as well as many of the B vitamins.

- Avoid sugar and sugary foods, as they may affect iron levels, and they contain no useful nutrients.

BENEFICIAL RECIPES & JUICES

Chilled watercress soup
(see page 155)

●

Nut & seed savoury cakes
(see page 172)

●

Griddled liver & bacon with grilled potatoes (see page 179)

Iron pick-me-up
(see page 149)

●

Soothing tonic
(see page 157)

●

Watercress, carrot & celery juice
(see page 157)

Most women cease menstruating (the menopause) in their early 50s, as a result of declining oestrogen levels. This is a natural and inevitable event. Nevertheless, there can be some upsetting symptoms during the preceding and subsequent years, as well as long-term health implications.

Above: Osteoporosis is a high risk for women going through the menopause. Ideally women should begin doing bone-loading exercises in their early twenties to build up bone strength.

- **hot flushes** Waves of heat sweep across the body and are accompanied by sweating, especially at night. They are caused by dilation of the blood vessels and can be relieved by blood-pressure medication.

- **mood changes** Irritability, emotional instability, worsening memory, depression (see page 58) and tiredness often accompany the menopause. It is difficult to determine whether these are hormone-related or psychological.

- **physical changes** The breasts become smaller, thinner and will change shape as fatty tissue is reabsorbed. The vaginal walls become thin and drier, leading to discomfort on intercourse and sometimes slight bleeding. An oestrogen cream will reduce vaginal dryness, but should not be used for more than a few years. A non-hormone lubricating gel may suffice and regular intercourse will reduce dryness without need for hormones. Recurrent cystitis may occur.

- **heart disease** Oestrogen exerts a protective effect on the heart until the menopause. Afterwards, women's risk of heart disease rises rapidly until it equals that of men.

- **osteoporosis** Loss of bone mass is especially rapid at the menopause and for several years afterwards. There may be a general stiffening of the joints and aching, which is due partly to ageing but also to oestrogen deficiency. (See also osteoporosis, page 52.)

Hormone replacement therapy (HRT) replaces natural oestrogen. It can be administered as a tablet, a pellet implanted in the abdomen, a patch, or a gel. In addition, a woman who still has her womb has to take progestogen tablets for 10–12 days each month to reduce the risk of womb cancer.

Hormone replacement therapy (HRT) alleviates many of the distressing symptoms, such as hot flushes and vaginal dryness. It also gives a sense of well-being and improves skin texture. Less obviously, it prevents osteoporosis and protects against heart disease. Side-effects include weight gain, breast tenderness and nausea. It also slightly increases the risks of thrombosis and possibly breast cancer. On balance, if taken for two to five years, the benefits outweigh the disadvantages.

choosing beneficial foods

Symptoms which affect women in the time leading up to the menopause and while it is taking place are largely due to the declining levels of the female hormone oestrogen, so foods which can help balance this loss can play an important role. Adjustments to your diet can also help to ease other menopause-related symptoms such as depression and hot flushes.

Many plant-based foods contain their own versions of oestrogen – known as phyto-oestrogens – which, although far less powerful than the human hormone, nevertheless can play a valuable role. They tend to nudge levels back towards the norm, so they are helpful both when oestrogen levels are fluctuating pre-menopausally and when the ovaries finally shut down production altogether. The best sources are soya beans and foods made from them, lentils and pulses, but they are also present in many fruits, including rhubarb, plums, apples, bananas, cherries, papaya and pomegranates, among others, and in wholegrains, seeds, vegetables such as beetroot, broccoli and fennel, and seaweed such as kelp.

A diet of regular meals based around starchy vegetables and fruit, wholegrains and pulses, and low in sugar, will help to regulate blood-glucose levels and so minimize mood swings. This type of diet, which is low in saturated fats, will also help to protect against the risk of heart disease, which rises after the menopause. Polyunsaturated fats – from vegetable sources – and olive oil should be substituted for fats from animal sources, but these should still only be consumed in moderation in order to avoid unnecessary weight gain.

DIETARY TIPS

- A good calcium intake is especially important to help counter the loss of bone from the skeleton which can result in osteoporosis. Dairy foods and milk are very good sources, but opt for the low-fat varieties.

- The essential fatty acids omega-3 and omega-6 help to protect against heart disease and can also keep your skin supple and your joints mobile. Try to eat plenty of oily fish, such as salmon, mackerel, herrings and pilchards, as well as nuts and seeds and oils made from them.

- A glass or two of wine a day will do you no harm and may even protect against heart disease, but never use it to 'drown your sorrows', as this does not work.

Below: Seaweed, such as kelp, contains phyto-oestrogens, which may help with menopausal symptoms.

BENEFICIAL RECIPES & JUICES

Cranberry chicken stir-fry
(see page 119)

•

Spiced beetroot (see page 132)

•

Caldo verde & smoked tofu soup
(see page 184)

•

Tofu, cinnamon & honey pockets
(see page 186)

Cranberry & mango smoothie
(see page 123)

•

Breakfast smoothie (see page 121)

•

Blueberry & grapefruit juice
(see page 122)

•

Tomato & apple pick-me-up
(see page 153)

---

pre-menstrual
syndrome (pms)

Most women experience some effects from changing hormone levels during the menstrual cycle. In an estimated 10 per cent these effects are severe, while in 1–3 per cent they seriously affect the quality of life, disrupting relationships at work and at home.

Research into the relationships between hormone levels and symptoms of PMS has reached no generally accepted conclusion, although it appears that the level of oestrogen seems more important than that of other hormones. In addition, women vary in their tolerance of PMS. Surveys show that women in their 30s and 40s are the most affected.

The most frequent symptoms are bloating, depression, irritability, anxiety and headaches. A craving for sweet things is also common. In diagnosing PMS, it is essential to show that these symptoms fluctuate in a regular cycle. Symptoms should begin from mid-cycle onwards, reach a peak just before menstruation, and disappear within a few days of the onset of menstruation.

Treatment for PMS is controversial, and women should be prepared to try a variety of treatments in order to find one that works for them.

One scientifically validated treatment is vitamin B_6. This vitamin is essential for the enzymes that form serotonin and dopamine, the neurotransmitters that are associated with depression (see page 58). Although there appears to be no reason why women should become cyclically deficient in vitamin B_6, many benefit from taking a small dose.

Diuretics relieve bloating and breast tenderness by reducing fluid retention, but should only be taken for a few days. Drugs that suppress oestrogen and progesterone may also be effective, but side-effects such as nausea and weight gain make them unacceptable for many women.

Evening primrose oil, which is a rich source of gammalinoleic acid, theoretically reduces the level of prolactin, which some researchers believe causes breast tenderness and mood changes. Oestrogen in tablet form also helps to relieve symptoms in some women.

Small nutritional deficiencies may lead to PMS by affecting the production of oestrogen and progesterone and therefore the balance between them. This, in turn, may affect the levels of other vital hormones, such as insulin. These nutrients include essential fatty acids, zinc, magnesium and vitamin B_6.

Right: Evening primrose oil is thought to relieve breast tenderness and mood swings.

Below: Gentle massage strokes can relieve the pain of stomach cramps associated with PMS.

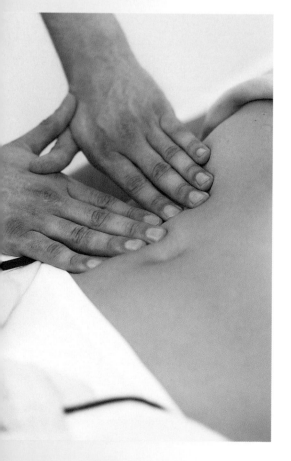

relieving symptoms with diet

This condition includes an enormous range of possible symptoms and, while changing your diet can definitely play a role in easing them, you may have to experiment a bit to find what works for you. Perhaps the most useful change is to incorporate more foods containing plant oestrogens into your diet as they can help to rebalance fluctuating oestrogen levels. These include soya-based foods, chickpeas, lentils, rhubarb, wholegrains, garlic, fennel, peas and celery.

Cut down on refined and processed foods and substitute wholefoods instead, including cereals, fruit, vegetables and juices, and eat as much freshly prepared food as you can.

Minerals are as important as vitamins – among them calcium, magnesium, chromium and zinc; some women with PMS have been found to have low levels, which may contribute to their symptoms. Dairy produce is a good source of calcium, but it is also found in muesli, prawns, Brazil nuts and some oily fish such as sardines and pilchards. Eating plenty of green, leafy vegetables and wholegrain cereals will ensure a good magnesium intake, while zinc is found in fish, shellfish, pork, turkey, peanuts, eggs, wheatgerm and pumpkin seeds. Chromium is needed to help balance out mood swings – opt for meat, including calves' liver, chicken, shellfish, hazelnuts, almonds, wholegrain cereals and eggs.

Essential fatty acids (omega-3 and omega-6) can help reduce pain, inflammation and cramps, and may alleviate problems with memory and concentration. Omega-6 is found in nuts, seeds and plant-based foods, as well as in evening primrose; omega-3 comes primarily from oily fish, and can also be found in seed oils.

DIETARY TIPS

Above: Eat plenty of watercress to ensure a reasonable magnesium intake.

- It is better not to use drinks containing caffeine, such as tea, coffee and cola as a stimulant, as they can exacerbate feelings of anxiety and irritability, and bring on headaches and migraines.

- Some women crave particular foods – predominantly carbohydrates and chocolate – in the pre-menstrual phase. However, it is healthier to opt for fruit, nuts, seeds and yogurt rather than sweet fatty treats.

- Vitamin B₆ has been used to treat some symptoms of PMS, including mood swings, insomnia and bloating. You will find high levels of this vitamin in many kinds of food, such as shellfish, meat, offal, green vegetables like broccoli, cabbages and spinach, lentils and bananas.

BENEFICIAL RECIPES & JUICES

Pan-fried oranges & bananas
(see page 116)

•

Butter bean & tomato soup
(see page 161)

•

Herrings with spinach & parmesan
(see page 180)

Blackberry & pineapple juice
(see page 131)

•

Juice medley
(see page 159)

•

Tofu fruit smoothie
(see page 187)

yeast infections
(candidiasis/thrush)

Above: Candida yeast fungus causes human thrush by affecting the moist mucus membranes of the body, such as skin folds and the mouth.

Babies can contract oral thrush from contact with their mother's skin. The organism forms small, white deposits on the inside of the mouth and, if these are scraped off, the surface below bleeds. The mouth is sore and there may be a reluctance to feed. The condition is treated with mouth drops.

Right: Watch out for signs that your baby may have developed oral thrush; if you are at all concerned, consult your doctor about the most appropriate treatment.

The yeast *Candida albicans*, which is a type of fungus, occurs naturally in all healthy bodies and thrives in warm, moist areas. It is found most often in the vagina, but also occurs in the mouth, bowel and, to a lesser extent, on the skin. It becomes a problem when, for some reason, the delicate balance between the naturally occurring organisms in the body is disturbed and the yeast is able to multiply excessively. About 70 per cent of women suffer from at least one attack of candidiasis during their lifetime. On the rare occasions that it affects men, there are usually no symptoms, although men may pass it on to female partners.

A number of factors cause excessive growth of candida. Treatment for other illnesses with antibiotics and immuno-suppressive drugs destroys the organisms that compete with candida for space and food. Excess sugar (as in diabetes) or refined carbohydrate in the body act as a food source for the yeast and encourage its growth.

Hormonal changes, mechanical abrasion during intercourse and poor hygiene may be contributory factors to vaginal thrush, which produces a thick, cheesy, white discharge. A swab of the discharge may be taken in order to confirm the diagnosis. The vulva may be sore and itchy and there may be stinging on urinating and soreness during intercourse. If the skin is affected, there may be an itchy, red rash beneath the breasts or on the inner thighs, sometimes extending around the anus.

Treatment includes antifungal drugs in the form of ointments, creams or pessaries. If this treatment is unsuccessful, an antifungal agent can be taken by mouth. It is wise to avoid any possible source of irritants, such as scented bath preparations and biological washing powders. Wearing loose-fitting cotton underwear allows air to circulate, cooling the skin and evaporating sweat.

adapting your diet

When changing your diet to fight the symptoms of candidiasis, you need to plan carefully, as the range of foods you might want to exclude can be quite wide. It is important that you do not miss out on vital nutrients and, in particular, that you keep your immune system in good working order to maximize its ability to fight the infection. This means ensuring that you get adequate amounts of minerals such as zinc, iron and magnesium, as well as anti-oxidant vitamins A, C and E and flavonoids.

The other important change is designed to deprive the candida organisms of the favourable environment in which they thrive and multiply; effectively this means cutting your intake of all forms of sugar and foods containing it. Avoid all refined foods as far as possible, and do not consume foods with a high level of natural sugars, such as milk, fruit and fruit juice, until you have recovered. Remember that alcohol contains sugar as well, so you should cut it out completely for the time being.

Fresh, green, leafy vegetables, meat, offal, chicken, wholegrain cereals, oats and pulses should all feature regularly in your diet because they contain B vitamins and other vitamins and minerals that will help fight the infection. Live yogurt, which contains lactobacilli organisms, will help to rebalance your gut flora and displace the candida organisms – you should try to eat it every day, or even more often if you can.

Food and drink containing yeast could encourage the growth of candida, so try to avoid bread, alcohol, yeast-based spreads, vinegar, dried fruit and mushrooms.

Above: Most types of bread contain yeast, and should be avoided, but sourdough bread makes a good substitute.

- People who are sensitive to particular foods may be more vulnerable to candidiasis, so it is important to try to identify your own personal culprit foods and avoid them as far as possible.

- People with diabetes need to take extra care to keep their blood-glucose levels under control because, if these are above normal, they provide an ideal environment for candida to multiply.

- Vegetable juices are a better option than fruit juices because they have a high vitamin content but relatively few natural sugars.

BENEFICIAL RECIPES & JUICES

Broccoli & red pepper fettuccine (see page 134)	*Green vegetable juice* (see page 137)
Greens soup (see page 140)	*Iron pick-me-up* (see page 149)
Spinach & lemon risotto (see page 148)	*5-vegetable juice* (see page 163)

cystitis

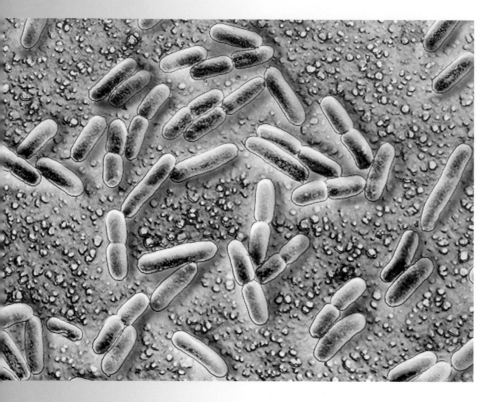

Above: The *E. coli* bacteria (*Escherichia coli*) is one of the bacterias known to cause infection in the bladder.

Over-the-counter remedies relieve the stinging and slow the growth of the bacteria by making the urine more alkaline. A teaspoonful of sodium bicarbonate dissolved in water may be just as effective. Cranberry juice also helps by preventing bacteria from adhering to the bladder walls, so that they can be washed out more easily.

Cystitis is an inflammation of the bladder, usually caused by a bacterial infection around the neck of the bladder or within the bladder itself. It is more common in women than men because the urethra (the passage leading from the bladder) is shorter: 3–4cm (1¼–1¾in) compared with 15–20cm (6–8in). Consequently, bacteria can more easily spread from the anus or vagina into the bladder. Diabetics and post-menopausal women are particularly prone to cystitis and it commonly occurs in pregnancy and after sexual intercourse.

Symptoms include an overwhelming and frequent urge to pass urine and a burning sensation when doing so. The amounts of urine passed are small and the urine feels hot and stings. It may also be foul-smelling and cloudy, or contain blood. There is a dull ache in the lower abdomen over the bladder and occasionally stress incontinence. Men may have an additional ache in the perineum.

To reduce the likelihood of infection, it is best to avoid any foods that are known to provoke cystitis, and to refrain from using vaginal deodorants and douches, which remove natural lubricants. Passing urine before and after sexual intercourse and washing carefully after opening the bowels also help.

Minor episodes of cystitis may settle down without treatment, and it helps to drink plenty of fluids to wash out the bladder. If treatment is necessary, a urine test will indicate the appropriate antibiotic to use.

Recurrent infections may be due to an abnormality, such as a tumour or a stone, in the bladder or ureter. In men, infections are most frequently due to an obstruction, such as an enlarged prostate gland (see page 96). Both require further investigation, as does the presence of blood in the urine. Hormone replacement therapy (HRT) may help post-menopausal women to avoid cystitis.

changing your eating habits

Your first priority during an attack of cystitis is to drink as much as you can to flush out the kidneys and dilute your urine so as to reduce the irritation when you empty your bladder. Try to drink as many glasses of plain water as you can.

Cranberry juice is now accepted as having a beneficial effect on the bacterial infection which is often, though not always, the cause of cystitis, because it prevents the bacteria from adhering to the inner walls of the bladder. Opt for the unsweetened variety, or make your own if possible. Other good juices which encourage the flow of urine are watermelon and cucumber; combined with cranberry juice, they help to cleanse the system as well as containing many useful nutrients, including vitamins A and C, potassium, iron and calcium.

You need to follow a diet which will enhance the ability of your immune system to fight off infection in future. This means a diet rich in the anti-oxidant vitamins A, C and E as well as zinc, with particular emphasis on vitamin C. Opt for blackcurrants, strawberries, citrus fruit (add the zest to juices), pineapples, kiwi fruit, and all red, orange and yellow fruit and vegetables, including less common ones such as sweet potatoes and mangoes. Garlic is also said to have anti-infective properties, so add it to meals whenever you can.

BENEFICIAL RECIPES & JUICES

Strawberry & cucumber salad
(see page 118)
•
Cranberry chicken stir-fry
(see page 119)
•
Tomato & orange soup
(see page 152)

Cranberry & mango smoothie
(see page 123)
•
Orange & raspberry juice
(see page 127)
•
Mixed fruit smoothie
(see page 131)

DIETARY TIPS

- Yogurt will be a useful addition to your diet. Not only does it contain a rich supply of calcium, but the lactobacilli in live yogurt help to rebalance your gut flora, which is especially important if your cystitis has been treated with antibiotics. It protects against bacterial infection, especially in the urinary tract.

- Steer clear of sugar and sugary foods which have little or no nutritional value, and leave you less of an appetite for more nourishing food.

- Avoid alcohol, tea, coffee and cola while you have cystitis, as they may cause further irritation to the bladder and urinary tract.

Above left: As well as drinking plenty of plain water, try drinking unsweetened cranberry juice.

Below: Even unrefined sugar, such as brown sugar should be avoided at the time of an infection.

EATING FOR ENERGY

There are any number of reasons why you may lack energy and zest for life and it is a wise precaution to have a check-up with your doctor to ensure you are not suffering from a condition that needs to be diagnosed and treated. Very often, however, the cause will be found to be related to aspects of your lifestyle rather than to a specific condition. Before considering your diet, make sure that you are getting enough of the right kind of sleep (see page 46) and try to get at least some exercise every day.

fuelling your system

You cannot expect your energy levels to be high unless you supply your body with the fuel it needs to power all your activities, both physical and mental. As far as physical energy is concerned, the most important source is carbohydrates, which come in two forms, sugar and starch. Ordinary sugar, and foods that contain lots of it, will not meet your need for a sustained energy supply, and therefore they should be avoided as far as possible.

Starchy carbohydrates from all kinds of plant foods not only provide a constant source of energy but also contain many valuable nutrients without which you cannot function effectively. These include important vitamins and minerals and, equally importantly, high levels of fibre. Also known as NSP (non-starch polysaccharides), fibre is needed for a healthy digestive system and helps to ensure that energy is released into your bloodstream, and thence into your cells, at a measured and consistently steady pace rather than in a sudden rush.

Above: Even a quick ten minutes of light weight-lifting can make a difference to your overall fitness. Ensure that you combine daily exercise with a well-balanced diet.

filling that gap

To avoid energy dips, when you eat is as significant as what you eat. Never miss out on breakfast because, if you do, your blood-glucose levels will be low in the morning; wholegrain cereal and/or bread, fruit and yogurt, together with fruit or vegetable juice, will set you up for the day and make it less likely that you will succumb to a fatty or sugary snack in the middle of the morning. If you find it difficult to stick to a regular three meals a day, there is nothing wrong with having more frequent, smaller meals or snacks, provided that you choose healthy options like fruit, low-fat, wholemeal sandwiches, salads, soups and smoothies, for example.

MINIMIZING AGEING

As we get older, it is hard, if not impossible, to ignore the manifestations of ageing: joints become stiffer, skin becomes drier and begins to wrinkle, hair becomes coarser and may thin, the senses become less sharp and the memory starts to go. These changes may be hardly noticeable to begin with, and some people are less affected than others. It is easier to accept these things if you are generally in good health but, unfortunately, we also become more vulnerable to certain illnesses in later life. Osteoarthritis, heart disease, diabetes, certain types of cancer and dementia are just some of the conditions which occur more frequently in older people; but, while there are no guarantees, eating the right kind of diet may make you less susceptible to some of them.

In general, this means eating a wide range of foods, concentrating on whole rather than highly refined foods, with plenty of fruit and vegetables and a minimum of sugary, processed and fatty foods, especially those high in saturated fats. You may also want to increase your intake of certain nutrients to guard against specific age-related conditions and symptoms.

protecting your joints

There is now a lot of evidence that fish oils can be helpful in reducing inflammation in the joints associated with various kinds of arthritis because they contain an essential fatty acid known as omega-3. The richest sources are oily fish such as salmon, trout, herrings, mackerel, pilchards and halibut, so try to eat these at least two or three times a week.

feeding your skin

Make sure that your diet contains plenty of foods rich in vitamins and minerals, especially beta-carotene, vitamin E and zinc. These will help your skin to retain moisture, protect skin cells and repair cell damage. This effectively means increasing your intake of red, yellow and orange fruit and vegetables, wholewheat, apples, eggs, broccoli, seafood such as oysters and clams, parsley and pumpkin seeds.

combating heart disease

For a healthy heart, cut down on saturated fats and eat a high-fibre diet with lots of fruit and vegetables; also opt for lentils, pulses and oily fish as your main sources of protein rather than meat or high-fat dairy produce (for more on this, see page 12).

Above: Many fruit, including strawberries and blueberries, are excellent sources of vitamin C.

Below: Eating fish, the oily varieties in particular, at least two or three times a week can help to reduce inflammation around the joints caused by arthritis.

Above: If you fancy a snack between meals, it is always better to eat a piece of fruit rather than a proprietary confection that will provide you with no nutrients whatsoever.

combating diabetes

Although it is not true that people develop diabetes in later life because they consume too much sugar, being overweight is a risk factor. You can reduce your chances of developing the condition by losing excess pounds on a nutritionally sound diet and by taking regular exercise. For more on this, see Obesity (page 44) and Diabetes (page 36).

reducing the risk of cancer

Experts have estimated that around one in three cases of cancer is diet-related, so eating the right foods may well reduce your risk. It is well worth adopting a healthy diet that is rich in anti-oxidants, flavonoids and other plant chemicals, high in fibre and low in highly refined foods. In practice, this means the more fruit and vegetables you eat, the better, and you should also eat lots of complex carbohydrates, such as unrefined cereals, and non-animal protein in the form of lentils, pulses and soya.

combating memory loss

Brain cells are particularly vulnerable to damage from free radicals, which are chemicals produced in the body in response to a wide range of triggers, including smoking, pollution, ultra-violet light and radiation. Fortunately, it is possible to limit their effects by ensuring that your diet is rich in anti-oxidant nutrients which mop up free radicals and impede their capacity to attack cells. The most powerful anti-oxidants are the ACE vitamins and compounds called anthocyanidins, found in all kinds of berries, cherries and grapes. Fruit and vegetables are the best sources of vitamins A and C, while eating plenty of wholewheat and rye foods, apples, broccoli, eggs, nuts and seeds will boost your intake of vitamin E. You also need a good supply of B vitamins to meet your brain's energy requirements: so include such foods as liver, wholegrains and brewer's yeast on your menu as often as you possibly can.

FOOD ALLERGIES & SENSITIVITY

There is no doubt that food can affect some people's health adversely, but it is often difficult to pinpoint what exactly is happening and which foods are responsible. A straightforward allergy – to strawberries, seafood or peanuts, for example – usually results in symptoms developing very soon after you have eaten the culprit food, and can often be diagnosed through skin or blood tests. Intolerance to a particular food – such as gluten or milk protein – usually causes symptoms because the individual concerned lacks the enzymes necessary to digest the culprit food. In both cases, the solution is to identify any trigger foods and avoid them.

Food sensitivity is more difficult to recognize and deal with. The symptoms, which may include digestive problems, headache and general malaise, may not appear for several hours or even days after you have eaten the trigger food, and there is no reliable diagnostic test. Often, people actually crave the food which is causing problems and so eat it frequently; or their symptoms may be a reaction to an ingredient which is not immediately obvious, such as the flavour-enhancer monosodium glutamate, which is added to many processed foods, including stock cubes, and is often a constituent of Chinese food.

identifying the culprits

The first step is to keep a detailed diary of everything you eat and drink, with notes on what symptoms develop and when. After a few weeks, any connection between your diet and symptoms may become apparent. The next stage is to exclude a suspect food or group of foods from your diet for about three weeks and record whether you still get symptoms. If you do not, try consuming the suspect food again and see whether your symptoms come back. You do need to be careful when excluding any major food groups – such as dairy produce – from your diet to ensure that you are not missing out on any important nutrients. It can also be difficult to do an elimination diet on your own, which is why it is worth getting advice from a dietician before going ahead.

HEALTH 'ROBBERS'

You will not get the maximum benefit from eating a health-boosting diet unless you also cut out those elements which may undermine its positive effects – and if you find it hard to give them up completely, at least try to cut down, gradually if necessary.

caffeine

Coffee, tea and cola may give you a temporary lift, but too much can increase feelings of anxiety and nervousness as well as interfering with your

TIME TO EXPERIMENT:

• *Do not be put off trying a food because you have never come across it before – you will not know whether you like it until you have tried it! Unusual fruit such as papaya, mangoes, fresh lychees and kiwi fruit, for example, are all good sources of ACE vitamins.*

• *Instead of relying on packaged fruit juices, try making up some new and interesting combinations of your own using a wide range of different fruit and vegetables.*

• *Add variety to your diet with staples from other countries, such as couscous, sweet potatoes or soya, and try some of the more unusual vegetables such as pak choi and squashes.*

Below: Health 'robbers' such as alcohol or caffeine can give you instant symptoms like a headache, as well as storing up long-term problems for the future.

sleep and reducing your ability to absorb certain important nutrients. If you are a heavy consumer, reduce your intake gradually so as to avoid withdrawal symptoms such as headaches.

alcohol

Drinking in moderation is unlikely to do you any harm and may even help to protect against heart disease, but more than one or two drinks a day can rob your body of important nutrients, cause dehydration, low blood-sugar levels and hangovers. Excessive drinking damages the brain and other important organs such as the liver, and is a major 'health robber'.

salt

Never add salt to your food either when cooking or at the table; a varied diet will supply all your body's needs. Excessive salt intake has been linked to raised blood pressure.

sugar

It is bad for your teeth, can contribute to weight gain and contains no nutrients whatsoever. This applies to both white and brown varieties, and even honey contains only tiny amounts of nutrients. While sweet foods may provide an energy 'rush', the effect is quickly countered as your pancreas responds by releasing more insulin, resulting in an equally rapid fall in your blood-glucose level.

refined foods

When grains such as wheat or rice are refined, many of the nutrients they contain are lost, along with virtually all the fibre. Always avoid white versions of all cereals and products that are made from them, and opt for wholegrain varieties instead.

'bad' fats

As a general rule, you should avoid all saturated fats – that is, hard fats that are found mainly in animal products such as red meat, butter and hard cheeses – because these can raise your cholesterol levels and contribute to the 'clogging up' of your arteries. You also need to avoid trans-fats – these are produced during manufacturing by a technique called hydrogenation, which is used to solidify fats and oils in many processed foods such as margarines, cakes, biscuits and pies.

Above: Alcohol in moderation, such as a glass of punch at a party, will do you little harm, but you should always control it rather than let it control you.

recipes

APRICOTS

Apricots are a good source of beta-carotene (vitamin A), which helps prevent some cancers. Fresh apricots are also rich in vitamin C needed for immunity and general health. Dried apricots provide iron and potassium. Iron is needed to form haemoglobin in blood cells, and potassium is vital for cell growth and has a beneficial effect on blood pressure. The non-soluble fibre is a laxative, while sweet alcohol, sorbitol helps to soften stools. The soluble fibre, pectin, helps to regulate the gut's muscle, making apricots ideal for constipation sufferers, and helps to lower blood cholesterol.

poached apricots with oatmeal cream

SERVES 4

Preparation time: *5 minutes*

Cooking time: *10 minutes*

500 g (1 lb) fresh apricots

2 tablespoons light muscovado sugar

½ teaspoon ground ginger

5 tablespoons water

40 g (1½ oz) medium or coarse oatmeal

200 ml (7 fl oz) Greek yogurt

2 tablespoons double cream

2 tablespoons clear honey

1 Halve and quarter the apricots, discarding the stones. Heat the sugar, ginger and water in a saucepan until the sugar has dissolved.

2 Add the apricots and cover the pan. Simmer gently, stirring once, for about 10 minutes, until tender. Cool slightly, then spoon into 4 serving glasses or bowls.

3 Lightly toast the oatmeal in a dry frying pan over a medium heat for about 30 seconds, shaking the pan frequently. Remove from the heat and cool slightly.

4 Stir the toasted oatmeal into the yogurt, with the cream and honey. Spoon over the fruit and serve warm, or chill before serving if preferred.

● **Tips:**
● Try using ripe peaches, nectarines, plums or greengages.
● Ready-to-eat dried apricots can be substituted for fresh ones. Use 250 g (8 oz); halve, then poach as above, using 200 ml (7 fl oz) water and only 1 tablespoon of sugar.

NUTRITIONAL VALUES
calories: 253 Kcal (1060 Kj)
●
fat: 13 g
●
carbohydrate: 31 g
●
fibre: 3 g
●
vitamin A: 237 mcg (789 i.u.)

apricot smoothie

Place all the ingredients in a blender or food processor and process until smooth. Add a couple of ice cubes and drink immediately.

● **Good for:** Calcium. This smoothie will provide almost a third of our daily requirement. Calcium is essential for helping to build and maintain good bone health, and is also involved in nerve transmission, blood clotting and muscle function. The canned apricots are a handy standby item to have in your store cupboard and provide an additional source of carbohydrate.

NUTRITIONAL VALUES
calories: 130 kcal (550 kj) ● fat: 2 g ● carbohydrate: 24 g
● fibre: 1 g ● calcium: 219 mg

SERVES 2

Preparation time: *2–3 minutes*

Makes: *400 ml (14 fl oz)*

200 g (7 oz) canned apricots in natural juice, drained

150 g (5 oz) apricot yogurt

150 ml (¼ pint) ice-cold semi-skimmed milk

apricot & pineapple smoothie

Roughly chop the apricots into small pieces and place in a bowl. Pour the pineapple juice over them, cover with clingfilm and allow to stand overnight. Place all the ingredients in a blender or food processor and process until smooth. Add a couple of ice cubes and drink the juice immediately.

● **Good for:** Calcium. Dried apricots also have an increased concentration of beta-carotene, potassium and iron, making them attractive to athletes. Drunk after exercise, this juice helps to refuel the muscles and to boost energy levels. This is particularly so after endurance activities, such as long-distance running. Many brands of dried apricots are preserved using sulphur dioxide, which can trigger asthma attacks – always check the packaging to avoid this.

● **Try the following variation:**
orange & apricot juice: wash and remove the stones from 300 g (10 oz) apricots; peel and divide 1 large orange into segments. Juice the fruit together and then add 300 ml (½ pint) water. Pour into a glass and add a couple of ice cubes. This will make 300 ml (½ pint) and serves 1.

SERVES 1

Preparation time: *5 minutes, plus standing*

Makes: *350 ml (12 fl oz)*

65 g (2½ oz) ready-to-eat dried apricots

350 ml (12 fl oz) pineapple juice

NUTRITIONAL VALUES
calories: 240 Kcal (1024 Kj)
●
fat: 1 g
●
carbohydrate: 59 g
●
fibre: 11 g
●
vitamin A: 59 mcg (196 i.u.)

BANANAS

These energy-rich fruit have a high fibre content, making them mildly laxative, although very ripe bananas can help to alleviate diarrhoea. Bananas contain the amino acid tryptophan, which may reduce symptoms of PMS, anxiety and insomnia. The high levels of potassium help cellular growth, the functioning of the nervous system and controlling blood pressure. Bananas are full of vital anti-oxidants, notably beta-carotene, which converts naturally within the body to vitamin A; vitamin C, which boost the immune system, and protects against heart disease and some cancers; and vitamin B6, which protects against heart disease, regulates the nervous system and helps promote healthy skin.

pan-fried oranges & bananas

SERVES 4

Preparation time: *5 minutes*

Cooking time: *5 minutes*

2 oranges

25 g (1 oz) unsalted butter

1 cinnamon stick, halved

25 g (1 oz) light muscovado sugar

4 bananas, each cut diagonally into 4 pieces

5 tablespoons fresh orange juice

25 g (1 oz) broken walnuts, toasted

1 Using a sharp knife, cut the peel from the oranges, removing the white pith too. Thinly slice the oranges into rounds, discarding any pips; reserve the juice.

2 Melt the butter in a frying pan. Add the cinnamon stick and sugar and heat gently, stirring until the sugar has dissolved.

3 Add the bananas to the syrup and cook gently for 2 minutes, stirring frequently. Add the orange slices and juice and cook until the syrup is bubbling. Serve warm, scattered with toasted walnuts.

NUTRITIONAL VALUES

calories: 245 Kcal (1030 Kj)

•

fat: 10 g

•

carbohydrate: 38 g

•

fibre: 5 g

•

vitamin A: 63 mcg (210 i.u.)

banana & almond smoothie

Peel and slice the bananas, put into a freezerproof container and freeze for at least 2 hours or overnight. Place all the ingredients in a blender or food processor and blend until thick and frothy. Pour into glasses and serve immediately.

● **Good for:** Endurance athletes. Bananas are a popular carbohydrate and can be eaten before, during or after exercise, making them hugely versatile. Make sure that you use very ripe bananas (very yellow skin with black spots), as less ripe ones are largely indigestible. Almonds are an excellent source of vitamin E, along with the minerals calcium, magnesium, phosphorus and copper. They also help to increase the protein content of this drink. This smoothie is an excellent source of vitamins C, E, B1, B2, B6, niacin, folic acid, copper, potassium, zinc, magnesium and phosphorus, and provides useful amounts of calcium.

● **Try the following variations:**

avocado & banana smoothie: Peel, stone and roughly chop 1 small ripe avocado, and place it in a blender or food processor with 1 small sliced, ripe banana and process until smooth. Pour into a glass, add a couple of ice cubes and drink immediately. This will make 400 ml (14 fl oz) and will serve 1.

banana & peanut butter smoothie: Peel and slice 1 ripe banana, place in a freezerproof container and freeze for at least 2 hours or overnight. Place 300 ml (½ pint) semi-skimmed milk and 1 tablespoon smooth peanut butter or 2 teaspoons tahini paste in a blender or food processor and process until smooth. Pour into a glass and serve immediately. This will make 400 ml (14 fl oz) and will serve 1.

SERVES 2

Preparation time: *10 minutes*

Makes: *600 ml (1 pint)*

2 ripe bananas

450 ml (¾ pint) soya milk

40 g (1½ oz) ground almonds

pinch of ground cinnamon

a little honey to sweeten (optional)

NUTRITIONAL VALUES
calories: 330 Kcal (1370 Kj)
●
fat: 16 g
●
carbohydrate: 34 g
●
fibre: 8 g
●
vitamin C: 11 mg

BERRIES

Berries contain most of the anti-oxidant vitamins A, C and E, which protect against infections, premature ageing and degenerative diseases. All berries have high levels of phyto-oestrogens and are helpful for erratic periods, PMS and menopausal problems. Arthritis may be eased by strawberries. Mildly laxative, raspberries are good for indigestion and effective for menstrual problems. Sore throats and chesty coughs can be helped by blackberries and cranberries, while the pain of kidney and bladder infections and cystitis can be soothed by cranberries and blackcurrants.

strawberry & cucumber salad with balsamic dressing

SERVES **4–6**

Preparation time: *10 minutes, plus chilling*

1 cucumber, halved lengthways, deseeded and thinly sliced

250 g (8 oz) strawberries, halved or quartered if large

Balsamic dressing:

1 tablespoon balsamic vinegar

1 teaspoon coarse-grain mustard

1 teaspoon clear honey

3 tablespoons olive oil

pepper

1 Place the cucumber and strawberries in a shallow bowl.

2 To make the dressing, put all the ingredients in a screw-top jar and shake well.

3 Taste the dressing for seasoning and adjust if necessary before pouring it over the cucumber and strawberries. Toss lightly to coat and chill for 5–10 minutes before serving.

● **Tips:**
● Balsamic vinegar has a mellow, aromatic flavour and a dash added to all kinds of salads and vegetable dishes enhances the taste. This can be helpful if you are finding it difficult to do without additional salt.
● Strawberries macerated in balsamic vinegar are a traditional Italian dessert.

NUTRITIONAL VALUES
calories: 107 Kcal (440 Kj)
●
fat: 9 g
●
carbohydrate: 7 g
●
fibre: 2 g
●
vitamin C: 49 mg

cranberry chicken stir-fry with ginger

SERVES **4**

Preparation time: *20 minutes*

Cooking time: *10 minutes*

2 tablespoons vegetable oil

2 shallots, finely chopped

2.5 cm (1 inch) piece of fresh root ginger, peeled and thinly sliced into julienne strips

2 garlic cloves, crushed

4 skinless chicken breasts, about 75 g (3 oz) each, thinly sliced

2 tablespoons hoisin sauce

2 tablespoons oyster sauce

1 tablespoon light soy sauce

150 g (5 oz) dried cranberries

4 spring onions, diagonally sliced

125 g (4 oz) beansprouts, sliced green or red pepper or carrot strips

To garnish:

handful of basil leaves

1 large red chilli, deseeded and thinly sliced

vegetable oil, for deep frying

1 Heat the 2 tablespoons of oil in a wok and stir-fry the shallots, ginger, and garlic over a medium heat for 30 seconds. Add the chicken and stir-fry for 2 minutes or until golden brown.

2 Add the hoisin, oyster, and soy sauces and the cranberries and stir-fry for a further 2 minutes. Check that the chicken is cooked all the way through, then add the spring onions and beansprouts or other vegetables, if using, and toss together for 3–4 minutes.

3 In a small saucepan containing 1 cm (½ inch) of oil, deep-fry the basil leaves and red chilli in 2 batches for 10–30 seconds, until crisp. Use the basil and chilli as a garnish for the stir-fry.

NUTRITIONAL VALUES
calories: 230 Kcal (970 Kj) ● fat: 10 g ● carbohydrate: 8 g
● fibre: 5 g ● iron: 3 mg

figs with blackberries on toast

SERVES 4

Preparation time: *5–10 minutes*

Cooking time: *8–10 minutes*

12 ripe figs

125 g (4 oz) blackberries

pared rind and juice of 2 oranges

2 tablespoons crème de cassis

1 tablespoon caster sugar

½ teaspoon cinnamon

25 g (1 oz) butter, melted

4 slices of brioche or white bread

*fromage frais or Greek yogurt,
to serve (optional)*

NUTRITIONAL VALUES
*(not including fromage
frais or yogurt)*
calories: 246 Kcal (1040 Kj)
•
fat: 6 g
•
carbohydrate: 43 g
•
fibre: 7 g
•
vitamin A: 100 mcg (333 i.u.)

1 Cut the figs into quarters, slicing almost, but not all the way through, so that the quarters fall back like flower petals. Cut out 4 squares of double-thickness foil and place 3 figs and a quarter of the blackberries on each piece.

2 Cut the orange rind into julienne strips. Place in a bowl, stir in the orange juice and the crème de cassis and divide between the fig parcels. Bring up the edges of the foil and press to seal.

3 Mix the sugar, cinnamon and melted butter in a bowl and brush over 1 side of each brioche or bread slice.

4 Cook the fig parcels in a preheated oven, 200°C (400°F), Gas Mark 6, for about 8–10 minutes, or until the figs are hot and slightly soft. Towards the end of the cooking time, add the brioche or bread slices to a medium hot griddle pan, with the buttered side up, and toast until golden.

5 Serve the cinnamon toast on individual plates, topped with the figs and blackberries. Add a spoonful of fromage frais or Greek yogurt, if liked.

breakfast smoothie

Juice the strawberries and kiwi fruit and process in a blender or food processor with the banana, spirulina, linseeds and a couple of crushed ice cubes. Pour into a glass and decorate with redcurrants, if liked. Serve immediately.

● **Good for:** Fast, nutritious food. Don't you feel more energetic after eating a healthy fruit breakfast rather than grabbing a cup of coffee? These fruits, in particular the banana, create a feeling of fullness as well as helping to rebalance your sugar levels and thus your energy levels. Your sugar levels will also be helped by the protein in the linseeds. The high levels of vitamin B in this juice will also increase your energy. High in potassium, vitamin C, vitamin B$_{12}$ and essential fatty acids, this is a thick shake with a punch that will take you through the morning and keep you going without any cravings for unhealthy snacks.

SERVES 1

Preparation time: *4–5 minutes,*

Makes: *200 ml (7 fl oz)*

250 g (8 oz) strawberries

125 g (4 oz) kiwi fruit

100 g (3½ oz) banana

1 tablespoon spirulina

1 tablespoon linseeds

NUTRITIONAL VALUES

calories: 340 Kcal (1420 Kj)
●
fat: 8 g
●
carbohydrate: 55 g
●
fibre: 4 g
●
iron: 8 mg

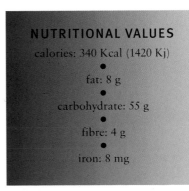

blueberry & grapefruit juice

SERVES 1

Preparation time: *2 minutes*

250 g (8 oz) blueberries

125 g (4 oz) grapefruit

250 g (8 oz) apple

2.5 cm (1 inch) cube fresh root ginger, peeled and roughly chopped

Juice all the ingredients and serve in a tall glass with ice cubes. Decorate with thin slices of ginger, if liked.

● **Good for:** Reducing blood cholesterol levels. High cholesterol levels are caused by eating a diet containing too much saturated fat, which leads to a build-up along the inside walls of the arteries. Grapefruit is particularly recommended for its rich source of vitamin C and bioflavonoids, which protect the health of the arteries. Blueberries are also extremely potent anti-oxidants and, along with apples, can help prevent atherosclerosis, hardening of the arteries, and reduce blood cholesterol levels.

NUTRITIONAL VALUES
calories: 230 Kcal (985 Kj)
●
fat: 1 g
●
carbohydrate: 56 g
●
fibre: 0 g
●
iron: 2 mg

cranberry & mango smoothie

Peel, stone and roughly chop the mango, then place the flesh in a blender or food processor with the remaining ingredients. Process until smooth. Pour into a glass, add a couple of ice cubes and drink immediately.

1 ripe mango

200 ml (7 fl oz) cranberry juice

150 ml (¼ pint) peach–flavoured yogurt

● **Good for:** Vitamins A, C, B₁, B₂, B₆, B₁₂, folic acid, calcium, zinc, potassium, magnesium and phosphorus. It will also provide useful amounts of iron. Containing high levels of carbohydrate for energy and calcium for bone health and strength, this smoothie is ideal for many different athletes and people worried about the onset of osteoporosis and iron deficiency.

NUTRITIONAL VALUES

calories: 319 Kcal (1360 Kj)
●
fat: 2 g
●
carbohydrate: 71 g
●
fibre: 4 g
●
vitamin A: 489 mcg (1628 i.u.)

CITRUS FRUIT

Oranges, lemons, limes, grapefruit and the other citrus fruit are renowned for their high levels of the anti-oxidant vitamin C, which helps white blood cells fight infection, boosts immunity in general and helps maintain mental alertness and a retentive memory. It is also needed for healing wounds. Other anti-oxidants found in citrus fruit, called flavonoids, work with vitamin C to boost immunity and strengthen blood vessel walls, reducing the risk of stroke. Oranges are a very good source of folates, which are essential for the healthy development of a baby's brain and spinal cord in early pregnancy; they help to reduce the risk of spina bifida. In adults, folates protect against heart disease by lowering blood levels of the amino acid homocysteine. In addition, folic acid is essential for the formation of red blood cells to prevent fatigue and anaemia.

lemon & basil penne

SERVES 4

Preparation time: *10 minutes,*

Cooking time: *10–12 minutes*

2 garlic cloves

large handful of basil leaves

4 tablespoons olive oil

grated rind and juice of 2 lemons

175 g (6 oz) dried penne

50 g (2 oz) freshly grated Parmesan cheese

pepper

NUTRITIONAL VALUES
calories: 309 Kcal (1297 Kj)
•
fat: 16 g
•
carbohydrate: 33 g
•
fibre: 2 g
•
calcium: 174 mg

1 Bring a large saucepan of water to the boil.

2 Meanwhile, using a pestle and mortar or a food processor, blend the garlic, basil, olive oil and lemon rind and juice until smooth.

3 Place the penne in the boiling water, bring back to the boil and cook for 10–12 minutes, or according to the package instructions.

4 Add the grated Parmesan to the basil mixture, blend well and season with pepper to taste.

5 Drain the penne thoroughly. Add the pesto and toss thoroughly so that the sauce is distributed evenly throughout the penne. Serve immediately.

● **Tips:**
● Although Parmesan cheese is a relatively high-fat dairy product, it has such an intense flavour that you need use only a little. Buy it in a block and grate it freshly when required. Ready-grated Parmesan quickly loses its flavour and you will end up using much more.
● Besides its use as a favourite culinary herb, basil has a reputation in traditional herbal medicine for soothing pain, nervous stress and headaches.
● Many wholemeal pasta shapes are widely available. If you prefer to use wholemeal pasta, cook it for about 12 minutes, timing it from when the water returns to the boil after the pasta has been added to the pan.
● Bring lemons to room temperature and roll them over the work surface before squeezing to maximize the yield of juice.

spiced orange & avocado salad

1 Peel the oranges, then cut away the white pith. Working over a bowl to catch the juices, cut between the membranes to remove the segments. Slice the avocados and toss gently with the orange segments. Pile on to serving plates.

2 Reserve a few whole cardamom pods for decoration. Crush the remaining pods using a mortar and pestle to extract the seeds, or place in a small bowl and crush with the end of a rolling pin. Pick out and discard the pods. Mix the seeds with the olive oil, honey, allspice, lemon juice and reserved orange juice. Season to taste with pepper.

3 Garnish the salads with the watercress sprigs and serve with the dressing spooned over the top.

● **Tips:**
● For a sharper flavour, substitute 2 pink grapefruit for the oranges.
● Besides being delicious, avocados are energy rich and contain the anti-oxidant vitamins C and E, as well as useful amounts of potassium and folic acid. Although high in fat compared with other fruit and vegetables, half of the fat is monounsaturated and there is no dietary cholesterol.

SERVES 4

Preparation time: *10 minutes*

4 large juicy oranges

2 small ripe avocados, halved, stoned and peeled

2 teaspoons cardamom pods

3 tablespoons light olive oil

1 tablespoon clear honey

good pinch of ground allspice

2 teaspoons lemon juice

pepper

watercress sprigs, to garnish

NUTRITIONAL VALUES

calories: 265 Kcal (1100 Kj)
●
fat: 18 g
●
carbohydrate: 24 g
●
fibre: 4 g
●
vitamin C: 117 mg

fresh lime sorbet

Preparation time: *20 minutes, plus freezing*

Cooking time: *6 minutes*

3 limes

175 g (6 oz) caster sugar

600 ml (1 pint) water

1 egg white, stiffly whisked

1 Pare the rinds of the limes with a potato peeler, reserve and squeeze the juice. Dissolve the sugar in the water and bring to the boil. Boil for 3 minutes. Add the lime rinds and boil rapidly, uncovered, for a further 3 minutes. Remove the lime rinds with a slotted spoon and set aside.

2 Cool the syrup, then add the lime juice. Strain into a freezerproof container and freeze until mushy. Stir thoroughly, mixing the sides into the centre, then carefully fold in the stiffly whisked egg white. Refreeze, covered, until firm.

3 Serve in bowls, decorated with the reserved lime rinds, and with biscuits such as tuiles d'amandes.

NUTRITIONAL VALUES
calories: 187 Kcal (798 Kj)
•
fat: 1 g
•
carbohydrate: 48 g
•
fibre: 0 g
•
vitamin C: 16 mg

orange & raspberry juice

SERVES 1

Preparation time: *5 minutes, plus freezing*

2 large oranges

175 g (6 oz) raspberries

250 ml (8 fl oz) water

Peel the oranges and divide the flesh into segments. Wash the raspberries. Juice the fruit, then add the water. Pour into a glass and add a couple of ice cubes.

● **Good for:** Drinking during endurance, extra-energy or general fitness activity. It will give a good boost of vitamin C, plus potassium and folate. An excellent isotonic drink containing plenty of calcium.

● **Try the following variations:**

horseradish pick-me-up: Pulverize 1½ teaspoons grated horseradish by juicing it and mixing the juice and the pulp. Put it into a shot glass and stir in the juice of ½ lemon. Take twice a day.

Watermelon & Orange: Remove the skin and seeds from ¼ watermelon or use 300 g (10 oz) chopped watermelon flesh. Peel 2 oranges and divide the flesh into segments. Juice the fruit, pour into a glass and add a couple of ice cubes. This will make 300 ml (½ pint) and will serve 1.

NUTRITIONAL VALUES

calories: 199 Kcal (854 Kj)
●
fat: 1 g
●
carbohydrate: 44 g
●
fibre: 0 g
●
vitamin C: 283 mg

DATES & PRUNES

Dates are renowned as a laxative, because of their high levels of NSP (fibre), and this also slows down the speed at which energy from their sugars is released, so that, like bananas, they make a good snack food. Dates contain beta-carotene, vitamin B₆ and Niacin (B₃), which help maintain healthy skin, nervous and digestive systems. Fresh dates contain some vitamin C. Their mineral content includes potassium, which maintains the sodium balance in cells and regulates blood pressure, magnesium, which is vital for bones, muscles and the heart, and iron and copper, which are both vital for forming haemoglobin in the blood, preventing fatigue and anaemia. Prunes also have laxative qualities, boost energy and have a reputation for curing hangovers.

date & orange fool

SERVES 4

Preparation time: *10 minutes, plus chilling*

Cooking time: *10 minutes*

*freshly squeezed juice of
2 large oranges*

125 g (4 oz) stoned dates

300 ml (½ pint) natural bio yogurt

1 banana, sliced, to serve

NUTRITIONAL VALUES
calories: 168 Kcal (714 Kj)
•
fat: 2 g
•
carbohydrate: 36 g
•
fibre: 3 g
•
calcium: 127 mg

1 Make the orange juice up to 275 ml (9 fl oz) with water and put into a small pan with the dates. Bring to the boil, cover and simmer for 10 minutes, until soft. Allow to cool slightly, then process in a food processor or blender until smooth. Set aside until completely cooled.

2 Put alternate spoonfuls of date purée and yogurt in 4 small serving dishes, then swirl together attractively, using a small knife or skewer. Chill in the refrigerator until required.

3 Top the fruit fools with sliced banana just before serving.

● **Tips:**
● Prunes, figs or dried apricots may be used instead of dates.
● As a variation, the date purée and yogurt can be layered in small plastic or glass dishes.
● Encourage your children to brush their teeth after a meal, especially after a dessert. Although there is no added sugar here, the natural sugar in the dates and the acid in the oranges can cause problems for tooth enamel.
● Date and orange purée also makes a great spread for toast, or a filling for a simple Victoria sandwich, and it has a much lower sugar content than jam. Make as above, but add only enough water in step 1 to make up to 250 ml (8 fl oz). Store in a sealed plastic container or screw-top jar in the refrigerator for up to 1 week.

really fruity flapjacks

Preparation time: *10 minutes*

Cooking time: *20 minutes*

75 g (3 oz) ready-to-eat dried prunes

*75 g (3 oz) ready-to-eat
dried apricots*

100 g (3½ oz) unsalted butter

100 g (3½ oz) light muscovado sugar

5 tablespoons clear honey

375 g (12 oz) porridge oats

75 g (3 oz) raisins or sultanas

2 eggs

1 Lightly grease a 28 x 23 cm (11 x 9 inch) shallow baking tin, or a tin with similar dimensions. Chop the prunes and apricots into small pieces.

2 Melt the butter with the sugar and honey in a small saucepan. Remove from the heat and stir in the oats, prunes, apricots and raisins or sultanas until evenly mixed. Beat in the eggs.

3 Turn the mixture into the prepared tin and level the surface. Bake in a preheated oven, 180°C (350°F), Gas Mark 4, for 20 minutes, until turning pale golden. Leave in the tin until almost cold, then cut into fingers and finish cooling on a wire rack. The flapjacks can be stored in an airtight container in a cool place for up to 5 days.

● **Tips:**
● When you take them out of the oven, the flapjacks will still be soft in the centre. They firm up on cooling. Don't be tempted to cook them for longer or they will turn brittle.
● Other dried fruit, such as chopped figs or dates, can be used as alternatives to those listed above. For an extra tang, add the grated rind of 1 lemon with the melted butter.
● Make sure the fruit and oat mixture has cooled a little before you add the eggs or they will scramble in the heat.

NUTRITIONAL VALUES
calories: 217 Kcal (915 Kj)
●
fat: 8 g
●
carbohydrate: 35 g
●
fibre: 3 g
●
iron: 2 mg

PINEAPPLE

> This fruit is rich in beta-carotene and vitamin C, which protect against the free radicals that damage cells. Its potassium helps to regulate blood pressure. It is also a good vegetarian source of manganese, which is needed for protein and fat metabolism, helping protect against hardening of the arteries, and is vital for formation of bones and cartilage and maintaining a good immune system. It also maintains fluid in the joints, so helping prevent some forms of arthritis.

stir-fried chicken with pineapple

SERVES **2**

Preparation time: *10 minutes*

Cooking time: *12–14 minutes*

about 750 ml (1¼ pints) oil, for deep-frying

50 g (2 oz) tempura flour or self-raising flour

5 tablespoons water

125 g (4 oz) chicken, skinned and cut into bite-sized pieces

150 g (5 oz) pineapple, cut into chunks

1 tomato, cut into 8 pieces

1 tablespoon tomato purée

1 tablespoon palm sugar or light muscovado sugar

50 g (2 oz) cashew nuts

1½ tablespoons light soy sauce

To garnish:

1 spring onion, diagonally sliced

coriander sprigs

1 Heat all but 1 tablespoon of the oil in a wok and, while it is heating, mix the flour and water together thoroughly to make a coating batter.

2 When the oil is hot enough, coat half the chicken pieces in the batter and deep-fry them until they are golden brown. Remove from the oil and drain them on kitchen paper. Repeat the process with the rest of the chicken.

3 Pour off the oil, wipe the wok clean with kitchen paper and then heat the remaining oil in it. Add the pineapple, tomato, tomato purée, sugar and cashews and stir-fry for 2 minutes.

4 Add the soy sauce and stir, return the batter-coated chicken to the wok. Stir again over a high heat then serve, garnished with spring onion slices and coriander sprigs.

● **Tips:**
● Pineapple contains the enzyme bromelain, which not only helps prevent blood clots and promotes the healing of minor injuries, but it also acts as a tenderizer for meat and thus aids digestion.
● Always buy nuts in small quantities and store them in an airtight container in a cool place. They will keep only a few weeks before turning rancid.
● Removing the skin from chicken before cooking gets rid of almost all the fat. Trim off any remaining visible fat before cutting it into pieces to ensure a healthy, low-fat meal.
● Low-sodium soy sauce is available from health food shops.

NUTRITIONAL VALUES

calories: 530 Kcal (2216 Kj) ● fat: 31 g ● carbohydrate: 43 g
● fibre: 3 g ● iron: 4 mg

mixed fruit smoothie

Juice the grapefruit, kiwi and pineapple. Process in a blender or food processor with the frozen berries. Decorate with raspberries, if liked.

● **Good for:** Immune system. The best anti-oxidants are found in citrus fruit, pineapple, kiwi fruit, raspberries and blueberries. This drink may help prevent or treat urinary infections, provide the fibre necessary to ward off colon cancer and aid weight loss as these fruits are all low in calories.

● **Try the following variation:**
blackberry and pineapple juice: Juice 375 g (12 oz) blackberries first, then add 375 g (12 oz) pineapple, to push through the pulp. Blend the juice with a couple of ice cubes and serve in a tall glass, decorated with a pineapple sliver, if liked. This will make 200 ml (7 fl oz) and will serve 1.

SERVES 1–2

Preparation time: *3–4 minutes*

Makes: *200 ml (7 fl oz)*

150 g (5 oz) grapefruit

50 g (2 oz) kiwi fruit

175 g (6 oz) pineapple

50 g (2 oz) frozen raspberries

50 g (2 oz) frozen cranberries

NUTRITIONAL VALUES
calories: 160 Kcal (688 Kj)
●
fat: 1 g
●
carbohydrate: 37 g
●
fibre: 3 g
●
vitamin C: 127 mg

BEETROOT

Beetroot has a very high anti-oxidant content (beta-carotene and vitamin C) and helps fight off infection. It also contains vitamin B$_6$, folic acid, calcium, iron, manganese, magnesium, phosphorus and potassium. It helps the functioning of the kidneys, gall bladder and liver, and contains minerals vital for healthy bones, teeth and muscles (including the heart). Its iron content helps to prevent fatigue. Its iron and manganese help to alleviate menstrual problems, particularly low haemoglobin levels caused by very heavy periods, and menopausal problems.

spiced beetroot

SERVES **4**

Preparation time: *8 minutes*

Cooking time: *10 minutes*

1 tablespoon vegetable oil

2 garlic cloves, finely chopped

1 teaspoon grated fresh root ginger

1 teaspoon cumin seeds

1 teaspoon coriander seeds, roughly crushed

½ teaspoon dried red chilli flakes

625 g (1¼ lb) freshly cooked and peeled beetroot, cut into wedges

150 ml (¼ pint) coconut milk

¼ teaspoon ground cardamom seeds

grated rind and juice of 1 lime

handful of chopped fresh coriander

pepper

1 Heat the oil in a large frying pan and when hot, add the garlic, ginger, cumin, coriander seeds and chilli flakes. Stir-fry for 1–2 minutes then add the beetroot. Fry, stirring gently, for 1 minute and then add the coconut milk, ground cardamom, lime rind and juice and cook over a medium heat for 2–3 minutes.

2 Stir in the chopped coriander, season with pepper to taste and serve hot, warm or at room temperature.

NUTRITIONAL VALUES

calories: 110 Kcal (468 Kj) ● fat: 3 g ● carbohydrate: 18 g

● fibre: 4 g ● iron: 2 mg

beetroot risotto

SERVES **4**

Preparation time: *5 minutes*

Cooking time: *25 minutes*

4 tablespoons olive oil

1 large red onion, chopped

3 garlic cloves, crushed

400 g (13 oz) risotto rice

1.3 litres (2¼ pints) hot
vegetable stock

425 g (14 oz) freshly cooked
beetroot, peeled and finely diced

4 tablespoons coarsely chopped dill

1–2 tablespoons grated fresh
horseradish or 1 tablespoon hot
horseradish from a jar

50 g (2 oz) salted macadamia nuts
or almonds

pepper

mixed salad leaves, to serve

1 Heat the oil in a large, heavy-based saucepan. Add the onion and garlic and fry gently for 3 minutes. Add the rice and cook for 1 minute, stirring.

2 Add 2 ladlefuls of the hot stock and cook, stirring frequently, until almost absorbed. Add a little more stock and continue cooking, stirring frequently, until almost absorbed. Continue in the same way until all the stock is used and the rice is creamy but still retaining a little bite. This will take a total of about 20 minutes.

3 Stir in the beetroot, dill, horseradish and nuts. Season to taste with pepper and heat through gently for 1 minute. Spoon on to serving plates and serve scattered with mixed salad leaves.

- **Tips:**
- This dish could also serve 6–8 as a starter.
- If you can find fresh horseradish, use it in place of the bottled variety. The flavour is far superior, but beware of its heat intensity.

NUTRITIONAL VALUES
calories: 630 Kcal (2650 Kj)
•
fat: 22 g
•
carbohydrate: 103 g
•
fibre: 6 g
•
iron: 2 mg

BROCCOLI

Both calabrese and purple sprouting broccoli contain the anti-oxidants beta-carotene, vitamin A and vitamin C, which combine with fibre and the substance sulfuraphane, which detoxifies and helps secrete carcinogens and so is a major force in protecting against cancer of the bowel. Broccoli also protects against heart disease and a range of infections, particularly those affecting the respiratory system. It stimulates the liver, which makes the whole body function better, including the skin. Its B vitamins are vital for turning food into energy. Broccoli is a good source of folic acid and so protects against spina bifida in unborn babies. Like iron, it is vital for haemoglobin formation, and so helps to prevent anaemia. Folic acid also promotes the production of the neurotransmitter serotonin, so it may also be beneficial for people suffering from depression, insomnia and difficulty in going to sleep. Broccoli also contains tryptophan, an amino acid which the brain converts into serotonin.

broccoli & red pepper fettuccine

SERVES **4**

Preparation time: *10 minutes*

Cooking time: *15 minutes*

---

300 g (10 oz) fresh fettuccine

---

3 red peppers, cored, deseeded and halved

---

250 g (8 oz) small broccoli florets

---

5 tablespoons olive oil

---

2 tablespoons balsamic vinegar

---

pepper

---

basil leaves, to garnish

NUTRITIONAL VALUES
calories: 425 Kcal (1715 Kj)
•
fat: 19 g
•
carbohydrate: 57 g
•
fibre: 1 g
•
vitamin A: 490 mcg (1630 i.u.)

1 Bring at least 1.8 litres (3 pints) water to the boil in a large saucepan. Add the pasta, bring back to the boil and cook for 4–6 minutes, until just tender but still with a little bite.

2 Drain, rinse under cold running water in a colander and drain again. Set aside in a large salad bowl.

3 Grill the peppers, skin side up, until the skins have blackened and blistered. Remove from the heat and leave to cool for 5 minutes.

4 Meanwhile, bring a large saucepan of water to the boil, add the broccoli florets and blanch for 3 minutes. Drain, rinse under cold running water and drain well again.

5 Peel the peppers and slice the flesh into strips. Add to the pasta with the drained broccoli florets, olive oil and the balsamic vinegar. Season with pepper to taste and toss well. Serve immediately, garnished with basil leaves.

- ● Tips:
- ● This dish is the perfect pick-me-up when you are feeling a bit fed up. Quite apart from its delicious flavour, the presence of high-carbohydrate pasta increases the brain's take-up of tryptophan, resulting in greater production of the feel-good chemical serotonin.
- ● Do not overcook the broccoli, as not only will you destroy valuable vitamins, but it will also become soggy and tasteless.
- ● The peppers will be easier to peel if you cool them in a sealed plastic bag.

mixed vegetable risotto

1 Heat the oil in a large, heavy-based saucepan, add the garlic and rice and cook, stirring constantly, for 1 minute. Pour in the stock and bring to the boil. Reduce the heat and simmer gently for 15–20 minutes, stirring frequently, until the mixture is creamy, the stock has been absorbed and the rice is just tender.

2 Cut the broccoli into small florets and slice the stalks. Add to the risotto with the peas and cook for a further 5 minutes, stirring frequently to prevent the rice from sticking to the pan. Add a little more water if the risotto becomes dry.

3 Stir in the spinach and cook for 1–2 minutes until it is wilted. Stir in the grated Parmesan and season lightly with pepper. Spoon on to warmed serving plates and sprinkle with Parmesan shavings. Serve immediately.

● **Tip:**
● Add 150 g (5 oz) lean, rindless bacon rashers to the risotto to make a meat-eaters alternative. Dry-fry the bacon in a small, heavy-based frying pan until crisp. Remove and drain on kitchen paper, then cut into strips. Top the risotto with the bacon and serve immediately.

SERVES 4

Preparation time: *15 minutes*

Cooking time: *about 25 minutes*

2 tablespoons olive oil

1 garlic clove, crushed

300 g (10 oz) risotto rice

1 litre (1¾ pints) vegetable stock

250 g (8 oz) broccoli

125 g (4 oz) frozen peas

150 g (5 oz) baby spinach

25 g (1 oz) Parmesan cheese, freshly grated

pepper

Parmesan shavings, to garnish

NUTRITIONAL VALUES
calories: 480 Kcal (2020 Kj)
●
fat: 16 g
●
carbohydrate: 70 g
●
fibre: 5 g
●
vitamin A: 326 mcg (1085 i.u.)

stir-fried broccoli with sesame seeds & red rice

SERVES **4**

Preparation time: *15 minutes*

Cooking time: *about 40 minutes*

500 g (1 lb) broccoli florets

125 g (4 oz) sugar snap peas

125 g (4 oz) mangetouts

250 g (8 oz) red or brown rice

10 cm (4 inch) piece of dried kombu seaweed (optional)

3 tablespoons groundnut oil

2–3 garlic cloves, crushed

3 tablespoons soy sauce

1 tablespoon tahini paste

1 tablespoon sesame oil

2 tablespoons sesame seeds, toasted

pepper

NUTRITIONAL VALUES
calories: 453 Kcal (1900 Kj)
•
fat: 20 g
•
carbohydrate: 57 g
•
fibre: 4 g
•
iron: 5 mg

1 Bring a pan of water to the boil. Plunge the broccoli into the water for 1 minute, then remove with a slotted spoon and immediately add to a bowl of cold water to refresh and prevent any further cooking.

2 Trim the sugar snaps and mangetouts and blanch them in the boiling water for 30 seconds. Remove them from the boiling water with a slotted spoon and refresh in the bowl of cold water for 5 minutes, then drain well. Reserve the pan of vegetable water.

3 Add the red or brown rice to the pan of vegetable water with the kombu, if using, and return to the boil. Reduce the heat a little and cook at a fast simmer for 30 minutes. When the rice is just cooked and still retains a little bite, drain well, reserving a little of the water. Discard the seaweed.

4 Heat the groundnut oil in a wok or large frying pan, add the garlic and cook gently, stirring constantly, for 1 minute to flavour the oil. Do not allow the garlic to burn.

5 Add the drained vegetables to the oil and stir-fry for 1–2 minutes. Mix together the soy sauce, tahini, sesame oil and 8 tablespoons of reserved vegetable water, add to the vegetables and stir-fry for 1 further minute.

6 Remove the wok from the heat and toss the cooked red or brown rice through the vegetables. Spoon into serving bowls and top with toasted sesame seeds and black pepper. Serve immediately or chill and serve cold.

● **Tips:**
● Red rice has a flavour rather like buckwheat and looks quite spectacular. Semi-cultivated varieties, such as Camargue and the Californian Wehani, are widely available from supermarkets. If you substitute brown rice, you may need to cook it for 5–10 minutes longer.
● Kombu is a variety of kelp that is particularly popular in Japan. It is available from some supermarkets and specialist stores. It is used for making sushi and also helps to soften dried pulses during cooking.
● Middle Eastern tahini paste or tahina is made from pulped sesame seeds. It is the essential flavouring for the dip hummus, where it is combined with chickpeas, and can be added to salads or simply spread on toast.

mixed vegetable juice

Juice all the ingredients and serve in a tall glass. Decorate with a coriander sprig, if liked.

● **Good for:** Immune system. The immune system is your body's inner protection system, designed to fight bacteria, infection, viruses or any foreign substances which may have entered your body. In order to fight the potential illnesses in your system, it is necessary to increase your intake of anti-oxidants, which can help to rebalance your immunity. High in selenium, this is an ideal juice for smokers, to help guard against lung cancer.

● **Try the following variation:**

green vegetable juice: Juice 100 g (3½ oz) broccoli, 25 g (1 oz) parsley, 200 g (7 oz) apples and 50 g (2 oz) celery and serve in a glass over ice. Decorate with kale, if liked.

SERVES **1**

Preparation time: *3–4 minutes*

Makes: *200 ml (7 fl oz)*

250 g (8 oz) broccoli

175 g (6 oz) carrot

50 g (2 oz) beetroot

NUTRITIONAL VALUES

calories: 160 Kcal (675 Kj)

●

fat: 3 g

●

carbohydrate: 22 g

●

fibre: 0 g

●

vitamin A: 2600 mcg (8658 i.u.)

CABBAGE & KALE

All cabbages are highly nutritious and benefit the digestive and immune systems. Raw cabbage detoxifies the digestive system, working to soothe indigestion and the after-effects of stomach upsets. It encourages peristalsis, so is helpful for treating constipation. Cabbage contains high levels of the anti-oxidant vitamins A, C and E, so protecting against free radicals and improving skin conditions such as acne. Its high vitamin C content helps to build up resistance to coughs, colds and other infections. It is an important source of iodine, which is vital for thyroid function, energy and growth. Magnesium is needed for healthy muscles and nerves. Calcium is required for bones and teeth, the nervous system, muscles and preventing blood clotting. Potassium and phosphorus are both vital for a healthy heart and kidneys. Kale has many of the benefits of cabbage, as well as being a rich source of folic acid.

colcannon

SERVES 4–6

Preparation time: *15 minutes*

Cooking time: *20 minutes*

500 g (1 lb) kale or green leaf cabbage, stalks removed, and finely shredded

500 g (1 lb) potatoes, unpeeled

6 spring onions or chives, finely chopped

150 ml (¼ pint) milk or cream

125 g (4 oz) butter

pepper

NUTRITIONAL VALUES
using whole milk
calories: 390 Kcal (1630 Kj)
●
fat: 29 g
●
carbohydrate: 25 g
●
fibre: 6 g
●
iron: 3 mg

1 Bring a pan of water to the boil. Add the kale or cabbage and cook for 10–20 minutes, until very tender. Meanwhile, bring another pan of water to the boil, add the potatoes and cook until tender. Place the spring onions or chives and the milk or cream in a pan and simmer over a low heat for about 5 minutes.

2 Drain the kale or cabbage and mash. Drain the potatoes, peel and mash well. Add the hot milk and spring onions or chives, beating well to give a soft fluffy texture. Beat in the kale or cabbage, season with pepper and add half the butter. The colcannon should be a speckled, green colour. Heat through thoroughly before serving in individual dishes or bowls. Make a well in the centre of each serving and put a knob of the remaining butter in each. Serve the colcannon immediately as a main dish with a glass of buttermilk or as an accompanying vegetable.

● **Tips:**
● Try blending the kale in a food processor along with the hot milk and spring onions or chives before adding it to the potatoes. This produces an even texture and overall green colour and makes an interesting alternative.
● There are many variations of this traditional Irish recipe. For a more substantial dish add 50 g (2 oz) finely chopped celery to the milk with the spring onions or chives in step 1. You could substitute 2 tablespoons finely grated onion for the spring onions or, if you omit any kind of onion, then the dish is known as Rumbledethumps.
● Traditionally, Colcannon is served at Halloween and contains the silver charms more usually associated with Christmas pudding – coin, ring, horseshoe, bachelor's button and old maid's thimble. Sadly, there is no charm that predicts good health.

cabbage bhaji

1 Place the cabbage in a large saucepan with the measured water, cover and cook over a medium heat for 10 minutes, stirring occasionally. Drain, return to the pan, set aside and keep warm.

2 Meanwhile, heat the oil in a small nonstick frying pan and when hot, add the urid dhal, mustard seeds and dried chilli. Stir-fry for 1–2 minutes and, when the dhal turns light brown, add the curry leaves and fry, stirring constantly, for 2 minutes. Pour this spiced oil over the cabbage, stir in the coconut, season with pepper and serve hot.

● **Tips:**
● Also known as black gram, urid dhal is a fairly small type of lentil. It is available with or without its dark husk.
● Whole black mustard seeds are widely used in Indian cooking, usually with vegetable dishes and pulses. Adding them to hot oil releases their aroma and nutty flavour.
● Curry leaves look a little like bay leaves and have a pronounced curry flavour. They are generally fried in hot oil until crisp.

SERVES 4

Preparation time: *10 minutes*

Cooking time: *10 minutes*

500 g (1 lb) white cabbage, roughly chopped

150 ml (¼ pint) water

1 tablespoon vegetable oil

2 teaspoons urid dhal

1 teaspoon black mustard seeds

1 dried red chilli, finely chopped

6–8 curry leaves

2 tablespoons grated fresh coconut

pepper

NUTRITIONAL VALUES
calories: 93 Kcal (385 Kj)
●
fat: 6 g
●
carbohydrate: 7 g
●
fibre: 4 g
●
vitamin C: 44 mg

greens soup

SERVES 6–8

Preparation time: *15–20 minutes*

Cooking time: *about 1¼ hours*

500 g (1 lb) kale, stems discarded

500 g (1 lb) greens, chopped, stems discarded

250 g (8 oz) leeks, trimmed, cleaned and sliced

1 teaspoon caraway seeds

3 garlic cloves, crushed

1 tablespoon olive oil

1.8 litres (3 pints) water

150 ml (¼ pint) dry white wine

125 g (4 oz) ricotta cheese

125 ml (4 fl oz) crème fraîche

125 ml (4 fl oz) natural yogurt

white pepper

NUTRITIONAL VALUES
calories: 176 Kcal (733 Kj)
•
fat: 10 g
•
carbohydrate: 8 g
•
fibre: 9 g
•
calcium: 388 mg

1 Combine the kale, greens, leeks, caraway seeds, garlic and olive oil in a large saucepan. Pour in the water, partially cover the saucepan, and bring the mixture to the boil. Lower the heat and simmer for 45 minutes.

2 Drain the vegetables through a colander or sieve. Reserve the liquid and place the vegetables in a blender or food processor. Process until fairly smooth, but not puréed.

3 In a large saucepan combine 600 ml (1 pint) of the reserved cooking liquid with the wine. Cook over a low heat for 3 minutes, then whisk in the ricotta cheese, crème fraîche and yogurt. Stir well and continue to simmer for a further 3 minutes before adding the finely chopped greens. Stir in most of the remaining liquid to make a fairly thick soup.

4 Simmer the soup, partially covered, for 20 minutes. Do not bring it to the boil or it will curdle. Stir occasionally. Season to taste with white pepper. Serve the soup in warmed soup bowls or plates.

● **Tips:**
● Bacon and croûtons would make a wonderful garnish for this tasty soup. Heat 1 tablespoon sunflower oil and fry 4 rashers of rindless, smoked streaky bacon over a low heat until crisp. Remove from the pan with a slotted spoon and set aside. Remove the crusts from 2 slices of wholemeal bread and cut them into 1 cm (½ inch) squares. Add them to the frying pan and cook, turning frequently and adding a little more oil if necessary, until crisp and golden brown all over. Remove from the pan and drain on kitchen paper. Crumble the bacon, mix with the croûtons and then sprinkle over the bowls of soup before serving.
● This soup would taste even richer and be still more nutritious made with homemade vegetable stock instead of water. However, do not use a stock that originally included any members of the cabbage family – cabbage, kale, spring greens, kohlrabi, Brussels sprouts or even turnip tops – as the flavour could then become unpleasantly overpowering.
● Caraway seeds have an affinity with greens, especially kale and cabbage and are said to have digestive properties that help to counteract flatulence. However, their flavour is very distinctive and some people dislike it intensely. If you prefer, you could use a milder spice, such as dill seeds or fennel seeds.

kale & wheatgrass energizer

Juice the kale and the wheatgrass, stir in the spirulina powder. Serve in a small glass decorated with wheatgrass blades.

● **Good for:** Vitamin B_{12}. Spirulina is one of the best plant sources of vitamin B_{12}, which is essential for the functioning of all cells. Wheatgrass is high in chlorophyll, which combats anaemia. Kale has as much usable calcium as milk. Need we say more? This juice is a great energy booster with nutritional benefits that far outweigh its flavour.

● **Try the following variation:**
cabbage & carrot juice: Juice 250 g (8 oz) carrot and 250 g (8 oz) white cabbage and serve in a tall glass over ice. Both juices are renowned for having a healing effect on stomach ulcers.

SERVES 1

Preparation time: *3–4 minutes*

Makes: *50 ml (2 fl oz)*

25 g (1 oz) kale

100 g (3½ oz) wheatgrass

1 teaspoon spirulina

NUTRITIONAL VALUES
calories: 48 Kcal (200 Kj)
●
fat: 1 g
●
carbohydrate: 2 g
●
fibre: 0 g
●
iron: 6 mg

CARROTS

The beta-carotene in carrots has beneficial effects on the respiratory and digestive systems and skin, and is vital for building strong teeth, hair and bones. It is also believed to lead to improved night vision and healthy eyes. The carotenoids may help to protect the eyes from ultra-violet light and reduce the risk of cataracts. The anti-oxidants in carrots are vital for the immune system and also offer protection against various cancers. Carrots are also thought to protect against heart and arterial diseases and to help reduce blood cholesterol levels.

chunky carrot & lentil soup

SERVES 4

Preparation time: *10 minutes*

Cooking time: *30–35 minutes*

2 tablespoons vegetable oil

1 large onion, chopped

2 celery sticks, sliced

500 g (1 lb) carrots, sliced

1 garlic clove, crushed

150 g (5 oz) split red lentils, rinsed

1.4 litres (2¼ pints) vegetable stock

pepper

Spiced butter (optional):

40 g (1½ oz) lightly salted butter, softened

2 spring onions, finely chopped

¼ teaspoon dried chilli flakes

1 teaspoon cumin seeds

finely grated rind of 1 lemon

handful of fresh coriander, chopped

a few mint sprigs, chopped

1 First make the spiced butter, if serving. Put all the ingredients in a bowl and beat together until combined. Transfer to a small serving dish, cover and chill until ready to serve.

2 To make the soup, heat the oil in a large saucepan. Add the onion and celery and cook over a low heat, stirring occasionally, for 5 minutes until softened. Add the carrots and garlic and fry for 3 minutes.

3 Add the lentils and stock and bring just to the boil. Reduce the heat, cover the pan and cook gently for 20–25 minutes, until the vegetables are soft and the soup is pulpy. Season lightly to taste with pepper. Divide the soup between warmed soup bowls. Serve the spiced butter, if using, at the table so diners can stir in as much as they like.

● **Tips:**
● If you omit the spiced butter, serve the soup topped with toasted French bread and cheese, for a robust meal.
● Wrap any leftover spiced butter in clingfilm, store in the refrigerator and use as a topping for baked potatoes.

NUTRITIONAL VALUES
without spiced butter calories: 105 Kcal (440 Kj) ● fat: 3 g ● carbohydrate: 16 g
● fibre: 4 g ● vitamin A: 753 mcg (2508 i.u.)

carrot & banana booster

Juice the carrot and orange. Process in a blender with the banana, apricot and some cracked ice cubes. Decorate with chunks of banana, if liked.

SERVES 1

Preparation time: *10 minutes*

Makes: *200 ml (7 fl oz)*

150 g (5 oz) carrots

100 g (3½ oz) orange

100 g (3½ oz) banana

1 ready-to-eat dried apricot

● **Good for:** Children. Full of iron, calcium and potassium, this is an all-round booster that is great for bones and teeth and keeping colds at bay. Juices are the quickest and easiest way to make sure your kids not only receive vital nutrients, but also enjoy their food at the same time. Juicing is so easy that you can ask your child to do it – this way they'll feel more involved.

● **Try the following variations:**

carrot & kiwi juice: Scrub about 200 g (7 oz) carrots. Cut the carrots and 1 kiwi fruit into even-size pieces and feed into the juicer. Juice, then pour into a glass, add a couple of ice cubes and drink immediately.

carrot, apple & ginger juice: Scrub 200 g (7 oz) carrots. Cut the carrots, 1 tart apple and 1 cm (½ inch) piece fresh root ginger into even-size pieces, add to the juicer and juice. Pour into a glass, add a couple of ice cubes and drink immediately. This will make 250 ml (8 fl oz) and will serve 1.

NUTRITIONAL VALUES
calories: 203 Kcal (860 Kj)
●
fat: 1 g
●
carbohydrate: 48 g
●
fibre: 5 g
●
vitamin A: 2047 mcg (6817 i.u.)

RED PEPPER

Peppers contain high levels of the anti-oxidants vitamin C, beta-carotene, vitamin E and zinc so they fight off free radicals and protect against heart disease, strokes and some cancers. They are vital for maintaining a strong immune system and for energy production. Vitamin C is needed for the production of adrenaline, which stimulates the heart, and this is boosted by the magnesium they also contain. Substances in peppers stimulate the digestive system and help to prevent constipation, especially if drunk in fresh juice or eaten raw. They also improve the blood circulation.

roasted pepper soup

SERVES 4

Preparation time: *30 minutes*

Cooking time: *50–60 minutes*

6 large red or yellow peppers

4 leeks, white and pale green parts only, thinly sliced

3 tablespoons olive oil

750 ml (1¼ pints) chicken or vegetable stock

2 teaspoons black peppercorns

75 ml (3 fl oz) mascarpone cheese

75 ml (3 fl oz) milk

pepper

toasted country bread, to serve

NUTRITIONAL VALUES
calories: 230 Kcal (960 Kj)
•
fat: 18 g
•
carbohydrate: 14 g
•
fibre: 6 g
•
vitamin A: 1093 mcg (3640 i.u.)

1 Place the peppers in a large roasting tin and roast in a preheated oven, 240°C (475°F), Gas Mark 9, for 20–30 minutes, turning once, until they begin to char. Remove the peppers from the oven, put them into a plastic bag and close it tightly. Leave for 10 minutes to steam.

2 Put the leeks into a bowl of cold water to soak for 5 minutes.

3 Remove the peppers from the bag and peel off the skins, then pull out the stalks – the seeds should come with them. Halve the peppers, scrape out any remaining seeds and roughly chop the flesh. Swish the leeks around in the water to loosen any soil, then drain and rinse well.

4 Heat the oil in a large saucepan, add the leeks and cook gently, stirring occasionally, for 10 minutes until soft but not coloured. Add the peppers, stock and a little pepper. Bring the mixture to the boil, then turn down the heat and simmer for 20 minutes.

5 Pound or grind the black peppercorns as finely as possible. Beat the mascarpone with the milk and pepper. Chill until needed.

6 Process the soup in a blender, then pass it through a sieve back into the rinsed out pan. Reheat, taste and adjust the seasoning if necessary. Serve the soup in warmed bowls with spoonfuls of the pepper cream and slices of toasted country bread.

● **Tip:**
● Homemade stock is always the best choice, as not only does it taste better, but you also know precisely what went into it. If you have to use stock cubes or bouillon powder, look for a low-salt brand.

red pepper & tomato tonic

Juice the pepper, tomatoes and cabbage. Pour into a tall glass, stir in the parsley and decorate with a lime wedge, if liked.

● **Good for:** Skin disorders (see pages 70–79). There are many causes of skin disorders, ranging from stress to food allergies and vitamin deficiency. As the body's largest organ, your skin is the barometer of your body's health, being the first part to show any imbalances. It is also the first part to show the results of cleansing your system. All four ingredients in this juice contain bioflavonoids, which reduce inflammation.

● **Try the following variation:**

sweet & sour smoothie: Juice 100 g (3½ oz) red pepper, 50 g (2 oz) tomato and 125 g (4 oz) each of mango, watermelon and strawberries, process in a blender with 3 ice cubes and serve in a tall glass. Decorate with mango slices, if liked. This will make 200 ml (7 fl oz) and will serve 1.

SERVES **1**

Preparation time: *3–4 minutes*

Makes: *200 ml (7 fl oz)*

175 g (6 oz) red pepper

175 g (6 oz) tomatoes

100 g (3½ oz) white cabbage

1 tablespoon chopped parsley

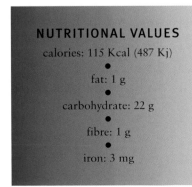

NUTRITIONAL VALUES

calories: 115 Kcal (487 Kj)
●
fat: 1 g
●
carbohydrate: 22 g
●
fibre: 1 g
●
iron: 3 mg

SPINACH

Spinach is a powerful source of anti-oxidants, containing high levels of beta-carotene (vitamin A), and vitamins C and E, strengthening the immune system and reducing the risk of heart disease and stroke, as well as some cancers. The carotenoids in spinach may protect against cataracts and macular degeneration, which causes blindness. Spinach is renowned for its high iron content, which prevents fatigue and anaemia, although its iron content is lower than was originally thought and some of the iron is inaccessible to the body. Its vitamin K and magnesium help to build healthy blood cells. Its calcium helps to build bones and teeth and in older people helps to work against osteoarthritis. It is a rich source of folic acid, which is essential for the healthy development of the nervous system in early pregnancy, protecting babies from spina bifida, while its high potassium content regulates high blood pressure. Spinach is a natural laxative, so it is great for people suffering from constipation.

WARNING: spinach should not be eaten or drunk as a juice on a daily basis, as its cleansing effect will be too strong and it should be avoided completely by people with kidney or bladder stones.

quick spinach

SERVES **4**

Preparation time: *10 minutes*

Cooking time: *10 minutes*

1 tablespoon olive oil

1 red onion, sliced

1 garlic clove, crushed and chopped

75 g (3 oz) pine nuts

4 tomatoes, skinned, cored, and coarsely chopped

1 kg (2 lb) spinach, washed and trimmed

50 g (2 oz) butter

pinch of freshly grated nutmeg

pepper

1 Heat the oil in a large saucepan, add the onion and garlic, and cook over a low heat, stirring occasionally, for 5 minutes.

2 Put the pine nuts into a heavy-based frying pan and dry-fry until browned, stirring constantly as they cook very quickly. Remove the pan from the heat and set aside.

3 Add the tomatoes, spinach, butter and nutmeg to the onion and season with pepper. Increase the heat to high and mix well. Cook for 3 minutes, until the spinach has just started to wilt. Remove the pan from the heat, stir in the pine nuts and serve immediately.

● **Tips:**
● The body's uptake of iron is increased if there is plenty of vitamin C present in the same meal. Why not have a glass of orange juice at the same time?
● Tea, coffee and milk contain substances which make it more difficult for the body to absorb iron. Don't drink them with or immediately after a meal. Wait about 30 minutes.

NUTRITIONAL VALUES
calories: 345 Kcal (1426 Kj) ● fat: 28 g ● carbohydrate: 12 g
● fibre: 12 g ● calcium: 450 mg

spinach & broccoli soup

1 Heat the oil and butter in a saucepan, add the onion and garlic and cook over a low heat, stirring occasionally, for 3 minutes.

2 Add the chopped potatoes, broccoli, spinach and stock, bring to the boil and simmer for 15 minutes.

3 This soup can be puréed in a blender or food processor or left with chunky pieces, according to taste. Add the Gorgonzola to the soup with the lemon juice, nutmeg and pepper to taste. Garnish with the toasted pine nuts and serve with plenty of warm crusty bread.

● **Tips:**

● When buying olive oil, look for extra virgin and virgin oils. These are made from the first cold pressings and have both the best flavour and the lowest acidity. They are also the most expensive – use extra virgin for salad dressings and special dishes and virgin for more general cooking. Olive oil simply labelled 'pure' is likely to have been heat treated.

● Gorgonzola has a very high fat content, but an inimitable flavour, so you need very little. However, if you are concerned, you could substitute Danish Blue, which has a fat content of just under two-thirds that of Gorgonzola.

SERVES 4

Preparation time: *10 minutes*

Cooking time: *20 minutes*

2 tablespoons olive oil

50 g (2 oz) butter

1 onion, diced

1 garlic clove, chopped

2 potatoes, chopped

250 g (8 oz) broccoli, chopped

300 g (10 oz) spinach, washed and trimmed

750 ml (1¼ pints) chicken or vegetable stock

125 g (4 oz) Gorgonzola cheese, crumbled into small pieces

2 tablespoons lemon juice

½ teaspoon freshly grated nutmeg

pepper

75 g (3 oz) toasted pine nuts, to garnish

NUTRITIONAL VALUES

calories: 470 Kcal (1944 Kj)
●
fat: 39 g
●
carbohydrate: 16 g
●
fibre: 4 g
●
iron: 4 mg

spinach & lemon risotto

SERVES 4

Preparation time: *5 minutes*

Cooking time: *20 minutes*

125 g (4 oz) butter

1 tablespoon olive oil

2 shallots, finely chopped

300 g (10 oz) risotto rice

900 ml (1½ pints) chicken or
vegetable stock

500 g (1 lb) spinach, chopped

grated rind and juice of 1 lemon

125 g (4 oz) Parmesan cheese,
freshly grated

pepper

grated lemon rind, to
garnish (optional)

1 Melt 4 tablespoons of the butter with the olive oil in a saucepan, add the shallots and cook over a low heat, stirring occasionally, for 3 minutes.

2 Add the rice and stir well to coat the grains thoroughly with butter and oil. Add a ladleful of the stock, enough to cover the rice, and stir well. Simmer gently and continue to stir as frequently as possible, adding more stock, a ladleful at a time, as it is absorbed.

3 Before you add the last of the stock, stir in the chopped spinach, lemon rind and juice and season with pepper. Increase the heat, stir well, then add the remaining stock and butter. Cook for a few minutes, then add half of the Parmesan and mix in well. Serve garnished with the remaining Parmesan and grated lemon rind, if liked.

NUTRITIONAL VALUES

calories: 700 Kcal (2928 Kj)

fat: 40 g

carbohydrate: 68 g

fibre: 7 g

calcium: 597 mg

iron pick-me-up

SERVES **2**

Preparation time: *3–4 minutes*

Makes: *200 ml (7 fl oz)*

250 g (8 oz) spinach

25 g (1 oz) parsley

250 g (8 oz) carrots

1 teaspoon spirulina

Juice the spinach, parsley and carrot and stir in the spirulina. Serve in a tumbler, decorated with carrot slivers, if liked.

● **Good for:** Iron deficiency (see page 40–41). If you lack iron in your diet (possibly owing to a vegetarian diet or a heavy menstrual cycle), then you may have anaemia which can leave you feeling lethargic, depressed, or prone to flu and colds. Folic acid builds up red blood cells, chlorophyll helps to combat fatigue, and spirulina provides a valuable boost of vitamin B12.

NUTRITIONAL VALUES

calories: 87 Kcal (360 Kj)
●
fat: 2 g
●
carbohydrate: 13 g
●
fibre: 0 g
●
iron: 5 mg

TOMATOES

The tomato is a fruit that figures prominently in the Mediterranean diet, which is renowned for its comparatively low incidence of heart disease. Tomatoes contain all the anti-oxidant vitamins – A (beta-carotene), C and E – plus the anti-oxidant mineral zinc, so they strengthen the immune system and reduce the risk of cataracts and age-related macular degeneration, heart disease, strokes and some cancers. The anti-oxidant lycopene occurs in large quantities in cooked tomatoes and may play an especially important role in protecting against prostate cancer. Tomatoes are also beneficial in preventing heart disease because they contain high levels of salicylates, which also prevent thickening of the blood. The zinc contained in tomatoes is vital for fertility, especially in men. Tomatoes may help to soothe inflammation of the liver and their high water content means that they help the digestive system to function. However, there are some conditions whose sufferers should avoid tomatoes: osteoarthritis, rheumatoid arthritis and asthma. Also hyperactive children should avoid tomatoes as eating them does sometimes aggravate the condition.

baked vine tomatoes

SERVES 4

Preparation time: *5 minutes*

Cooking time: *20 minutes*

500 g (1 lb) vine-ripened tomatoes

2 plump garlic cloves, thinly sliced

1 tablespoon coarsely chopped thyme

2 red chillies, halved lengthways

5 tablespoons extra virgin olive oil

4 tablespoons balsamic vinegar

pepper

NUTRITIONAL VALUES
calories: 149 Kcal (615 Kj)
•
fat: 14 g
•
carbohydrate: 5 g
•
fibre: 2 g
•
vitamin A: 160 mcg (533 i.u.)

1 Cut the tomatoes from the vine in clumps of 2 or 3. Make a deep slit in each tomato and insert a couple of garlic slices and a good pinch of thyme and season to taste with pepper. Pack into a shallow ovenproof dish.

2 Tuck the chilli halves around the tomatoes. Pour over the oil and vinegar, season to taste with pepper, then bake in a preheated oven, 220°C (425°F), Gas Mark 7, for 20 minutes until the tomatoes are softened but not falling apart.

● **Tips:**
● Vine tomatoes have usually been allowed to ripen naturally in the sun and have a sweeter, fuller flavour than those ripened under glass.
● Capsaicin, the substance that gives chillies their heat, stimulates the release of endorphins – feel-good chemicals – so they can give you a warm feeling in every sense. Most of the capsaicin is concentrated in the flesh surrounding the seeds, so if you prefer a milder flavour, deseeding the chillies will reduce the heat, although the seeds themselves do not contain it.

tomato, oregano & mozzarella tartlets

SERVES 6

Preparation time: *15 minutes*

Cooking time: *20 minutes*

250 g (8 oz) puff pastry

6 tablespoons sun-dried tomato paste

3 plum tomatoes, deseeded and coarsely chopped

125 g (4 oz) mozzarella cheese, coarsely diced

8 black olives, pitted and coarsely chopped

1 garlic clove, finely chopped

2 tablespoons coarsely chopped oregano

1 tablespoon pine nuts

olive oil, for drizzling

pepper

mixed salad leaves, to serve

1 Line a large baking sheet with nonstick baking paper. Roll out the pastry on a lightly floured board to 3 mm (⅛ inch) thick. Use a large round cutter to stamp out 6 circles, 12 cm (5 inch) across, and place them on the prepared baking sheet.

2 Spread 1 tablespoon sun-dried tomato paste over each pastry circle. In a small bowl, mix the tomatoes, mozzarella, olives, garlic, oregano and pine nuts, and season well with pepper. Divide this mixture between the pastry circles.

3 Drizzle a little olive oil over the tartlets and bake them in a preheated oven, 200°C (400°F), Gas Mark 6, for 20 minutes, or until the pastry is golden. Serve immediately with mixed salad leaves.

● **Tip:**
● Puff pastry is the richest of all pastries and it involves quite a long process to make it from scratch. Therefore, it is really convenient to buy it ready-made and some pastry even comes ready-rolled. It is best to use the pastry slightly chilled in order to achieve a light, flaky texture.

NUTRITIONAL VALUES
calories: 334 Kcal (1388 Kj)
●
fat: 25 g
●
carbohydrate: 20 g
●
fibre: 3 g
●
vitamin A: 106 mcg (353 i.u.)

tomato & orange soup

SERVES **6**

Preparation time: *15 minutes*

Cooking time: *30–35 minutes*

2 tablespoons olive or sunflower oil

1 onion, roughly chopped

2 garlic cloves, crushed

2 kg (4 lb) ripe tomatoes, skinned and chopped

2 tablespoons tomato purée

450 ml (¾ pint) vegetable or chicken stock

grated rind of 1 large orange

75 ml (3 fl oz) freshly squeezed orange juice

4 basil sprigs

1–2 teaspoons brown sugar

pepper

To garnish:

6 small basil sprigs

orange julienne (see Tips, right)

1 Heat the oil in a large saucepan and fry the onion and garlic until soft, but not coloured. Add the tomatoes along with their seeds and juice and stir in the tomato purée, stock, orange rind and juice and basil. Bring to the boil, reduce the heat, then cover and simmer gently for 20–25 minutes, until the vegetables are soft and pulpy.

2 Let the soup cool slightly, then process, in batches, in a food processor or blender and push through a plastic sieve into a clean saucepan to remove the seeds. Season with pepper and a little sugar. This will help counteract the acidity of the tomatoes without actually making the soup sweet. Return the pan to the heat and bring to the boil, then add a little extra stock or tomato juice, if necessary, to achieve the desired consistency.

3 To serve, pour the hot soup into warmed soup plates and garnish with tiny basil sprigs and orange julienne.

● **Tips:**
● To make orange julienne, remove a thin paring of rind from an orange using a swivel blade vegetable peeler. There should be very little white pith with the rind. Cut the rind into very thin strips – julienne – and drop them into a pan of boiling water for 30 seconds. Drain and refresh under cold water. Drain again and pat dry.
● To peel tomatoes, cut a cross in the skin at the blossom end using a sharp knife. Place in a bowl, cover with boiling water and leave to stand for about 30 seconds. Remove with a slotted spoon and, when cool enough to handle, peel off the skins.
● Use a sweet and juicy variety of orange for this soup. Blood oranges or Valencia would be a good choice.
● Plum tomatoes are perfect for cooking because they are less watery than standard tomatoes and have an intense flavour. Whatever type you use, remember that sun-ripened is best.

NUTRITIONAL VALUES

calories: 110 Kcal (460 Kj)
●
fat: 5 g
●
carbohydrate: 15 g
●
fibre: 5 g
●
iron: 2 mg

spicy tomato juice

Juice all the ingredients, blend with 2 ice cubes and serve in a tumbler. Decorate with celery slivers, if liked.

● **Good for:** Bronchitis (see page 32–33). Bronchitis occurs when the tissues of the lungs become inflamed, and can lead to a chesty cough and a lowered immune system. Strengthening the immune system and maintaining healthy lung tissue will help you to avoid such illnesses. Tomatoes and carrots provide large amounts of vitamin C, ideal for maintaining a healthy body. Garlic, ginger and horseradish are all powerful anti-oxidants – imperative for fighting off infections. Combined, they also deal a mighty anti-mucus punch.

● **Try the following variation:**

tomato & apple pick-me-up: Put 4 large, roughly chopped tomatoes, 1 cored and chopped apple, 1 chopped celery stick, 4 basil leaves and 1½ tablespoons lime juice into a blender and blend until smooth. Stir well. If you prefer a smooth juice strain the juice through a fine sieve into a glass. Serve over ice with lime wedges for breakfast, at lunch or as a virgin sundowner.

SERVES **1–2**

Preparation time: *5 minutes*

Makes: *200 ml (7 fl oz)*

300 g (10 oz) tomatoes

100 g (3½ oz) celery

2.5 cm (1 inch) piece of fresh root ginger, roughly chopped

1 garlic clove

2.5 cm (1 inch) piece of fresh horseradish, roughly chopped

175 g (6 oz) carrot

NUTRITIONAL VALUES
calories: 120 Kcal (514 Kj)
●
fat: 2 g
●
carbohydrate: 24 g
●
fibre: 0 g
●
vitamin A: 2696 mcg (8978 i.u.)

WATERCRESS

Watercress is a powerful detoxifier and contains the anti-oxidants beta-carotene (vitamin A) and vitamins C and E and zinc. These fortify the immune system and reduce the risk of heart disease, strokes, some cancers and cataracts. The carotenoids lutein and zeaxanthin prevent degenerative eye diseases, such as age-related macular degeneration and cataracts. Eating watercress can help to reduce blood cholesterol levels and it is a rich source of iron, which can prevent or reduce anaemia, and its high potassium content regulates blood pressure. Watercress is an appetite stimulant, making it useful for those with small appetites after illness, and helps the absorption of nutrients; it is also mildly diuretic and laxative, and stimulates all the excretory functions (it can also help to dissolve kidney and bladder stones). Watercress is a very good source of folates, which reduce the risk of spina bifida in unborn babies, and is also quite a good source of vitamins B_1, B_2, B_3, B_5 and B_6.

watercress & mushroom frittata

SERVES **3–4**

Preparation time: *5 minutes*

Cooking time: *15 minutes*

6 eggs

5 tablespoons freshly grated Parmesan cheese

1 bunch of watercress, tough stems removed

1½ tablespoons butter

250 g (8 oz) mushrooms, sliced

pepper

NUTRITIONAL VALUES

calories: 309 Kcal (1280 Kj)

fat: 25 g

carbohydrate: 0 g

fibre: 2 g

iron: 3 mg

1 Beat the eggs in a bowl with a fork to break them up. Stir in the Parmesan, watercress and plenty of pepper.

2 Melt the butter in a heavy-based frying pan. Add the mushrooms and sauté quickly, stirring occasionally, for 3 minutes. Pour in the egg mixture and gently stir the ingredients together.

3 Reduce the heat to its lowest setting and cook gently until the mixture is lightly set and the underside is golden when the edge of the frittata is lifted with a spatula. If the base of the frittata starts to brown before the top is set, place it under a moderate grill to finish cooking.

● **Tips:**
● Before placing the frying pan under the grill, wrap the handle in foil to prevent it from charring, unless it is made of a flameproof material.
● The role of mushrooms in a healthy diet is often overlooked. They contain no fat, no cholesterol and are low in salt. They do contain vegetable protein and some B vitamins and potassium.
● This frittata would taste even more delicious made with wild mushrooms. Try chanterelles, torn into pieces rather than sliced, oyster mushrooms or pieds de mouton, also known as hedgehog fungus. Many varieties of so-called wild mushrooms are now cultivated and available from supermarkets. If you are going to pick your own, be absolutely certain that you can identify them accurately, as some inedible or even toxic varieties look very similar to edible mushrooms.

chilled watercress soup

1 Melt the butter or margarine in a saucepan. Add the watercress and cook over a moderate heat for 3 minutes, stirring frequently. Add the stock, potatoes and nutmeg with pepper to taste. Bring to the boil, then lower the heat, cover and simmer for 15–20 minutes, or until the potatoes are soft. Remove from the heat and set aside to cool.

2 Pour the soup into a blender or food processor, in batches, and process until smooth, transferring each successive batch to a large bowl. Cover tightly with clingfilm and chill in the refrigerator for at least 3 hours.

3 Just before serving, fold in the chilled cream. Serve in chilled bowls, garnishing each portion with a few watercress leaves, a little oil, if using, and black pepper.

● **Tips:**
● Women taking oral contraceptives need to increase their intake of several B group vitamins and folic acid – and this soup is an ideal way to do it.
● Watercress is best eaten on the day of purchase, as it does not keep well. Avoid wilting or yellowing bunches.
● It is not advisable to pick wild watercress, even if it is quite clearly growing in a fast-flowing stream, as there is a risk of pollution.
● For an unusual and delicious variation, substitute 3 cored, peeled and sliced pears for the potatoes and stir in 2 tablespoons of lemon juice after processing the soup to a purée.

SERVES 4–6

Preparation time: *about 10 minutes, plus chilling*

Cooking time: *25 minutes*

50 g (2 oz) butter or margarine

2 bunches of watercress, tough stems discarded, coarsely chopped

1 litre (1¾ pints) chicken or vegetable stock

250 g (8 oz) potatoes, peeled and chopped

pinch of freshly grated nutmeg

150 ml (¼ pint) single cream, chilled

pepper

To garnish:
a few watercress leaves

1 tablespoon olive oil (optional)

NUTRITIONAL VALUES
(not including olive oil)
calories: 216 Kcal (896 Kj)
●
fat: 18 g
●
carbohydrate: 12 g
●
fibre: 1 g
●
vitamin A: 289 mcg (962 i.u.)

watercress & couscous filled cannelloni with tomato sauce

SERVES **4–6**

Preparation time: *30 minutes*

Cooking time: *45 minutes*

6 tablespoons olive oil

2 onions, finely chopped

75 g (3 oz) couscous

50 g (2 oz) watercress, tough stems discarded, chopped

12 no-pre-cook cannelloni tubes or sheets of fresh lasagne

2 garlic cloves, crushed

1 red chilli, deseeded and finely chopped (optional)

2 x 400 g (14 oz) cans chopped tomatoes

1 red or orange pepper, deseeded and finely chopped

2 tablespoons chopped basil or parsley

4 tablespoons freshly grated Parmesan cheese

pepper

1 Heat 2 tablespoons of the olive oil in a frying pan. Add 1 onion and cook over a low heat, stirring occasionally, for 8 minutes until soft and beginning to turn golden brown.

2 Meanwhile, put the couscous in a bowl and cover with boiling water. Leave for 3–4 minutes, then fluff up the grains using a fork. Season well with pepper and stir in the cooked onion and the watercress.

3 Using a teaspoon, fill the cannelloni tubes with the couscous filling and lay them in a lightly greased ovenproof dish. If using lasagne sheets, roll them into tubes, dampen the underside and press the sheets together or carefully secure with cocktail sticks. Fill as before.

4 Heat the remaining oil and cook the remaining onion with the garlic over a low heat, until softened. Add the chilli, if using, the tomatoes and peppers, and bring to a fast simmer. Cover and simmer for 10 minutes.

5 Season the sauce with pepper, add the chopped basil or parsley and pour evenly over the pasta tubes. Sprinkle the Parmesan over the dish and cook in the centre of a preheated oven, 190°C (375°F), Gas Mark 5, for 20–25 minutes, or until the pasta is cooked. Serve with a crisp green salad and a tomato and mozzarella salad.

● **Tips:**
● Couscous is a form of semolina that is a staple in North African cuisine. The grains are rolled, dampened and coated with finely ground wheat flour, so the only preparation they require is moistening to encourage them to swell.
● There is some evidence to suggest that organic produce contains more vitamins and minerals than conventionally grown crops, but this has not been proved. However, buying organic foods, including canned tomatoes, makes sure that there are no pesticide residues.

NUTRITIONAL VALUES

calories: 480 Kcal (2013 Kj) ● fat: 21 g ● carbohydrate: 60 g
● fibre: 4 g ● calcium: 195 mg

soothing tonic

Juice the ingredients and serve over ice. Add a twist of lemon, if liked.

● **Good for:** Haemorrhoids (see pages 16–17). The medical name for piles, haemorrhoids are caused by swollen veins inside or outside of the anus. They can cause itching and pain, and are the most common source of anal bleeding. Sometimes a blood clot or a thrombosis turns a pile into a hard, extremely painful lump. The watercress helps to dissolve the coagulated blood fibrin, and the pear helps to regulate bowel movement.

● **Try the following variation:**
watercress, carrot & celery juice: Wash 40 g (1½ oz) watercress well and juice with 3 carrots and 2 celery sticks. Pour into a glass, add a couple of ice cubes and drink immediately. This will serve 1. **Good for:** cleansing the system.

● **Tip:**
● Always combine watercress with sweet ingredients when making juices.

SERVES **1**

Preparation time: *3–4 minutes*

Makes: *50 ml (2 fl oz)*

250 g (8 oz) pears

125 g (4 oz) watercress

½ lemon

NUTRITIONAL VALUES
calories: 129 Kcal (545 Kj)
●
fat: 2 g
●
carbohydrate: 26 g
●
fibre: 0 g
●
calcium: 240 mg

GARLIC

Garlic is an antibiotic and taken regularly can build up resistance to infection. It is also a decongestant, helping to relieve the symptoms of colds, coughs and flu. It contains high levels of the anti-oxidants vitamin C and selenium, which combat free radicals and help prevent premature ageing, and cell degeneration, including some cancers. It contains sulphur, which is thought to slow or prevent the growth of tumours, as well as stimulating the liver. Garlic contains a substance called allicin, which thins the blood and dilates the blood vessels, so reducing the risk of clotting.

chicken with 40 garlic cloves

SERVES 4

Preparation time: *15 minutes*

Cooking time: *2¼ hours*

2 kg (4 lb) oven-ready chicken

1 bouquet garni

4 tablespoons olive oil

40 garlic cloves, unpeeled, separated

1 celery stick, chopped

pepper

rosemary, sage and thyme sprigs, to garnish

For sealing:
4 tablespoons plain flour

4 teaspoons water

NUTRITIONAL VALUES
calories: 834 Kcal (3498 Kj)
•
fat: 64 g
•
carbohydrate: 11 g
•
fibre: 1 g
•
iron: 3 mg

1 Wash and dry the chicken cavity, insert the bouquet garni and add pepper to taste. Truss the chicken with string.

2 Heat the oil in a large flameproof casserole into which the bird just fits. Add the garlic and celery, then the chicken and cook, turning frequently, until it is lightly coloured on all sides.

3 Cover the casserole with its lid. Make a paste with the flour and water and use to seal around the edge of the lid.

4 Place the casserole in a preheated oven, 180°C (350°F), Gas Mark 4, for 2¼ hours, without opening the oven door during cooking.

5 Break the flour and water seal, then lift out the chicken and place on a warmed serving platter. Arrange the garlic cloves around the chicken and garnish with sprigs of rosemary, sage and thyme. Serve hot, with mashed potatoes and a juicy vegetable dish such as ratatouille.

● **Tips:**
● Although the number of garlic cloves in this classic French dish sounds horrendous, in fact, cooking them in this way gives them a wonderfully mellow flavour and leaves surprisingly little trace on the breath.
● Use a fresh, free-range chicken for maximum flavour and nutrition. If it is also organically raised, it will be free of routine antibiotics and growth-promoting hormones.
● White-, pink- and purple-skinned varieties of garlic are available all year round. The purple-skinned type is said to have the best flavour. The fresh, new season's garlic is available in spring and early summer and its sweet flavour makes it the ideal choice for this dish. However, it still works well with the dried garlic available during the rest of the year.

juice medley

Juice the ingredients and serve in a tall glass. Decorate with beetroot leaves and watercress, if liked.

● **Good for:** Heart disease (see pages 10–15). This is one of the most preventable diseases in today's society. An increased intake of fried and fatty foods, a high salt intake, stress, smoking and lack of exercise are all contributory factors. Boosting your intake of vitamin C and vitamin E and taking regular exercise can add as many as ten years to your life. The onion and garlic thin the blood and help to lower blood cholesterol and blood pressure. Watercress oxygenates the blood and beetroot builds up the red blood cells.

● **Try the following variation:**
root juice: Juice 175 g (6 oz) each of carrots, parsnip, celery sticks and sweet potato with a handful of parsley and 1 garlic clove. Process in a blender with 2 crushed ice cubes and serve in a wide glass decorated with a wedge of lemon and a parsley sprig, if liked. This will make 200 ml (7 fl oz) and will serve 1.

SERVES 1

Preparation time: *10 minutes*

Makes: *200 ml (7 fl oz)*

125 g (4 oz) beetroot

125 g (4 oz) watercress

125 g (4 oz) red onion

250 g (8 oz) carrot

1 garlic clove

NUTRITIONAL VALUES
calories: 200 Kcal (860 Kj)
●
fat: 2 g
●
carbohydrate: 40 g
●
fibre: 0 g
●
iron: 5 mg

BEANS & LENTILS

As well as being good vegetable sources of protein and carbohydrates, pulses contain a wide range of minerals. They also contain phyto-oestrogens that mimic human oestrogens. These substances are thought to have a stabilizing effect on the menstrual cycle and to help in regulating erratic periods and tackling PMS. They are useful in stabilizing fluctuating oestrogen levels and so relieving distressing symptoms of the menopause such as night sweats, hot flushes and mood swings. They may also help to lower breast cancer risks and protect against fibroids. They help digestion by encouraging the friendly bacteria in the gut and are also often suggested as a means of lowering blood cholesterol. Rheumatoid arthritis sufferers should eat pulses regularly, and people with kidney stones could try chickpeas.

lentil, green peppercorn & mustard dip

SERVES 4

Preparation time: *7 minutes*

Cooking time: *10–15 minutes*

25 g (1 oz) Puy lentils

1–2 tablespoons green peppercorns in brine, drained

2 tablespoons Dijon mustard

4 tablespoons sunflower oil

1 tablespoon lemon juice

1 tablespoon warm water

NUTRITIONAL VALUES
calories: 513 Kcal (2120 Kj)
•
fat: 47 g
•
carbohydrate: 15 g
•
fibre: 2 g
•
iron: 5 mg

1 Bring a large saucepan of water to the boil, add the lentils and return to the boil. Cook for 10–15 minutes, until just tender and beginning to turn mushy. Drain and refresh under cold water until completely cold.

2 Crush the peppercorns until roughly broken using a pestle and mortar. Stir in the mustard and gradually beat in the oil, adding a little at a time. Stir in the lemon juice, warm water and cooked lentils. Pile into a serving bowl, cover with clingfilm and store in the refrigerator. The dip will keep for several days.

● **Tips:**
● Serve with crisp robust vegetables or grilled fish. This dip also goes well with crudités, vegetable kebabs or plain grilled vegetables.
● Lentils may be red, yellow, green or brown. The small grey-green lentils from Le Puy in France are said to have the best flavour and keep their shape well when cooked.
● Most pulses need to be soaked in cold water for some hours or even overnight before cooking. Lentils, however, do not require soaking, but the cooking time may vary depending on how long they have been in store.

butter bean & tomato soup

1 Heat the oil in a saucepan. Add the onion and cook over a low heat, stirring occasionally, for 3 minutes until softened. Add the celery and garlic and cook for a further 2 minutes.

2 Add the butter beans, sun-dried tomato paste, stock, rosemary or thyme and a little pepper. Bring to a boil, then reduce the heat, cover and simmer gently for 15 minutes. Serve sprinkled with Parmesan shavings.

● **Tips:**
● Serve with fresh, crusty bread or rolls and plenty of Parmesan for a robust main meal.
● Sun-dried tomato paste has an intense, sweet flavour and a slightly grainier texture than ordinary tomato paste. Not all so-called sun-dried tomatoes are prepared naturally; some are dried in ovens and the resulting flavour is not so good as the genuine article.
● Butter beans have a sweet flavour and a soft texture that goes especially well with tomatoes, but you could also use flageolets or haricot beans, if you like.

SERVES 4

Preparation time: *5 minutes*

Cooking time: *20 minutes*

3 tablespoons olive oil

1 onion, finely chopped

2 celery sticks, thinly sliced

2 garlic cloves, thinly sliced

2 x 425 g (14 oz) cans butter beans, rinsed and drained

4 tablespoons sun-dried tomato paste

900 ml (1½ pints) vegetable stock

1 tablespoon chopped rosemary or thyme

pepper

Parmesan cheese shavings, to serve

NUTRITIONAL VALUES
calories: 312 Kcal (1300 Kj)
●
fat: 16 g
●
carbohydrate: 31 g
●
fibre: 2 g
●
iron: 3 mg

bean & tomato couscous

SERVES **4**

Preparation time: *10 minutes*

Cooking time: *25 minutes*

3 tablespoons olive oil

1 large onion, chopped

2 celery sticks

2 garlic cloves

400 g (13 oz) can chopped tomatoes

1 teaspoon ground cumin

1 teaspoon ground coriander

1 tablespoon paprika

400 g (13 oz) can mixed beans (cannellini or haricot), rinsed and drained

400 g (13 oz) can chickpeas, rinsed and drained

50 g (2 oz) dried apricots, sliced

300 ml (½ pint) chicken or vegetable stock

250 g (8 oz) couscous

300 ml (½ pint) boiling water

pepper

celery leaves, to garnish (optional)

1 Heat the oil in a large saucepan. Add the onion, celery and garlic and cook over a low heat, stirring occasionally, for 5 minutes.

2 Stir in the tomatoes, spices, beans, chickpeas, dried apricots and stock and bring to the boil. Reduce the heat and simmer gently, uncovered, for about 20 minutes, until the vegetables are tender and the sauce is pulpy.

3 Meanwhile, put the couscous into a bowl with a little pepper. Add the boiling water and cover with foil. Set aside in a warm place for 5–10 minutes, until the water has been absorbed. Fluff up lightly with a fork.

4 Spoon the couscous on to warmed serving plates and top with the sauce. Garnish with celery leaves, if liked.

● **Tip:**
● You could also add extra roughly chopped vegetables with the chickpeas, or frozen beans or peas towards the end of cooking.

NUTRITIONAL VALUES
calories: 410 Kcal (1720 Kj) ● fat: 12 g ● carbohydrate: 64 g
● fibre: 8 g ● iron: 7 mg

5-vegetable juice

Wash all the vegetables and juice them with the lemon. Serve decorated with slivers of green bean and carrot, if liked.

● **Good for:** Diabetes (see pages 36–37). Unquenchable thirst and passing abnormal amounts of urine are among the first signs of diabetes. The disorder occurs when the pancreas fails to produce enough insulin – the hormone that regulates the blood-sugar level. (Warning: since diabetes is a serious illness, medical advice is imperative, especially if the sufferer is a child.)

SERVES 1

Preparation time: *5 minutes,*

Makes: *200 ml (7 fl oz)*

100 g (3½ oz) Brussels sprouts

100 g (3½ oz) carrot

100 g (3½ oz) Jerusalem artichokes

100 g (3½ oz) green beans

100 g (3½ oz) lettuce

½ lemon

NUTRITIONAL VALUES
calories: 160 Kcal (700 Kj)
●
fat: 3 g
●
carbohydrate: 28 g
●
fibre: 0 g
●
vitamin C: 158 mg

GRAINS

Most of the grains are very good sources of slow-release energy (although this is less true for couscous), preventing the fluctuating blood sugar levels that cause rapid demands for insulin. Buckwheat is also a good source of calcium, plus the B vitamins that allow the conversion of food into energy and potassium, which regulates blood pressure. Bulgar wheat and couscous are rich vegetable sources of iron, and so are very useful for those who have a low iron intake. Like buckwheat, they are good sources of B vitamins, as is quinoa, which also has high levels of calcium and iron. In addition, quinoa has only very low levels of gluten; some people with gluten intolerance may be able to use it. Other low-gluten or gluten-free grains include amaranth, cornmeal or polenta, and teff, which is a small variety of millet.

berry fruit scones

MAKES 15

Preparation time: *10 minutes*

Cooking time: *15–20 minutes*

50 g (2 oz) buckwheat flour

150 g (5 oz) brown rice flour

2 teaspoons baking powder

50 g (2 oz) margarine

50 g (2 oz) dried cranberries, blueberries, sour cherries or sultanas

125 g (4 oz) grated apple, with skin

about 6 tablespoons milk

1 Sift the flours and baking powder together into a large bowl. Add the margarine and rub it in with your fingertips. Add the dried fruit and grated apple and add enough milk to mix to a soft dough.

2 Drop spoonfuls of the mixture on to a greased baking sheet. Bake in a preheated oven, 230°C (450°F), Gas Mark 8, for 15–20 minutes, until a light golden colour. Transfer to a wire rack to cool.

3 Serve with butter or yogurt and fruit purées.

- **Tips:**
- This is a good recipe for anyone with a gluten intolerance, as both buckwheat and brown rice flour are gluten-free.
- Baking powder is a raising agent, consisting of 1 part bicarbonate of soda to 2 parts cream of tartar. While bicarbonate of soda can be used on its own, it leaves an unpleasant aftertaste.
- Most of the nutrients found in the fresh fruit are retained when it is dried, apart from vitamin C. Fruit that has been sun-dried has the best flavour. Sometimes, dried fruit is treated with sulphur dioxide to preserve it still further, but this must be clearly stated on the label.

NUTRITIONAL VALUES
calories: 87 Kcal (563 Kj) ● fat: 3 g ● carbohydrate: 14 g
● fibre: 1 g ● calcium: 9 mg

roasted peppers with millet & basil

SERVES **4–6**

Preparation time: *15 minutes,*

Cooking time: *2¼ hours*

3 large red peppers

175 g (6 oz) raw millet

5 tablespoons olive oil

1 onion, finely chopped

1 tablespoon chopped parsley

1 tablespoon harissa paste or pesto (optional)

450 ml (¾ pint) water

1 tablespoon pumpkin seeds, toasted

15 g (½ oz) basil leaves

6 cherry tomatoes

pepper

To serve:

thick slices of goats' cheese

basil leaves

extra virgin olive oil

1 Cut each red pepper in half and remove the seeds and white membrane. Pack the pepper halves tightly into a roasting tin with the skin side down.

2 Heat a frying pan until hot, add the millet grains and toast for 2–3 minutes, shaking the pan frequently.

3 In a separate saucepan, heat 2 tablespoons of the oil and lightly fry the onion until golden brown. Add the toasted millet grains, parsley and harissa or pesto, if using, and season to taste with pepper. Add the water, bring to the boil and boil for 5 minutes. Cover the pan, lower the heat and cook for a further 30 minutes, or until the millet grains are soft. Add more water if they begin to look like they are drying out.

4 Stir the toasted pumpkin seeds and basil into the millet, then spoon the millet into the pepper cups. Cut the cherry tomatoes in half, put 2 halves on top of each pepper and drizzle with the remaining olive oil.

5 Pour a cup of cold water over the base of the roasting tin, cover tightly with foil and cook in the centre of a preheated oven, 190°C (375°F), Gas Mark 5, for 1½ hours.

6 Top the hot peppers with goats' cheese and basil leaves and drizzle olive oil over and around them.

NUTRITIONAL VALUES
not including goats' cheese
calories: 363 Kcal (1508 Kj)
•
fat: 19 g
•
carbohydrate: 42 g
•
fibre: 3 g
•
vitamin A: 558 mcg (1858 i.u.)

mushroom, couscous & herb sausages

SERVES **4**

Preparation time: *15 minutes*

Cooking time: *10 minutes*

75 g (3 oz) couscous

6 tablespoons boiling water

3 tablespoons olive oil

1 onion, chopped

250 g (8 oz) chestnut mushrooms, coarsely chopped

1 red chilli, deseeded and thinly sliced

3 garlic cloves, coarsely chopped

small handful of mixed herbs, such as thyme, rosemary, parsley

200 g (7 oz) whole cooked chestnuts

75 g (3 oz) breadcrumbs

1 egg yolk

vegetable oil, for frying

pepper

NUTRITIONAL VALUES

calories: 425 Kcal (1770 Kj)
•
fat: 27 g
•
carbohydrate: 41 g
•
fibre: 6 g
•
iron: 3 mg

1 Place the couscous in a bowl with the boiling water and leave it to stand and swell for 5 minutes.

2 Meanwhile, heat the olive oil in a frying pan, add the onion, mushrooms, and chilli and sauté quickly for about 5 minutes, or until the mushrooms are golden and the moisture has evaporated.

3 Transfer to a food processor or blender with the garlic, herbs and chestnuts and process until finely chopped. Turn into a bowl and add the soaked couscous, breadcrumbs, egg yolk, and pepper to taste.

4 Using lightly floured hands, shape the mixture into 12 sausage shapes. Heat the vegetable oil for pan-frying and fry the sausages for about 5 minutes, turning frequently.

● **Tips:**

● A wide range of vegetable oils are available and most of them are high in unsaturated fats. While olive oil is high in monounsaturated fats, it is expensive and has a distinctive flavour. Rapeseed and groundnut oil are also high in monounsaturates and their bland flavour makes them good, all-purpose oils. Safflower, sunflower and corn oils, high in polyunsaturates, are also good all-purpose oils and have the additional benefit of high levels of essential omega-6 fatty acids. Soya oil contains both omega-3 and omega-6 fatty acids.

● Occasionally, the variety of chilli on sale is specified, giving you some idea of how hot it will be. Even then, you should still proceed with caution as fiery hot and quite mild chillies may grow on the same plant. As a general rule, green chillies are hotter than red ones, the darkest green ones being the most fiery. Thin pointed chillies are usually hotter than short, blunt ones. Nevertheless, there are exceptions. If you have sensitive skin, wear rubber gloves when preparing chillies and always wash your hands, the knife and chopping board thoroughly afterwards.

● Herbs have an association with health that pre-dates their use in the kitchen. Traditionally, parsley has been used to treat coughs, menstrual problems and urinary infections, while thyme is said to be good for coughs and digestive disorders and acts as a general tonic. Sage is thought to counteract depression and nervous anxiety. Whatever the case, fresh herbs have an indisputably important role in cooking. Dried herbs are a poor substitute and some herbs, such as parsley, are totally unsuitable for drying.

tabbouleh with fruit & nuts

1 Place the bulgar wheat in a bowl, cover with plenty of boiling water and leave for 15 minutes.

2 Meanwhile, place the pistachio nuts in a separate bowl and cover with boiling water. Leave to stand for 1 minute, then drain. Rub the nuts between several thicknesses of kitchen paper to remove most of the skins, then peel away any remaining skins with your fingers.

3 Mix the nuts with the onion, garlic, parsley, mint, lemon or lime rind and juice and prunes in a large bowl.

4 Drain the bulgur wheat thoroughly in a sieve, pressing out as much moisture as possible with the back of a spoon. Add to the other ingredients with the oil and toss together. Season to taste with pepper, cover with clingfilm and chill until ready to serve.

SERVES **4**

Preparation time: *10 minutes, plus soaking*

Cooking time: *15 minutes*

150 g (5 oz) bulgar wheat

75 g (3 oz) unsalted, shelled pistachio nuts

1 small red onion, finely chopped

3 garlic cloves, crushed

25 g (1 oz) flat leaf parsley, chopped

15 g (½ oz) mint, chopped

finely grated rind and juice of 1 lemon or lime

150 g (5 oz) ready-to-eat prunes, sliced

4 tablespoons olive oil

pepper

NUTRITIONAL VALUES
calories: 413 Kcal (1725 Kj)
•
fat: 22 g
•
carbohydrate: 46 g
•
fibre: 6 g
•
iron: 6 mg

WHEATGERM

Wheatgerm is probably the most nutritious part of the wheat kernel: it contains most of the oils from the grain and is rich in protein, vitamins B_1, B_2, B_3, B_6, folic acid, the anti-oxidants vitamin E and zinc, as well as iron and magnesium. The anti-oxidants help neutralize free radicals, and therefore reduce the risk of heart disease, strokes, cataracts and some cancers. Vitamin E is also particularly important for protecting cell membranes. It helps maintain healthy skin, heart and circulation, nerves, muscles and red blood cells.The folates in wheatgerm help to protect unborn children from spina bifida and work with iron, magnesium and zinc to prevent anaemia. B-complex vitamins are necessary for the conversion of food into energy.

wheatgerm, pineapple & banana booster

SERVES 4

Preparation time: *10 minutes*

Cooking time: *5 minutes*

2 tablespoons wheatgerm

1 tablespoon sesame seeds

2 bananas, peeled and roughly sliced

75 g (3 oz) pineapple pieces

450 ml (¾ pint) apple juice

300 ml (½ pint) natural yogurt

NUTRITIONAL VALUES
calories: 166 Kcal (700 Kj)
•
fat: 3 g
•
carbohydrate: 32 g
•
fibre: 2 g
•
calcium: 175 mg

1 Spread the wheatgerm and sesame seeds over a baking sheet and gently toast under a preheated grill, stirring a couple of times until the sesame seeds have begun to turn a golden brown colour. Remove from the grill and leave to cool.

2 Put the bananas in a blender with the pieces of pineapple and blend together to a rough purée.

3 Add the apple juice and blend once more until you have a fairly smooth juice. Add the yogurt and the cooled wheatgerm and sesame seeds, blend once again and pour into tall glasses to serve.

● **Tips:**
● Wheatgerm is also available ready toasted.
● Freshly made juices not only taste better, but also have a higher nutritional content than commercially produced ones. A limited range of fresh juices, including apple, is available from most supermarkets. Avoid concentrates.
● There are several types of yogurt available: live yogurt, which may or may not be set; low-fat yogurt (0.5–2 per cent fat), made from skimmed milk; very low-fat yogurt (less than 0.5 per cent fat); and Greek yogurt, which may be made from either ewes' or cows' milk, and has a high fat content of 9–10 per cent. Other yogurts include goat's milk yogurt and pasteurized or long-life yogurt.

wheatgerm tonic

Juice the melon and cucumber. Process in a blender with the avocado, apricots, wheatgerm and a couple of crushed ice cubes. Decorate with dried apricot slivers, if liked.

● **Good for:** Low fertility. With low sperm counts and lowered fertility levels, our reproductive abilities are one of the biggest causes of concern in today's society. Male fertility may be boosted by increasing intakes of vitamin E, zinc and iron. Women should look to increase their folic acid levels, as well as zinc and vitamin E.

SERVES **1–2**

Preparation time: *5 minutes*

Makes: *200 ml (7 fl oz)*

175 g (6 oz) melon

125 g (4 oz) cucumber

125 g (4 oz) avocado

50 g (2 oz) ready-to-eat dried apricots

1 tablespoon wheatgerm

NUTRITIONAL VALUES

calories: 400 Kcal (1680 Kj)

●

fat: 26 g

●

carbohydrate: 38 g

●

fibre: 11 g

●

iron: 4 mg

BROWN RICE

Brown rice is a good source of B vitamins, especially B₁, which helps in the transmission of messages between the brain and spinal cord. Lack of it can result in insomnia, poor concentration, mood swings and depression. It is essential for enzymes that convert food into fuel for the body, and chronic lack can lead to permanent nerve damage. Brown rice is also a good source of folates, the antioxidant vitamin E and NSP (fibre). It also contains potassium, which controls sodium levels in cells and so helps to regulate blood pressure, magnesium, which is important for the muscle function, the prevention of heart disease and cell maintenance, and zinc, which is now proving to be important in male fertility.

Mung bean & herb risotto

SERVES **4**

Preparation time: *15 minutes*

Cooking time: *about 50 minutes*

175 g (6 oz) mung beans, soked for 2 hours in cold water

15 g (½ oz) butter

1 tablespoon vegetable oil

1 large onion, chopped

250 g (8 oz) long grain brown rice

750 ml (1¼ pints) hot vegetable stock

3 tablespoons chopped mixed herbs, such as parsley, thyme, basil, mint

pepper

1 Drain and rinse the beans. Using a large pan with a well-fitting lid, heat the butter and oil and fry the onion for 3 minutes, then stir in the beans and rice. Pour on the hot stock and bring to the boil.

2 Cover the pan, lower the heat and simmer gently for 40 minutes until the beans and rice are tender and all the stock has been absorbed.

3 Add the herbs and pepper and gently fork them through the mixture. Spoon the risotto into a warm serving dish and keep warm.

● **Tips:**
● Alternatively, you could use soya margarine instead of the butter.
● Mung beans will probably be most familiar in their sprouted form, as bean sprouts. In dried form they may be bought whole, split and skinless. These minute olive green beans are known as moong dal in Indian cooking.
● You could try experimenting with different herbs in this dish. Try swapping the herbs suggested here for marjoram, coriander and chives for example.

NUTRITIONAL VALUES
calories: 463 Kcal (1954 Kj)
●
fat: 12 g
●
carbohydrate: 77 g
●
fibre: 9 g
●
iron: 3 mg

brown rice pudding

1 Lightly butter a 1.2 litre (2 pint) ovenproof dish.

2 Rinse the rice well and put it in a pan of water. Bring to the boil, cook for 15 minutes, then drain well. Return the rice to the pan with the milk and sugar and bring slowly to the boil.

3 Remove from the heat and pour into the prepared ovenproof dish. Add the sultanas and stir together. Sprinkle the nutmeg over the milk and dot the top with pieces of butter, if using.

4 Cook in the centre of a preheated oven, 180°C (350°F), Gas Mark 4, for 1½–2 hours, stirring twice. Once the rice is soft and tender, remove it from the oven and sprinkle the flaked almonds and stem ginger over the top.

5 When serving the pudding, stir the almonds and ginger into the rice. Serve with crème fraîche or fromage frais.

● **Tip:**
● Brown rice consists of the whole grain with only the outer, tough husk removed. It is available in long, medium and short grain.

SERVES **4–6**

Preparation time: *10 minutes*

Cooking time: *2–2½ hours*

75 g (3 oz) brown rice

900 ml (1½ pints) organic milk

25 g (1 oz) soft light brown sugar

75 g (3 oz) sultanas

15 g (½ oz) butter (optional)

3 tablespoons flaked almonds, toasted

50 g (2 oz) stem ginger, finely chopped

NUTRITIONAL VALUES
using whole milk and including butter
calories: 390 Kcal (1640 Kj)
●
fat: 16 g
●
carbohydrate: 54 g
●
fibre: 3 g
●
calcium: 290 mg

NUTS & SEEDS

Eating nuts seems to protect against heart disease, probably through a combination of their vitamin E and unsaturated fats (except coconuts), which help to lower blood cholesterol levels; omega-3 fats, which reduce blood clotting and irregular heartbeats; and arginine, which promotes relaxation of the arteries' linings and helps to make blood less likely to clot. Nuts also contain magnesium, potassium, NSP and vitamin E, the latter a component of many enzymes that give anti-oxidant protection to body cells. Many nuts contain other anti-oxidants, such as folic acid, vitamin C, beta-carotene (vitamin A), selenium or zinc, which are essential for a healthy immune system. Sesame, pumpkin and sunflower seeds are rich sources of the essential omega-3 fatty acids, while sesame and sunflower seeds also contain the omega-6 fatty acids. These are vital for cell regeneration and help protect against heart disease. Most seeds are also rich in the anti-oxidants folic acid, vitamin E, selenium, iron, magnesium and zinc. Sunflower seeds also contain vitamins A, B, D and K and calcium, as well as the unsaturated fats that lower blood cholesterol. Pumpkin seeds are a rich source of B vitamins, while sesame seeds are a good source of calcium.

nut & seed savoury cakes

SERVES **4**

Preparation time: *25 minutes, plus chilling*

Cooking time: *5 minutes*

250 g (8 oz) Brazil nuts, chopped

2 x 425 g (14 oz) cans chickpeas, drained and rinsed

25 g (1 oz) sunflower seeds

1 tablespoon chopped parsley

1 small onion, finely chopped

2 eggs

125 g (4 oz) wholemeal breadcrumbs

groundnut or vegetable oil, for brushing or shallow frying

pepper

1 Put the nuts in a blender with the chickpeas. Process until fairly smooth. Turn the mixture into a bowl, add the sunflower seeds, parsley and onion and mix together until well combined.

2 Beat 1 egg with pepper, add to the chickpea mixture and blend well. Take a tablespoon of the mixture, press into a flat patty and lay on a greased baking sheet. Repeat with the remaining mixture to make 8 large or 16 small patties. Beat the remaining egg, dip each patty into it, then coat in the breadcrumbs. Chill for 4 hours or overnight.

3 Either heat the oil until hot, and shallow-fry the cakes for 3–4 minutes on each side or until golden brown, or brush the nut cakes with a little oil and bake in a preheated oven, 200°C (400°F), Gas Mark 6, for 20 minutes, carefully turning once. Serve with steamed vegetables and a tomato sauce or with a mixed green salad and couscous.

NUTRITIONAL VALUES
calories: 970 Kcal (4036 Kj) ● fat: 75 g ● carbohydrate: 48 g
● fibre: 8 g ● iron: 6 mg

nut koftas with minted yogurt

Preparation time: *15 minutes*

Cooking time: *10 minutes*

5–6 tablespoons groundnut oil

1 onion, chopped

½ teaspoon crushed chilli flakes

2 garlic cloves, coarsely chopped

1 tablespoon medium curry paste

425 g (14 oz) can borlotti or cannellini beans, drained and rinsed

125 g (4 oz) ground almonds

75 g (3 oz) chopped honey-roasted or salted almonds

1 small egg

200 ml (7 fl oz) Greek yogurt

2 tablespoons chopped mint

1 tablespoon lemon juice

pepper

warm naan bread, to serve

mint sprigs, to garnish

1 Soak 8 bamboo skewers in hot water while preparing the koftas. Alternatively, use metal skewers which do not require soaking. Heat 3 tablespoons of the oil in a frying pan, add the onion and fry for 4 minutes. Add the chilli flakes, garlic and curry paste and fry for 1 minute.

2 Transfer to a food processor or blender with the beans, ground almonds, chopped almonds, egg and a little pepper and process until the mixture starts to bind together.

3 Using lightly floured hands, take about one-eighth of the mixture and mould around a skewer, forming it into a sausage about 2.5 cm (1 inch) thick. Make 7 more koftas in the same way.

4 Place on a foil-lined grill rack and brush with another tablespoon of the oil. Grill under a preheated moderate grill for about 5 minutes, until golden, turning once.

5 Meanwhile, mix together the yogurt and mint in a small serving bowl and season to taste with pepper. In a separate bowl, mix together the remaining oil, lemon juice and a little pepper.

6 Brush the koftas with the lemon dressing and serve with the yogurt dressing on warm naan bread, garnished with mint sprigs.

NUTRITIONAL VALUES

calories: 556 Kcal (2300 Kj)
•
fat: 49 g
•
carbohydrate: 11 g
•
fibre: 11 g
•
iron: 4 mg

lemon rice & wild rice salad with nuts, seeds & papaya

SERVES 6

Preparation time: *15 minutes*

Cooking time: *35 minutes*

50 g (2 oz) wild rice, rinsed

250 g (8 oz) long grain rice, rinsed

2 tablespoons lemon juice

1 teaspoon sugar

1 small papaya

1 bunch of spring onions, sliced

25 g (1 oz) pecan nuts, toasted and chopped

25 g (1 oz) Brazil nuts, toasted and chopped

25 g (1 oz) sunflower seeds, toasted

1 tablespoon poppy seeds

Dressing:

6 tablespoons extra virgin olive oil

1 tablespoon lemon juice or lime juice

2 tablespoons chopped parsley

pepper

1 Cook the wild rice in a large saucepan of boiling water for about 35 minutes, until tender.

2 Meanwhile, put the long grain rice in a pan with plenty of cold water, add the lemon juice and sugar, bring to the boil and simmer gently for 10–12 minutes, until cooked.

3 Drain both the wild and long grain rice and place in a large bowl. Blend all the dressing ingredients together, season to taste with pepper and toss with the rice. Set aside until cold.

4 Just before serving, cut the papaya in half, discard the seeds, peel and dice the flesh. Add to the rice with the spring onions, nuts and seeds. Taste and adjust the seasoning, if necessary, and serve immediately.

- **Tips:**
- Not a true rice, wild rice is an aquatic grass native to North America. The black grains are long and thin. It contains all the essential amino acids and is gluten-free. The cooking time varies from 35 minutes up to an hour, depending on the texture you prefer.
- Brazil nuts contain selenium and have been linked with protecting against some cancers, especially stomach cancer. However, unlike most nuts, they also contain high levels of saturated fats.
- Foods rich in vitamin E, such as nuts and seeds, enhance memory and are especially important in the diet of the elderly.
- The succulent orange flesh of papaya is very sweet. The small, black seeds clustered in the centre of the fruit are edible, but very peppery. It is best to scoop them out with a teaspoon.
- Buy nuts and seeds in small quantities and keep a note of the 'use by' date, as their high oil content means that they turn rancid quite quickly. You can store nuts in an airtight container in the refrigerator.

NUTRITIONAL VALUES
calories: 379 Kcal (1575 Kj) ● fat: 20 g ● carbohydrate: 45 g
● fibre: 1 g ● iron: 2 mg

cashew nut chicken

1 Put the onion, tomato purée, cashews, garam masala, garlic, lemon juice, turmeric and yogurt into a food processor or blender and process until fairly smooth. Set aside.

2 Heat the oil in a large nonstick frying pan and, when hot, pour in the spice mixture. Fry, stirring, for 2 minutes over a medium heat. Add half the coriander leaves, the apricots and chicken to the pan and stir-fry for 1 minute.

3 Pour in the stock, cover and simmer for 10–12 minutes, or until the chicken is cooked through and tender. Stir in the remaining coriander leaves and serve garnished with toasted cashew nuts and chopped coriander.

SERVES **4**

Preparation time: *10 minutes*

Cooking time: *20 minutes*

1 onion, roughly chopped

4 tablespoons tomato purée

50 g (2 oz) cashew nuts

2 teaspoons garam masala

2 garlic cloves, crushed

1 tablespoon lemon juice

¼ teaspoon ground turmeric

1 tablespoon natural yogurt

2 tablespoons vegetable oil

3 tablespoons chopped coriander leaves

50 g (2 oz) ready-to-eat dried apricots, chopped

500 g (1 lb) chicken thighs, skinned, boned and cut into bite-sized pieces

300 ml (½ pint) chicken stock

To garnish:

toasted cashew nuts

chopped coriander

NUTRITIONAL VALUES

calories: 279 Kcal (1166 Kj) ● fat: 16 g ● carbohydrate: 15 g

● fibre: 3 g ● iron: 3 mg

GAME

The term game is used here to mean animals and birds that live in the wild, rather than their farmed equivalents, because they are leaner and what fat there is is mainly monounsaturated. Game contains the correct proportions of the eight essential amino acids needed to build new tissues, blood, hormones and enzymes. It also contains selenium, zinc, iron, copper, chromium, phosphorus and magnesium. Selenium and zinc play pivotal roles in liver function and sex hormones. Lack of iron can cause anaemia, lack of muscle tone and reduced concentration. Chromium is essential for insulin activity. It helps to lower blood fat levels and increase the concentration of 'good' cholesterol. Magnesium, phosphorus and calcium are vital for the formation of bones, while potassium helps to prevent high blood pressure.

stuffed guinea fowl

SERVES **4**

Preparation time: *15 minutes*

Cooking time: *16–20 minutes*

125 g (4 oz) ricotta cheese

75 g (3 oz) sun-dried tomatoes in oil, drained and chopped

4 spring onions, chopped

4 guinea fowl breasts

pepper

1 In a large bowl, mix together the ricotta cheese with the chopped tomatoes and spring onions and season to taste with pepper. Heat a griddle pan.

2 To prepare each guinea fowl breast for stuffing, use a sharp knife and with the underneath of the breast facing you, carefully run the knife along the length of the breast and then inwards, making a long flat pocket.

3 Divide the stuffing between the 4 breasts and stuff the ricotta mixture into the pockets carefully.

4 Place the breasts on the griddle pan and cook for 8–10 minutes on each side, depending on the size of the breasts. To test, pierce the meat with a small, sharp knife at the thickest part – the juices should run clear when fully cooked. Serve either hot or at room temperature.

● **Tips:**
● Sun-dried tomatoes are available bottled in oil or in packets. Those in oil can be used straight from the jar and the oil can also be used in salad dressings or to replace some of the cooking oil in recipes to add extra flavour. Packet tomatoes need to be soaked in hot water to rehydrate them. The soaking water can be added to stock.
● Ricotta is an Italian whey cheese with a soft, creamy texture and a slightly sweet flavour. It is relatively low in fat, although it is sometimes enriched with milk. It should be used within 24 hours of purchase.
● These days, wild guinea fowl is not available, but it has been farmed successfully for over 500 years. Make sure you buy a free-range bird.

NUTRITIONAL VALUES
calories: 408 Kcal (1697 Kj)
●
fat: 29 g
●
carbohydrate: 2 g
●
fibre: 0.5 g
●
iron: 1 mg

venison steaks with red fruit sauce

SERVES 4

Preparation time: *10 minutes, plus marinating*

Cooking time: *20 minutes*

---

1 teaspoon crushed juniper berries

---

4 x 175 g (6 oz) venison steaks, from the fillet or loin

---

pepper

---

shredded orange rind, to garnish

Red fruit sauce:

125 g (4 oz) redcurrant jelly

---

125 g (4 oz) cranberries

---

grated rind and juice of 1 orange

---

2 tablespoons red wine

1 Mix the crushed juniper berries with pepper and spread over both sides of the venison steaks. Set aside to allow the flavours to mingle for at least 1 hour, but preferably overnight.

2 To make the sauce, place the ingredients in a small saucepan and simmer gently for 10 minutes, stirring constantly.

3 Heat a griddle pan. Add the venison steaks and cook for 3 minutes on each side for rare, or 5 minutes for well done. Serve immediately with the red fruit sauce poured over the top and garnished with the shredded orange rind.

- **Tip:**
- Venison steak from the loin or fillet is not always available, so ask your butcher if he can recommend another cut.

NUTRITIONAL VALUES

calories: 275 Kcal (1169 Kj)
●
fat: 3 g
●
carbohydrate: 24 g
●
fibre: 1 g
●
iron: 6 mg

LIVER

Liver is well-known as a rich source of iron that helps prevent or cure anaemia. It also contains vitamins B_1, B_2, B_6 and B_{12} (as well as the related chemical choline), which are necessary for the formation of haemoglobin and for brain function. The vitamin A levels in farmed liver are very high, and so pregnant women should not eat it or liver pâté as it could damage the developing foetus, but both are recommended after the birth, especially if the mother is breastfeeding. Liver is an excellent source of the anti-oxidant minerals zinc, selenium and copper, which protect against damage by free radicals, boost immune function and promote healthy skin, nails and hair. Liver contains higher amounts of fat than lean meat, but most of this is in the form of polyunsaturated fats, so it is not harmful and is unlikely to raise blood cholesterol levels.

penne with chicken livers

SERVES 4

Preparation time: *10 minutes*

Cooking time: *15 minutes*

1 yellow pepper, cored, halved and deseeded

300 g (10 oz) penne

2 tablespoons olive oil

50 g (2 oz) butter

1 red onion, sliced

250 g (8 oz) chicken livers, trimmed

1 rosemary sprig, chopped

pepper

75 g (3 oz) Parmesan cheese, freshly grated, to serve

1 Bring a large saucepan of water to the boil for the pasta.

2 Meanwhile, roast the yellow pepper in a hot oven or under a preheated hot grill for 5 minutes, until the skin is blistered and black. Allow to cool, then peel off the skin. Cut the flesh into long strips.

3 Add the pasta to the boiling water, bring back to the boil and cook for 4 minutes if fresh and 8 minutes if dried, or according to packet instructions.

4 Heat the oil and butter in a large frying pan, add the onion and chicken livers and cook over a high heat until browned all over. Add the rosemary and season with pepper. Do not overcook the chicken livers, as this dries them out and makes them hard; they are best when still pink in the middle.

5 Mix the chicken liver sauce with the pasta and toss well. Serve immediately with a bowl of freshly grated Parmesan.

● **Tips:**
● Penne are quill-shaped pasta tubes but other hollow short-cut pasta, such as chifferi, pipe or macaroni, could be used instead.
● You could also serve the chicken livers on toast as an appetizer.

NUTRITIONAL VALUES
calories: 579 Kcal (2428 Kj) ● fat: 27 g ● carbohydrate: 60 g
● fibre: 5 g ● vitamin A: 6275 mcg (20836 i.u.)

griddled liver & bacon with grilled potatoes

1 Boil the potatoes for 6–8 minutes, until just tender. Drain, refresh under cold water and halve. Mix with 3 tablespoons of olive oil and the rosemary.

2 Fry the thinly sliced onion in the remaining oil until golden brown. Add the sugar and stir until the onion is caramelized. Add the stock and bring to the boil. Reduce the heat, cover and simmer gently for 10 minutes.

3 Stir the cornflour paste into the gravy. Bring it slowly to the boil, stirring constantly until thickened. Season to taste. Place the potatoes on a baking sheet and grill for 8–10 minutes, turning frequently until golden brown.

4 Heat a griddle or large frying-pan until hot. Add the bacon and thickly sliced onion and cook over a medium heat for 6 minutes, turning once. Remove and keep warm. Add the liver to the pan and cook for 3–4 minutes on each side.

5 Serve the liver on a pile of grilled potatoes. Top with the griddled onions and bacon and pour the hot onion gravy over and around.

SERVES **4**

Preparation time: *15 minutes*

Cooking time: *35 minutes*

500 g (1 lb) salad potatoes

4 tablespoons olive oil

leaves from 1 rosemary sprig

2 large onions, 1 thinly sliced, 1 thickly sliced

2 teaspoons light muscovado sugar

450 ml (¾ pint) vegetable stock

1 tablespoon cornflour, mixed to a smooth paste with a little water

6 streaky bacon rashers

600 g (1¼ lb) lamb's liver, trimmed, thickly sliced and seasoned with pepper

pepper

NUTRITIONAL VALUES
calories: 574 Kcal (2400 Kj)
•
fat: 30 g
•
carbohydrate: 39 g
•
fibre: 3 g
•
iron: 12 mg

OILY FISH

Oily fish, such as salmon, trout, mackerel, tuna, herrings, sardines and anchovies, are highly nutritious because they contain the beneficial essential omega-3 fatty acids, which are vital for a large number of processes within the body, including brain function. Their main importance, however, lies in their effects on the heart and circulatory system. They lower blood cholesterol and blood pressure and make the blood less sticky, so reducing the risk of heart disease and strokes. Omega-3 fatty acids have recently been linked to reducing the effects of stress. They also help inflammatory conditions, such as rheumatoid arthritis, eczema and psoriasis. Fresh tuna also contains the anti-inflammatory agents biotin and vitamin B$_3$, making it especially good for easing the pain of rheumatoid arthritis. Always choose canned sardines and pilchards that have not been boned: they are rich in calcium, phosphorus and fluoride. Wild and organic salmon are preferred to farmed varieties because the flesh is leaner and firmer and they do not contain the dyes, anti-biotics or growth hormone residues that are given to many farmed fish.

herrings with spinach & parmesan

SERVES 4

Preparation time: *15 minutes*

Cooking time: *about 30 minutes*

2 tablespoons olive oil

2 streaky bacon rashers, rinded and chopped

1 small onion, chopped

25 g (1 oz) breadcrumbs

150 g (5 oz) baby spinach, trimmed

generous pinch of freshly grated nutmeg

25 g (1 oz) Parmesan cheese, freshly grated

8 herring fillets

pepper

1 Heat 1 tablespoon of the olive oil in a frying pan, add the bacon and fry for 3 minutes. Add the onion and fry for a further 3–4 minutes, until it is softened and the bacon is golden. Add the breadcrumbs and fry for 1 minute.

2 Stir in the spinach, nutmeg and a little pepper and cook until the spinach has wilted. Add the cheese and remove the pan from the heat.

3 Lay 4 herring fillets, skin side down, in a shallow ovenproof dish. Spoon the spinach mixture over the fish fillets then cover it with the remaining 4 fillets, placing them skin side up. Drizzle with the remaining oil and bake in a preheated oven, 180°C (350°F), Gas Mark 4, for about 20–25 minutes, until the fish is cooked through. Serve with new potatoes and grilled tomatoes.

● **Tips:**
● If you've bought a bag of spinach leaves and have some left over, combine them with other leaves to make a salad accompaniment.
● Herring is once again becoming a victim of over-intensive fishing and, consequently, its price is increasing. Mackerel might prove a less expensive but just as delicious substitute.

NUTRITIONAL VALUES
calories: 259 Kcal (1070 Kj) ● fat: 20 g ● carbohydrate: 5 g
● fibre: 2 g ● vitamin A: 267 mcg (889 i.u.)

boiled eggs with anchovy soldiers

1 Rinse the anchovies and pat dry with kitchen paper, then chop finely. Beat them into the butter and season to taste with pepper.

2 Boil the eggs for 4–5 minutes, until softly set. Meanwhile, toast the bread, butter one side with the anchovy butter and cut into fingers.

3 Serve the eggs with the anchovy toasts and some mustard and cress.

● **Tips:**
● Rinsing the anchovies gets rid of some of the salt, but if they are still too salty for your taste, soak them in a little milk for 5 minutes, then rinse and pat dry with kitchen paper.
● Eggshells are porous, so store eggs in a covered container, away from strong-smelling foods, in the refrigerator. This is better than the egg rack on the door. Store them pointed end downwards for up to 2 weeks, but not beyond their 'use by' date. Ideally, you should bring them to room temperature before cooking. Do not use cracked or dirty eggs, but you should never wash them.

SERVES 4

Preparation time: *5 minutes*

Cooking time: *5 minutes*

8 anchovy fillets in oil, drained

25 g (1 oz) unsalted butter, softened

4 large eggs

4 thick slices of white bread

pepper

mustard and cress, to serve

NUTRITIONAL VALUES
calories: 278 Kcal (1165 Kj)
●
fat: 15 g
●
carbohydrate: 25 g
●
fibre: 2 g
●
iron: 2 mg

tuna & red pepper chowder

SERVES 4–6

Preparation time: *10–12 minutes*

Cooking time: *35 minutes*

50 g (2 oz) butter or margarine

1 small red pepper, cored, deseeded and chopped

1 celery stick, thinly sliced

1 tablespoon dry white wine

1.2 litres (2 pints) fish stock

250 g (8 oz) potatoes, cut into 1 cm (½ inch) dice

1 teaspoon finely chopped fresh marjoram, or ½ teaspoon dried marjoram

375 g (12 oz) can sweetcorn, drained

200 g (7 oz) can tuna chunks in brine, drained and flaked

2 tablespoons finely chopped parsley

4 tablespoons double cream

pepper

marjoram sprigs, to garnish

1 Melt the butter or margarine in a saucepan. Add the red pepper and celery, cover the pan and cook for 8–10 minutes, stirring frequently. When the mixture gets a little dry, moisten it with the white wine.

2 Add the fish stock, potatoes and marjoram and cook over a moderate heat, partially covered, for 15 minutes.

3 Stir in the sweetcorn and tuna, season with pepper to taste and cook, uncovered, over a low heat for a further 10 minutes. Stir in the parsley and double cream. Pour the chowder into heated bowls, garnish with sprigs of marjoram and serve with crusty bread, if liked.

NUTRITIONAL VALUES

calories: 486 Kcal (2036 Kj) ● fat: 27 g ● carbohydrate: 37 g
● fibre: 5 g ● iron: 2 mg

salmon & courgette brochettes

SERVES 4

Preparation time: *15 minutes, plus marinating*

Cooking time: *5 minutes*

750 g–1 kg (1½–2 lb) salmon fillet, skinned and cut into 2.5 cm (1 inch) cubes

375 g (12 oz) courgettes, cut into 1 cm (½ inch) pieces

Marinade:

8 tablespoons sunflower oil

2 tablespoons light sesame seed oil

2 tablespoons sesame seeds

1 garlic clove, crushed

1–2 tablespoons lime juice

pepper

To serve:

rocket

whole chives

lime wedges

1 You will need 8 barbecue skewers. If they are wooden, put them to soak in cold water. Prepare the marinade by combining all the ingredients in a large bowl. Add the salmon and courgette pieces and toss to combine and coat. Cover and leave to marinate for about 30 minutes.

2 Thread the salmon and courgette pieces alternately on to the barbecue skewers and cook the kebabs under a preheated very hot grill or over a very hot barbecue for about 5 minutes, turning them frequently and brushing with the marinade to prevent the fish and courgettes from drying out. The fish is cooked when it is just beginning to look opaque. Take care not to overcook it or it will become dry and tough. Serve immediately on a bed of rocket, garnished with whole chives and lime wedges.

● **Tips:**
● These brochettes are equally delicious served on mashed potatoes flavoured with olive oil, with a salad served separately.
● Try making brochettes with fresh tuna or swordfish.
● Serve a speedy, low-fat sauce with these kebabs by mixing 150 ml (¼ pint) natural yogurt, 1 tablespoon lemon juice, grated rind of 1 lemon and 1 tablespoon chopped dill in a small bowl. Use set or Greek yogurt for the best flavour and texture or low-fat yogurt if you are watching the calories or your cholesterol levels.

NUTRITIONAL VALUES

calories: 639 Kcal (2650 Kj)
●
fat: 53 g
●
carbohydrate: 5 g
●
fibre: 1 g
●
iron: 2 mg

SOYA & TOFU

Soya is an excellent vegetable source of protein and, unlike most of the animal proteins, it lowers blood pressure and cholesterol levels. Soya beans are rich in fibre, which promotes the contractions of the bowel that prevent or improve constipation. Many minerals are found in soya, and tofu – mashed soya bean curd – is a particularly rich source of calcium because of how it is made. However, soya is now becoming known for the benefits of its phyto-oestrogens (plant hormones which mimic human oestrogen). Excessive oestrogens appear to promote hormone-related cancers, such as breast, cervical and ovarian cancers in women and prostate cancer in men. In some way phyto-oestrogens seem to protect against these diseases. Phyto-oestrogens also stabilize hormonal levels and so help relieve some menopausal symptoms and reduce some symptoms of PMS.

caldo verde & smoked tofu soup

SERVES **4–6**

Preparation time: *20 minutes, plus soaking*

Cooking time: *1¾ hours*

125 g (4 oz) dried cannellini beans, soaked overnight

1.2 litres (2 pints) water

1 small onion, roughly chopped

4 whole garlic cloves

250 g (8 oz) smoked tofu, cubed

2 tablespoons extra virgin olive oil

1 small potato, cubed

1 tablespoon chopped sage

175 g (6 oz) Savoy cabbage, roughly shredded

300 ml (½ pint) vegetable stock

pepper

1 Drain the soaked beans, rinse and place in a large saucepan. Add the water, bring to the boil and boil rapidly for 10 minutes, then reduce the heat and simmer gently for 45 minutes.

2 Meanwhile, toss the onion, garlic and tofu in half the oil and place in a roasting pan. Place in a preheated oven, 200°C (400°F), Gas Mark 6, for 35 minutes, turning occasionally until golden.

3 Heat the remaining oil in a large saucepan, add the potato and sage and fry for 10 minutes until browned. Stir into the beans with the roasted vegetables and tofu, cabbage, stock and seasoning. Bring to the boil, cover and simmer gently for 20 minutes until the potatoes and cabbage are cooked. Serve hot, with warm bread.

- **Tip:**
- Tofu is a staple of the vegetarian diet because it is so rich in protein. It has little flavour of its own, but readily absorbs the flavours of other ingredients. Silken tofu is a good substitute for dairy products, such as yogurt and cream, while firm tofu is useful in stir-fries. Smoked and dried are also available. These days, most supermarkets stock several types and Chinese food stores will carry the entire range, including tofu skins.

NUTRITIONAL VALUES
calories: 264 Kcal (1107 Kj) ● fat: 11 g ● carbohydrate: 25 g
● fibre: 2 g ● iron: 4 mg

lemon grass & tofu nuggets with chilli sauce

1 Coarsely chop the spring onions and place in a food processor with the ginger, lemon grass, coriander and garlic and process until mixed together and chopped, but still chunky. Add the sugar, soy sauce, tofu, breadcrumbs and egg, season to taste with pepper and process until just combined.

2 Take teaspoonfuls of the mixture and pat into flat cakes using lightly floured hands. Heat the oil in a large, nonstick, frying pan. Add half the tofu cakes and fry gently for 1–2 minutes on each side, until golden. Drain on kitchen paper and keep warm while frying the remainder. Serve with the chilli sauce.

● **Tip:**
● To make your own chilli dipping sauce, mix together 1 tablespoon clear honey, 2 tablespoons light soy sauce, 1 deseeded and sliced red chilli, 2 tablespoons freshly squeezed orange juice and 1 thinly sliced spring onion in a small serving bowl.

SERVES 4

Preparation time: *10 minutes*

Cooking time: *10 minutes*

1 bunch of spring onions

5 cm (2 inch) piece of fresh root ginger, chopped

2 lemon grass stalks, roughly chopped

small handful of fresh coriander

3 garlic cloves, coarsely chopped

1 tablespoon sugar

1 tablespoon light soy sauce

300 g (10 oz) tofu, drained

25 g (1 oz) breadcrumbs

1 egg

vegetable oil, for frying

pepper

chilli sauce, to serve

NUTRITIONAL VALUES
calories: 230 Kcal (960 Kj)
●
fat: 13 g
●
carbohydrate: 18 g
●
fibre: 1 g
●
calcium: 425 mg

tofu, cinnamon & honey pockets

SERVES 4

Preparation time: *15 minutes*

Cooking time: *15 minutes*

50 g (2 oz) butter

2 onions, chopped

50 g (2 oz) flaked almonds,
lightly crushed

1 tablespoon clear honey

1 teaspoon ground cinnamon

200 g (7 oz) tofu, drained and diced

150 g (5 oz) filo pastry

pepper

1 Melt half of the butter in a frying pan, add the onions and fry for 3 minutes, until softened. Stir in the almonds and fry for 2 minutes, until turning golden. Stir in the honey, cinnamon and tofu, and season to taste with pepper.

2 Melt the remaining butter in a small saucepan. Cut out 16 squares from the filo pastry, 18 cm (7 inches) across. Lay 8 squares on a work surface and brush with a little melted butter. Cover each with a second square placed at an angle to create a star shape. Pile the tofu mixture on to the centres of the squares.

3 Brush the edges of the pastry with a little butter. Bring the edges up over the filling and pinch together to make bundles. Repeat with the remaining pastry squares. Transfer to a baking sheet and brush with the remaining butter.

4 Bake in a preheated oven, 200°C (400°F), Gas Mark 6, for about 10 minutes, or until the pastry is golden. Serve warm.

- **Tips:**
- Filo pastry dries out very quickly, so keep the unused squares covered with a clean, damp tea towel until required.
- Use a clear, light honey, such as acacia, for this recipe. Darker honeys, such as sage or Hymettus, are too strongly flavoured.

NUTRITIONAL VALUES

calories: 368 Kcal (1536 Kj)
•
fat: 20 g
•
carbohydrate: 36 g
•
fibre: 3 g
•
calcium: 315 mg

banana tofu smoothie

1 Roughly chop the tofu and put it into a food processor or blender. Roughly chop the bananas and put them into the food processor with the raspberries, if using, and half of the fruit juice. Blend until smooth.

2 Roughly grind the linseeds in a coffee grinder or use a pestle and mortar, then add to the food processor or blender with the remaining fruit juice and blend until smooth. Serve immediately.

● **Good for:** Quick snack. Packed with protein, this smoothie is good to drink at any time of the day as a quick snack. The linseeds can be replaced with spirulina powder, if you prefer.

● **Try the following variation:**
tofu fruit smoothie: Put 300 g (10 oz) roughly chopped tofu, 50 g (2 oz) halved strawberries, 50 g (2 oz) blueberries, 1 chopped banana, 1 litre (1¾ pints) milk and 4 tablespoons clear honey into a food processor or blender and process until smooth. Pour into chilled glasses and serve immediately.

SERVES **4**

Preparation time: *10 minutes*

Makes: *1.2 litres (2 pints)*

300 g (10 oz) tofu

2 bananas

125 g (4 oz) raspberries (optional)

1 litre (1¾ pints) white grape or apple juice

2 teaspoons linseeds

NUTRITIONAL VALUES
calories: 217 Kcal (922 Kj)
●
fat: 5 g
●
carbohydrate: 38 g
●
fibre: 4 g
●
calcium: 411 mg

YOGURT

The *Lactobacillus acidophilus* bacteria in live yogurt support the friendly bacteria in the intestine. Conventional antibiotics destroy these gut flora and eating live yogurt restores the balance. Other problems caused by antibiotics, such as the yeast infection *Candida albicans,* can also be remedied by eating live yogurt regularly. Eating yogurt regularly can also protect against intestinal problems, including gastroenteritis, diarrhoea, food poisoning and travellers' tummy by ensuring that the digestive system is functioning at its best. Yogurt also protects against peptic ulcers and helps to heal them, and may even offer some protection against heart disease by lowering cholesterol levels. Its high calcium levels are good for bones and teeth.

chicken tzatziki

SERVES **4**

Preparation time: *15 minutes, plus marinating*

Cooking time: *about 20 minutes*

4 chicken portions or
8 chicken thighs

300 ml (½ pint) Greek yogurt

3 tablespoons virgin olive oil

2 garlic cloves, crushed

2 teaspoons dried mint

½ cucumber, peeled and
finely chopped

2 tablespoons finely
chopped mint

pepper

To garnish:
cucumber slices

mint sprigs

1 Score the chicken pieces deeply with a sharp knife, cutting right down as far as the bone.

2 Mix together half the yogurt with 2 tablespoons of the oil, half the garlic and dried mint and pepper to taste. Put the chicken in a shallow dish and spoon or brush the yogurt mixture over all the pieces. Cover and marinate in the refrigerator for at least 4 hours, preferably overnight.

3 Put the chicken on the grid over hot charcoal on the barbecue. Cook, turning frequently, for about 20 minutes, until the chicken is just charred on the outside, no longer pink on the inside and the juices run clear when the thickest part is pierced with the point of a sharp knife. Alternatively, cook under a preheated grill, turning frequently, for about 20 minutes.

4 Meanwhile, put the remaining yogurt, garlic and dried mint in a bowl and stir well to mix. Add the cucumber, fresh mint and pepper to taste and stir again. Turn into a serving bowl, drizzle with the remaining oil and garnish with cucumber slices and mint sprigs, if using.

5 Serve the chicken hot, with the tzatziki salad. Hot pitta bread and a tomato salad make good accompaniments.

NUTRITIONAL VALUES
calories: 311 Kcal (1296 Kj) ● fat: 19 g ● carbohydrate: 2 g
● fibre: 0 g ● calcium: 136 mg

cranberry yogurt smoothie

Juice the apples and process in a blender with the other ingredients. Serve in a tumbler over ice cubes.

● **Good for:** Thrush (see pages 104–105). *Candida albicans* is a common yeast which lives harmlessly in all of us. However, in some cases of low immunity, it can travel through the vaginal tract and cause thrush. Symptoms include mood swings and depression, recurrent vaginal yeast and chronic digestive problems. Cut out junk food, fats, sugar and highly processed foods to discourage the growth of yeast. All the ingredients in this juice have antibacterial properties. It is particularly effective if you are taking antibiotics.

● **Try the following variation:**

yogurt & buttermilk fruit medley: Put 2 roughly chopped bananas, 100 g (3½ oz) frozen cranberries and 125 ml (4 fl oz) live natural yogurt in a blender or food processor and process until smooth. Pour into a glass and stir in 125 ml (4 fl oz) buttermilk. Serves 1.

SERVES 1–2

Preparation time: *3–4 minutes*

Makes: *200 ml (7 fl oz)*

250 g (8 oz) apples

100 g (3½ oz) frozen cranberries

100 ml (3½ fl oz) live natural yogurt

1 tablespoon clear honey

NUTRITIONAL VALUES

calories: 258 Kcal (1090 Kj)
●
fat: 1 g
●
carbohydrate: 59 g
●
fibre: 4 g
●
calcium: 213 mg

INDEX

Acknowledgements in Source Order

Getty Images/Stone 22 top left, 68 top left, 96

Octopus Publishing Group Limited 49 right/Colin Bowling 102 right/Jean Cazals 22 bottom right, 38/Stephen Conroy 3 centre, 67 bottom right, 95, 121, 122, 131, 137, 141, 143, 145, 149, 153, 157, 159, 163, 169, 189/Jeremy Hopley 13 centre left, 15 bottom right, 21 bottom right, 53, 59, 75 centre right, 85 bottom right, 109 top, 113, 165, 186, 187/David Jordan 21 top left, 23 top left, 33, 35, 45 top, 49 left, 63 bottom right, 91 bottom right, 93, 97, 114, 116, 129, 135, 142, 162/Sandra Lane 103, 183/Gary Latham 6 top, 6 bottom/William Lingwood 7 top, 11 bottom right, 13 top right, 15 top left, 17 top right, 19, 25 top left, 45 bottom, 47 top, 47 bottom, 55 top, 55 bottom right, 61 bottom, 71 top left, 72 centre right, 73 top centre, 75 top left, 79, 88 left, 99, 105/David Loftus 82 bottom, 88 right, 147, 148/James Merrell 120/Neil Mersh 3 left, 118, 151/Diana Miller 155/Peter Myers 16 centre right, 34, 69, 76, 98/Sean Myers 57, 72 bottom left/Peter Pugh-Cook 16 top left, 44, 46 bottom right, 64 top left, 94 right, 104 bottom right, 108/William Reavell 7 bottom, 11 top left, 17 centre, 23 bottom right, 29 top left, 31 top right, 37 bottom right, 39, 41, 43 left, 46 centre left, 61 top right, 65, 66 top right, 81 top, 81 bottom, 82 top, 83, 84 bottom, 87, 107 top left, 107 bottom right, 112, 125, 132, 133, 139, 161, 167, 171, 172, 173, 175, 179, 185/Gareth Sambidge 14, 28, 40, 62 top left, 62 bottom right, 68 bottom right, 92 bottom right, 102 left/Niki Sianni 100/Simon Smith 7 centre, 51, 77, 84 top, 126/Karen Thomas 27, 117, 123, 127/Ian Wallace 8, 12, 18 top left, 20, 29 bottom right, 31 top left, 43 right, 48 right, 56 left, 56 right, 63 top left, 71 bottom right, 73 bottom right, 78, 85 top left, 89, 91 top centre, 92 centre left, 94 left, 101, 111, 181/Philip Webb 9, 67 top left, 109 bottom, 119, 177, 182/Mark Winwood 110

Photodisc 1, 3 right, 25 bottom right, 36, 37 centre, 48 left, 50 top, 58, 70

Science Photo Library 50 bottom/Mike Bluestone 26/BSIP Ducloux 10 top, 60 left/BSIP 106/BSIP, Fife 54 bottom left/Dr Jeremy Burgess 30 bottom left/Oscar Burriel 32, 64 centre right, 74/Dr. W. Crum, Dementia Research Group, TIM, Beddow 60 right/Custom Medical Stock Photo 24 top left/Dept. of Clinical Radiology, Salisbury, District Hospital 86/E. Gueho, CNRI 104 top left/P. Hawtin, University of Southampton 90/Damien Lovegrove 31 bottom right/Prof. P. Motta, Dept. of Anatomy, University, 'La Sapienza,' Rome 52 top, 52 bottom/David Nunuk 80/Alfred Pasieka 24 centre right, 42, 54 centre right/Chris Priest 18 bottom right/Saturn Stills 66 bottom left

Jacket Acknowledgements

Octopus Publishing Group Limited/Stephen Conroy front cover centre, back cover centre left, back cover top 2, spine centre top/Neil Mersh front cover centre left/William Reavell back cover centre

Photodisc/front cover background, front cover centre right, back cover background, back cover centre right, back cover top 1, back cover top 3, back cover top 4, spine top, spine centre bottom, spine bottom